Pelican Books
Allen Lane The Penguin Press
My War with the CIA

KU-256-241

Norodom Sihanouk was born in 1922 and succeeded to the throne of Cambodia in April 1941. In 1947 he introduced a new constitution with an elective assembly and manhood suffrage, except for Buddhist priests and soldiers who were disenfranchised. In March 1955 the King abdicated in favour of his parents, entered politics and founded the Sangkum (Popular Socialist Community) Party. In the elections of 1955, '58, '62 and '66 the Sangkum won all the seats in the assembly. His father died in April 1960 and the royal powers were then vested in a Council of Regency until June 1960 when Sihanouk became Head of State without becoming king. He was deposed in March 1970 and now lives in exile.

Wilfred Burchett was born in 1911 in Australia and has been recognized over the last thirty years as a specialist in Asian affairs and has spent nineteen years in South-East Asia and in China. During the war he was war correspondent for the *Daily Express* reporting for the Asian and Pacific theatres. In 1955 the Australian government revoked his passport because of his opinions on the Korean and Vietnam wars. Wilfred Burchett is the author of sixteen books which have been translated into several languages and sold all over the world. He speaks six languages and now lives in Paris with his wife and three children.

Norodom Sihanouk
as related to Wilfred Burchett

My War with the CIA

Cambodia's Fight for Survival

Penguin Books · Allen Lane The Penguin Press

Penguin Books Ltd, Harmondsworth,
Middlesex, England
Allen Lane The Penguin Press
74 Grosvenor Street, London W1
Penguin Books Inc., 7110 Ambassador Road,
Baltimore, Maryland 21207, U.S.A.
Penguin Books Australia Ltd, Ringwood,
Victoria, Australia

Published in Penguin Books
and Allen Lane The Penguin Press, 1973
Reprinted 1973

Hardback ISBN   0 7139 0449 X
Paperback ISBN 014.02.1689 8

Made and printed in Great Britain by
Cox & Wyman Ltd, London, Reading and Fakenham
Set in Monotype Baskerville

Contents

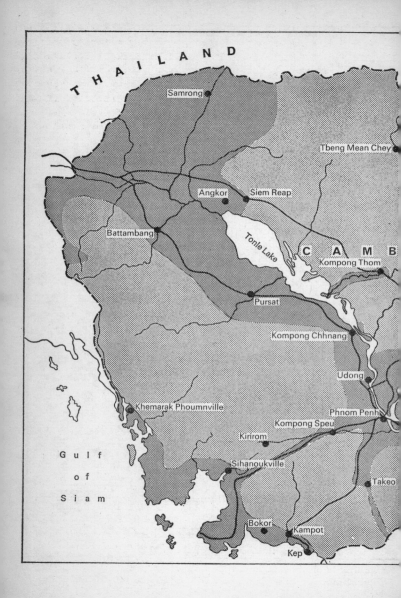

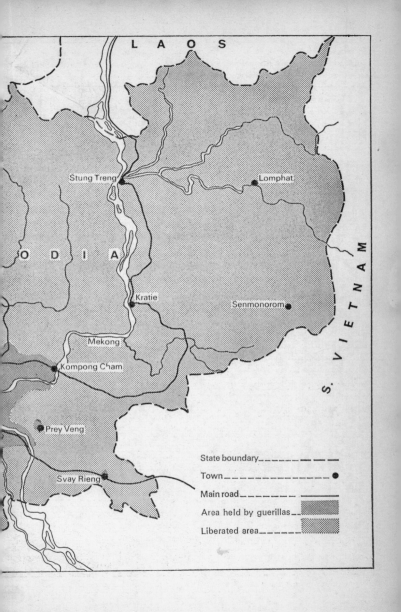

Introduction

My War with the CIA

Prince Norodom Sihanouk's *My War with the CIA* is much more than a book of political memoirs. It is a revealing account of the tactics used by the ruthless imperialist power of the West, the United States of America, to infiltrate, corrupt, subvert, colonize and subjugate an independent, neutral and peace-loving nation. It is also a deeply moving account of the determined and heroic response of a proud people, under the inspired leadership of a great patriot, to the plunder and massive genocide that was unleashed by the Pentagon and its puppets against Cambodia, when the subtle techniques of take-over and domination failed.

The current phase of open military confrontation between the military machine of the United States and the peoples of Indo-China is there for all to see. Sihanouk writes: 'It is worse than what Hitler did . . . what is the difference between burning and gassing people in ovens and doing it to a whole nation out in the open? That is just what the United States of President Nixon is doing today. Everyone knows the horrors of Auschwitz and other extermination camps. But Nixon is waging a war of extermination against the entire people of Indo-China . . . In Cambodia, it is happening before our eyes, as part of deliberate US policy . . . to destroy present and future generations of Cambodians by destroying our environment. Once nature dies, man also dies.'

For Cambodia this phase of open, barbaric aggression by the world's mightiest military machine begins with the CIA-sponsored coup by Lon Nol and his gang on 18 March 1970. The events that preceded this coup – events that span a period of over fifteen years – represent the first phase of US

9

intervention in Cambodia, a phase characterized by economic, political and cultural infiltration, subversion and intrigue. These events, when examined against the historical experience of many third-world countries, reveal a pervasive standardized pattern of subversion – both in respect to goals and in respect to techniques and tactics.

The goal in all instances is clear. It is the complete economic, political, cultural, military subjugation of a country to the interests, economic and military, of US imperialism. A necessary condition for success – in all cases other than those involving military aggression from the start – is the infiltration of the machinery of the state – both the civilian and military branches – and the 'softening-up' of the political and intellectual elites. This process goes hand in hand with a variety of military, economic and educational 'assistance' programmes that are extended on conditions favouring 'private enterprise', an open-door policy to foreign investment, and a militant anti-communist stand. Economic assistance, military aid, etc. are the baits – often quite attractive at the time they are extended – for propagation of increasing dependence of the developing country on the US. Political, economic, cultural, military and clandestine operations are intertwined according to a blueprint that is hard to decipher by the leadership of a country, undergoing the process until the point of open confrontation.

'The only thing I had not anticipated,' says Prince Sihanouk, 'was that the United States would take part directly in trying to take our country to pieces . . . We were being punished, humiliated, and prepared for the chopping-block because we had stood on our dignity. We refused to become US puppets, or join in the anti-communist crusade. We spurned the billion-dollar rewards for such a role. That was our crime in the eyes of successive US administrations.'

This phrase could easily have been written by a Greek. Our government had 'spurned' President Johnson's offer of economic aid in return for our participation side by side with Turkey, in the subjugation and partition of Cyprus. And Greece had to be 'punished' because it had insisted that 'Greece is an ally but not a satellite of the US', that 'Greece belongs to the Greeks'. Lon Nol had been groomed for administering the 'punishment' in Cambodia, as Papadopoulos had been groomed for the same role in Greece. With only a slight difference. Papadopoulos, having collaborated directly with the Nazi occupation troops in the forties, had achieved greater prominence in the ranks of the CIA than Lon Nol.

Papadopoulos's reputation was further enhanced when he pulled off a successful coup in Greece. Now a faithful and capable US puppet, he can school others in the techniques of coup-making. This explains Lon Nol's stopover in Athens from France prior to his coup. Similar activities have been reported to be occurring in Italy – a direct contact between Papadopoulos and neo-fascist elements in the Italian army and political world.

There is another parallel in the stories of Cambodia and Greece that is worth mentioning. The overt military coup had become necessary in both countries because the leadership had exposed American designs, and had created a militant popular climate. Prince Sihanouk writes that 'my strategy of bringing out into the open before the eyes of the people' these designs 'had succeeded'. It is exactly what we did in Greece in the fateful period between 15 July 1965 and 21 April 1967 – when the colonels struck. After George Papandreou was ousted by the King, acting on instructions from the US, and deputies had been bought off by the CIA to collaborate with the right in a new government, our party took the issues to the people, unveiled the power structure and showed how it was strangling our dreams of independence and sovereignty. Prince Sihanouk and I both received similar snubs from the American Embassy! He received his snub when the US Ambassador strode off the platform as he went to make his opening report to the Cambodian National Congress in 1956, and I when two members of the political section of the American Embassy walked out in the midst of my speech to the Foreign Press Association in February 1967. They claimed I had 'attacked the US'.

Prince Sihanouk says that at the time he was laying bare American designs he 'could not guess the terrible cost in maintaining such a stand. Even had I known, however, I don't think I could have acted otherwise.' This expresses exactly our own feelings about our stand in Greece.

But all this relates to the past. What about the future? 'In the end it was the Americans who drove home the bitter lesson that imperialists leave only one road to freedom, once they have marked a country down as their prey; and that is the road of armed struggle as defined by Ho Chi Minh.' This is the fundamental, inescapable conclusion to which all the victims of American imperialism are drawn. We too in Greece have reached the same conclusion as Prince Sihanouk and the Cambodian people. And for this reason we have forged the Panhellenic Liberation Movement (PAK).

In the difficult, long and costly struggle for liberation, national self-determination, socialism, democracy and popular sovereignty, the nations that have fallen prey to aggressive American imperialism must coordinate their actions on a global basis – since the aggressor himself operates on a global basis. But beyond this, the third-world liberation movements need, in their struggle against US imperialism, the active support of the anti-imperialist camp. There is the widespread concern in our ranks that the increasingly complex nature of superpower relations and politics may tend to limit the willingness or the capability of anti-imperialist nations to contribute actively to the liberation struggles of peoples in Asia, in Latin America, in Africa, and in southern Europe. Such a development would be no less than tragic. Not only for the already 'occupied' nations of the third world, but also for the anti-imperialist superpowers themselves. If the hawks of the US are met with subservience and passivity by the other giants of the world, then their positions will become more and more hawkish. There should be no doubt in anyone's mind about the nature of American imperialism. It constitutes a global threat not only to the independence of nations and the dignity of life, but a direct and immediate threat to human survival. Unless the anti-imperialist forces coalesce in the common struggle against a 'clear and present' danger, they will be paving the way not to Pax Americana but to a global American-generated holocaust.

In closing I should like to state that the Greek people deeply admire the peoples of Indo-China. It is they who have borne the main burden – a spectacular and appalling burden – in the struggle for independence and self-determination. They have shown the way. We will follow.

Andreas G. Papandreou
Panhellenic Liberation Movement (PAK)
July 1972

Foreword

For sixteen years, Cambodia lived under the shadow of that which happened on 30 April 1970, when United States tanks rolled across her frontiers and United States bombers started the systematic process of reducing Cambodian towns and villages to rubble and ashes. In the pages that follow, the Cambodian Head of State, Prince Norodom Sihanouk, chronicles the background, from his first fateful meetings in the mid-1950s with the brothers Dulles, heading the US State Department and the CIA respectively, until the coup of 18 March 1970.

The account is classic for its description of the total nature of the means employed by the world's mightiest military-economic power to force a small country away from its chosen policy, and to get rid of the architect and chief executant of that policy. At Sihanouk's first meetings with the brothers Dulles, there was ominous insistence that he should abandon his neutralist ideas. When diplomatic, political and economic pressures accompanied by military threats failed, there was a period of plots and assassination attempts. When they in turn failed, it was finally, with well-financed treason at the top, a miltary coup and armed intervention by the United States and its Saigon satellite to maintain the usurpers in power that the deed was done. The USA, by the Lon Nol coup of March 1970, had succeeded in exporting to Indo-China the well-tried methods of Latin America.

For those of us who have followed this cruelly unequal struggle from the time of the signing of the 1954 Geneva Ceasefire Agreements on Indo-China, there seemed to be an inevitability of sequence and denouement in the unfolding drama. The scenario was only too familiar. Friends of Cambodia, supporters of Norodom Sihanouk's neutrality-for-peace policies often held their breath in anguished concern when it seemed he must back down or fall, either to an assassin's bullet or by well-paid treachery. Those who knew him best, however, were convinced he would never back down.

A point which zealots for US policies in South-East Asia should ponder is the standard pattern which renders military dictatorships essential to implement those policies. This proves true for South Vietnam, for Cambodia and for Thailand. No shade of political deviation, nothing less than total devotion to the US line can be tolerated. Only when their implementation is thwarted by force of arms does the United States yield any ground. The 1970 coup in Cambodia, for instance, had its counterpart in the 17 November 1971 coup in neighbouring Thailand. The mere rumour that Thailand was flirting with China and North Vietnam, and that Foreign Minister, Thanat Kohman, was meditating over the advantages of neutralism, was sufficient for a military coup to install Field-Marshal Thonam Kittikachorn as military dictator. His first acts were to dissolve the government, both houses of parliament and the constitution, just as Lon Nol had done soon after seizing power in Cambodia. In Thailand, as in Cambodia, US air power was soon engaged in propping up the new dictator.

Norodom Sihanouk has analysed in depth, and documented in detail, the sordid saga of Washington's underground war against his country until it erupted above ground on 30 April 1970. It is an account which is bound to be studied with special interest in the third world, where innumerable countries are entangled, at some stage or another, in the web of intrigues and pressures woven by the CIA and other US agencies, as a prelude to encompassing their downfall.

The material in the following pages was dictated by Norodom Sihanouk in French, transcribed by myself into English, divided up according to agreed chapter titles, and corrected by Prince Sihanouk. The fact that he used a language other than his own, translated into a third language, means the material lacks some of the pungency and vigour when Norodom Sihanouk is translated direct from his native Cambodian. The main part of the work was done at the Head of State's Peking residence during the second half of December 1971 and January 1972. It was more or less completed at further working sessions in Shanghai and Peking in March 1972, with fresh material added as the situation in Cambodia developed.

One aspect of the coup in human terms was evident from the moment I set foot in Prince Sihanouk's headquarters. The first to greet me to arrange working schedules was Sihanouk's Head of Protocol, Prince Sisowath Méthavi, brother of Sirik Matak, the co-author with Lon Nol of the coup. Present at the residence in January 1972, to welcome two Cambodia ping-pong champions who had given the slip to Lon Nol's security agents in Hong Kong, while returning home from matches in South Korea, was the younger sister of Cheng Heng, who replaced Sihanouk as Head of State immediately after the coup.

A ping-pong champion herself, she now studies medicine in Peking. Two of her brothers are also there as engineering students. Even the chief plotters are thus seen to be in a minority within their own families. As for their status in Cambodian society as a whole, the narrative of Norodom Sihanouk is eloquent.

The present work is viewed by the author as a weapon in the struggle to regain his own country's independence, and as a warning to other countries marked down as future victims.

W. G. Burchett
Paris
30 June 1972

Preface

There have been numerous accounts of the events leading up to the *coup d'état* of 18 March 1970, intended to depose me as Head of State of the Kingdom of Cambodia. Some of the accounts have been sympathetic, some unfriendly, some objective, others tendentious. Accounts were written by persons exploiting confidences shared with them when they were in my employ, to claim 'inside knowledge' of what were, more often than not, insignificant or irrelevant events, and were published to establish the authors' reputations as experts on the matter. The absurd scenarios which these persons have concocted served also to cover up their own perfidy.

Others, who came to Cambodia after the coup, sincerely tried to reconstruct the scene. But, viewing the events through their own optics, using their own weights and measures, they attempted to shed light on matters of which they had neither the knowledge nor the objectivity necessary to make accurate appraisals.

Many of the articles and books by Western writers have one thing in common: patronizing overtones of 'West knows best'. Asians have grown understandably sensitive to assumptions of Caucasian intellectual superiority, for we have suffered too long the humiliations of colonialism for it to be otherwise.

There have been accounts written from afar with benign intent, but which suffer from lack of factual information and from ignorance of our history. Because of the world-wide interest in the drama in which my Cambodian people have been cast as unwilling actors, such accounts risk acceptance as actual history.

Absent from almost all of these books and articles is the vital central issue to which all other factors are subordinate: the struggle to maintain peace and independence; the sovereignty and neutrality of our country. It is only through this optic that my leadership of Cambodia for three decades should be judged – not on the basis of the vagaries of internal politics upon which so many writers love to dwell. Too many could not see the Cambodian forest for its trees; others did not want to see the forest. Despite their experiences in many lands, and their academic distinctions, many observers proved less enlightened than the lowliest of our peasants. The peasants' consciousness of the difference between independence and colonialism, between peace and war, was soon heightened by American bombs.

It is to set the record straight that I am, in this book, relating the salient facts of the Cambodian drama as I lived it, often as the principal actor. Alas, I am hindered by lack of documents. When I left our oasis of peace, as it was in January 1970, for medical treatment in France, I took the minimum baggage necessary for such a purpose. Historical records were obviously not included.

Enough evidence is available, however, to prove the unceasing and determined intervention of the United States in the internal affairs of my country, and particularly the role of the Central Intelligence Agency, in a series of plots which culminated in the military coup of 18 March 1970.

I have chosen to relate this story to one of a small group of writers who have consistently shown sympathy, comprehension, and respect for our national dignity, for the aspirations of my people, and for my own part in defending those aspirations.

Norodom Sihanouk
Peking
June 1970

Chapter 1

Moscow—Peking

'You mustn't go, Samdech. It's Friday and the 13th.' These words were uttered half in jest by one of my aides on the way to the airport to catch the plane which was to take me from Paris to Moscow. It was the morning of 13 March 1970. I am not superstitious so I laughed and flew off to meet the Russian leaders. Five days later, while still in Moscow, I was deposed – and the Soviet government has still not recognized the Royal Government of National Union set up in Peking less than two months later. So Friday the 13th was an unlucky day after all!

President Podgorny greeted me at the Moscow airport. There were no elaborate welcoming ceremonies, because mine was a political, not a state, visit. After welcoming me, President Podgorny said there was a plane waiting to take me straight home to Phnom Penh.

'Take an overnight rest in Moscow if you like,' he said, 'and fly on to Phnom Penh in the morning. We have confidence in you, Prince Sihanouk. You are really the indispensable leader of your people. But it's important that you fly straight back and take charge of Cambodia's affairs. See they don't fall into the hands of Lon Nol and Sirik Matak. You must ensure that Cambodia doesn't drift into an American take-over. You must prevent Lon Nol and Sirik Matak from creating difficulties for the South Vietnamese people who are waging a heroic struggle for the liberation of their country.'

I replied that I would have to think things over very carefully. There was much to think about. On 8 March there had been anti-Vietnamese demonstrations in Svay Rieng province,[1] and reports reaching me showed that Lon Nol, at the time Prime Minister, was behind them. On 11 March a mob, ostensibly of students and schoolchildren, attacked the Embassy of the Provisional Revolutionary Government of the Republic of South Vietnam and, a few hours later, that of the Democratic Republic of Vietnam (Hanoi). Again, my reports showed it to be the work of the army – specifically Lon Nol. The nucleus of the attackers was, in both cases, some fifty military men in civilian clothes, commanded by Lon Nol's younger brother, Colonel Lon Non. This was a far cry from the 'spontaneous demonstrations' naively reported in the European press and on American television. Signs had been prepared in English, a language rarely used in public display in my country. Photographers and crews had been alerted. Everything pointed to a scenario drawn up well in advance.

As soon as I heard of the attack on the embassies, I sent a cablegram to my mother, the Queen,[2] condemning the violence as 'acts of personalities attaching greater importance to their individual and clan interests than to the country's future and the fate of the people'. I warned of the possibility of a rightist coup and said that I would return for a confrontation with those responsible, but I added that, if the people chose to follow them 'along a path that will turn Cambodia into a second Laos, they will compel me to resign'.

On 10 March I appeared on French television in Paris and said that right-wingers in Phnom Penh had 'taken advantage of my long absence to try and change Cambodia's political orientation. They would like us to enter the American camp.'[3] I said that there had been contacts between the rightists and the CIA and again warned of the danger of a coup, saying that: 'Everything depends on the army.'

At the time I was thinking exclusively in terms of Sirik

1. Known in the West as the 'Parrot's Beak' area where Cambodian territory comes close to Saigon.
2. Queen Sisowath Kossamak Nearireath, widow of former King Norodom Suramarit, my father.
3. I had been at Grasse, in the south of France, for medical attention.

Matak, the deputy Prime Minister and his group of rightists. I still had complete confidence in Lon Nol, and thought that he would use the army to deal with any attempt at an overthrow. I knew that Sirik Matak had been in close touch with the US embassy from the time diplomatic relations had been re-established in June 1969, and I predicted in the Paris TV interview that the future would be very dark if I were defeated.

The answer to my message to the Queen came in the form of further demonstrations and outrageous attacks against the Vietnamese community, including their churches. This was something quite foreign to our Buddhist culture and to our traditions of tolerance. Further reports reaching me from my own sources repeated that the ringleaders were military personnel in civilian clothes. I began to ask myself if it were possible that Lon Nol had turned against me. I was loath to believe this for we had been together most of our lives and I had always considered him as my 'right arm'. His declarations of loyalty – too profusive, I think, in retrospect – were always more emphatic than those of my other ministers. I remember that he had reiterated his affirmations of loyalty a few weeks earlier in France.

The official pretext for the demonstrations and the sacking of embassies was the presence of Vietcong and Vietminh troops in the border areas. No one knew better than Lon Nol that, even if NLF units came from time to time in the border areas, they did us no harm. If they had 'sanctuaries' these were in the sparsely populated forests in the north-east. There were none in the 'Parrot's Beak' – the flat ricelands which provided no cover. In any case the NLF looked towards Saigon, not Phnom Penh. They were fighting to liberate their own country, not to aggress ours. For years we had officially winked at their presence, just as the Moroccans and Tunisians had ignored the presence of Algerian resistance fighters in their territories during the Algerian resistance struggle. The Vietnamese resistance fighters came and went without disturbing the life of the frontier people. If they needed something and our people had it and wanted to sell, they bought and paid for it. They stayed away from our women. Our people were to have monstrously different experiences with

23

other types of Vietnamese when Lon Nol brought in Saigon troops!

It was from American bombs and shells that our peasants suffered in the frontier areas – not from the occasional presence of the Vietcong. And in the areas most frequently and most heavily bombed, there had never been any trace of the Vietcong. The corpses found after the bombings in Svay Rieng and other frontier areas were those of Cambodian peasants, including a high proportion of women and children. This is confirmed by scores of reports after investigations by the International Control Commission.[1]

In any case, if the Americans, with well over a million troops at their disposal, including over half a million of their own, could not seal off the frontier from their side, how could we be expected to do it from ours when we had a total of only 30,000 troops to guard all our frontiers, including the continually threatened border with Thailand? Lon Nol had always shared my views on this. If he was now using Vietcong presence as a pretext to reverse our policies, and to defy me, there must be something much more serious going on!

It was with these thoughts in mind that I told President Podgorny that I would go ahead with the original itinerary of my visit to Moscow, and then continue on to Peking as planned. In any case, I needed more time to watch developments in Phnom Penh. Later, people said I had missed my chance. Had I flown back immediately, I could have taken charge of things. We shall see whether this was correct or not.

The press reported that I had gone to Moscow to seek Soviet aid in expelling the Vietcong. This was not so. I had gone primarily to enlist their support for strengthening our military position. I wanted to negotiate a military aid agreement. There had been increasing incursions by US-Saigon forces from the east, and by the CIA-sponsored Khmer Serei (Free Khmer) traitor groups coming from their Thailand bases in the west. There were daily air violations. These were

1. Set up to supervise the implementation of the 1954 Geneva Ceasefire Agreements and composed of India as chairman, Canada and Poland. The ICC, in hundreds of investigations, never found any trace of Vietcong in the frontier areas.

the real threats, recognized as such by the Cambodian people. There had been no replacements of US military equipment since I had repudiated American military aid in 1963, so there was a lack of everything, especially transport. The army officers were restless, and there was a real risk that they would demand the restoration of US military aid unless something were done quickly. I even suggested that the Soviet Union send a small MAAG-type[1] military aid mission to Phnom Penh to evaluate our needs and instruct our armed forces in the use of Soviet weapons.

After a few days of talks, the Russians agreed to supply everything we needed. But by then it was too late.

Premier Kosygin gave me a splendid lunch at the Kremlin shortly before I left. He placed me opposite himself at the table and, with the coffee, we spoke of the situation in Cambodia:

'You must prevent Lon Nol and Sirik Matak from stabbing the NLF in the back,' he said. 'If they do this we will never forgive them. It is a difficult historical moment for our Vietnamese comrades. They are fighting for the liberation of their country. Get rid of Lon Nol and Sirik Matak! You have already given proof of your anti-imperialism. You have given precious support to the NLF. You have played a glorious role and we count on you in the future too.' I promised that my support for the NLF and their struggle for independence would never waver.

By that time I had received a telegram from Premier Chou En Lai expressing concern about events in Phnom Penh. On 17 March, after the discussion with Premier Kosygin, I immediately sent the following message to the Queen Mother:

The socialist camp considers recent events to be a direct threat to the balance of forces between the United States and itself. Premier Chou En Lai has asked our ambassador to inform me of the concern of China which, for the moment, is maintaining its calm regarding the provocations threatening its Phnom Penh embassy.

1. From the US Military Aid and Advisory Group which had performed a similar function in Saigon at the start of American involvement there.

25

The highest Soviet leaders have not refrained from telling me that they consider the present policy of our right wing to be extremely dangerous for the future of our country. The Russians have offered me aid of many kinds to restore order and neutrality in Cambodia, but, while thanking them, I have told them that I reserve the right to act according to my conscience as a Cambodian and in the behalf of what I believe to be the medium-and long-term interests of my country and my people.

One remark from Premier Kosygin seems to me to be particularly pregnant with meaning. I quote: 'Your Vietnamese allies have good memories. Just as they will never forget the support you have given them during a very difficult period of their struggle, so they will remember at an appropriate moment the foul blow which your extreme right has struck at an even more difficult and decisive moment in their struggle against American imperialism. If the right continues to strike such blows at our allies, it will inevitably mean war between Cambodia and Vietnam.' I hope our leaders who are playing the sorcerer's apprentice will meditate at length on these Soviet words.

The Queen Mother had already convoked Lon Nol and Sirik Matak, demanding that they call off the anti-Vietnamese riots. They countered with a proposal to send a delegation to negotiate with me. The Queen, on my behalf, justly refused. There was nothing to negotiate. It was a question of ceasing to violate policies embodied in our constitution, policies which had kept the war away from our frontiers. The Queen Mother expressed strong indignation at the sacking of the embassies and ordered Lon Nol and Sirik Matak to send written apologies and to pay for the damages.

After sending the telegrams, discussions resumed with the Soviet leaders, among whom appeared for the first time Leonid Brezhnev, First Secretary of the Soviet Communist Party's Central Committee. The talks again centred on the situation in Phnom Pehn and the effect this would have on the struggle in Vietnam. I received news of the arrest of some officers, known to be loyal to myself, and heard rumours of an attempt to arrest Lon Nol and Sirik Matak. This confirmed my fears of a grave crisis.

I left for Peking on the afternoon of the 18th. In the car, on the way to the airport, Premier Kosygin turned to me and said:

'There has been a vote in your National Assembly to strip you of your powers. What does that mean?' By this time we were almost at the airport. As I discovered later, members of my suite had heard the news on the radio, but could not bring themselves to tell me at that moment.

'What does it mean? It means that I have been deposed,' I replied.

'What do you intend to do about it?' he asked.

'I'll fight back, of course,' I replied.

Premier Kosygin then said: 'You can have absolute confidence in the Soviet Union's backing of your struggle. We will always support you – and to the end. You will see how it will be with the Chinese. They helped you while you were in power in Phnom Penh but now that you are no longer in power, you will see what they will do!'

I thanked him and said: 'I will continue on to Peking and get the support of my old friend, Chou En Lai. Then I shall return to Moscow.'

'Whatever you do, you can count on us,' replied Kosygin.

I told members of the Cambodian community who had come to see me off that I had just been deposed, but that since Moscow and Peking would not recognize the new régime, I would consider setting up a government to organize resistance.

President Podgorny had placed his own plane at my disposal – a very comfortable plane with plenty of room to work.

I hardly need describe my feelings in those first moments! My worst suspicions confirmed! Lon Nol turned traitor. That Sirik Matak acted as he had was no great surprise. He had hated me from childhood days because he thought his uncle, Prince Sisowath Monireth, should have been placed on the throne instead of myself. He even had a notion that he himself should have been chosen. I knew of his contacts with the CIA when he was ambassador in Tokyo, and later in Manila. But that Lon Nol had allied himself with Sirik Matak was a shock. There were still graver shocks to come regarding Lon Nol's treachery. What was to be done?

We held a meeting with Penn Nouth[1] and other members of

1. Elder statesman, several times Prime Minister.

my suite as soon as the plane was air-borne, and it was unanimously decided that we would appeal to our people to launch a resistance struggle.

My wife, Monique, who had consoled some of the other family members while the meeting was being held said: 'You have done so much, you have devoted your whole life to your country and now they have deposed you. It would be better, perhaps, if we retired to France.'

'No,' I said. 'Of all times, this is not the moment to hide ourselves. We would be condemned by history if we permitted Cambodia to become not only a military dictatorship but once more a colony. All my life I have dreamed and fought for my country's independence. I did not win it from France in order to abandon it now. The monarchy must not now stand aside. It is certain that U S imperialism will be beaten in Indo-China and we must participate in that struggle. The Americans will be beaten by the Vietnamese and our own Khmers Rouges,[1] together with us. And the Pathet Lao will win in Laos. It is the duty of the monarchy to remain with the people.'

Monique understood immediately. We sat down at a work table, Monique at my side, Penn Nouth opposite me. While our plane cruised 10,000 metres above the Siberian wastes I started drafting the Proclamation and Appeal to resistance, a document which has since attained historical significance like the famous 18 June Appeal of General de Gaulle which sparked the French resistance against the Nazi invaders. I think none of us slept on that flight; some of us were in a state of emotional turmoil which forbade rest, while Monique, Samdech Penn Nouth and myself worked without respite to finish the Proclamation. It was not actually broadcast until 23 March, because we had to study developments inside Cambodia before I could put the last touches to it. But, by the time our plane touched down at Peking airport, the major part of it had been completed.

1. Khmers Rouges (Cambodian Reds) is a loose description of communists and other leftists, at one time in opposition to the Royal Government, now an important component in the Cambodian National United Front and the resistance.

In Peking, Chou En Lai embraced me warmly as I stepped out of the plane. He knew me well enough to take it for granted that I would put up a fight and he had already acted on that assumption. He had convoked the entire diplomatic corps, which was lined up for my arrival. 'You remain the Head of State,' he said. 'The only one. We will never recognize another.' He said he was going to publish the name of every ambassador and chargé d'affaires, who had turned up for my arrival, in the official Hsinhua news service and Chinese newspapers, to emphasize the continuing recognition of myself as the Cambodian Head of State. By this time it was towards midday of the 19th and the news that I had been deposed was one day old. Some of the diplomats present still thought I might be able to redress the situation, and later abandoned me when I could not do so. But, with one or two exceptions, they were all there that morning – from forty-one countries altogether.

Then another memorable conversation held in a car. Almost the first words of Chou En Lai as we drove out of the airport were: 'Yesterday I discussed the situation with Chairman Mao. I have only one question: Are you going to fight?'

I replied: 'I am going to fight, and fight till the end.'

'Then we will give you every support,' declared Premier Chou. He then asked me to think it over for twenty-four hours. 'The way would be long and arduous,' he warned me, before the inevitable, final victory. There would be setbacks along the way.

'I know that my thinking is that of all Khmer patriots,' I replied. 'They will be with me and we will fight side by side against the US imperialists and their puppets.' I confirmed my decision the next day.

Reports in the Western press were to the effect that China hesitated for some days – according to Lon Nol's absurd version, weeks even – before deciding to assist me. But within twenty-four hours of my final decision I had issued my first statements over Radio Peking. How could I have done that had the Chinese not decided to support me? My first statements were on 20 and 21 March and the Proclamation was read on 23 March.

The day after I arrived in Peking, Premier Pham Van Dong arrived from Hanoi. He greeted me with fervour, and exclaimed: 'From now on we are comrades-in-arms. We are proud to have you in our camp in the struggle against US imperialism.' Western press reports spoke of some 'negotiations' with Pham Van Dong and 'mediation' by Chou En Lai. This was nonsense! Our solidarity had always been there. Now it was moved up to a higher level and buttressed by the force of events.

One of my first official acts in Peking was to receive the Soviet Chargé d'Affaires. I related my conversation with Premier Kosygin, and said that now I was assured of Chinese support and would welcome a public statement from the Soviet Union along the lines of Kosygin's *unofficial* assurances. The reply from the Soviet Chargé was that, because I was now on Chinese soil, it would be better first for the Chinese to make a public statement. The Soviet Union would follow suit. (I had thought that I was giving the Soviet Union a deserved political advantage in letting them be first to announce their official support, in return for them being ahead of China in giving me their unofficial pledge. But nothing came of this.)

The opening conversation with Pham Van Dong went something like this:

'How can we help?'

'Military instructors,' I replied. 'We have no lack of man-power and the Chinese have already promised arms. We lack trained cadres. You have the best in the world for the type of war we have to fight.'

'I'll tell Giap[1] to send you a couple of thousand of the best we have,' replied Premier Pham Van Dong. We discussed at length the best ways of coordinating the struggle of the three peoples of Indo-China and it was during that discussion that the first germs of the idea of a Summit Conference of the Peoples of Indo-China was generated.[2]

1. General Vo Nguyen Giap, Minister of Defence of the Democratic Republic of Vietnam, better known in the West as the 'victor of Dien Bien Phu'.

2. The Summit Conference of the Peoples of Indo-China was held, at

Later, I spoke with Chairman Mao for a couple of hours before he mounted the tribune at Tien An Men for the 1 May (1970) celebrations. He questioned me at length about Lon Nol, whom he had met during the previous 1 October festivities to mark the twentieth anniversary of the founding of the People's Republic of China, but who had made little impression on him. Mao was interested in everything going on in Cambodia and in my role in Cambodian affairs.

'I would rather shake the hand of a prince like you, who is a patriot,' he said, 'than with the so-called "sons-of-the-people" like certain other heads of state. You have played a splendid role. You deserve to be a communist.' This was the greatest tribute Mao could pay. He went on: 'You must tell us what you need. If we've got it, you'll have it. Anything we give you is nothing compare to what you give us by heading the struggle of the Cambodian people.'

During my first days in Peking in March, Premiers Chou En Lai and Pham Van Dong gave me categoric assurances that, after victory, Cambodia would be 'independent, sovereign, neutral and free of any Vietnamese military presence'.

'China is one country; Cambodia is another,' said Chou En Lai. 'China will remain communist, Cambodia should remain neutral.'

From the beginning, the Chinese government respected my independence of thought and action, my royalism, my nationalism, my Buddhism, my dignity. They offered generous financial aid and, out of respect for my feelings, they delicately call it a 'loan', repayable thirty years after victory.

The French Ambassador presented me with a message from his government, to the effect that if I retired to France, they would place a villa, a car and a chauffeur at my disposal. I thanked him and said: 'The Chinese government just offered me these things. But they were only the first instalment. The second part consists of support for my cause. So I must accept their two-part offer and refuse yours.'

---

my initiative, on 24–25 April 1970 in a border area between China and Indo-China. The main aim was to coordinate the resistance struggles of the three peoples of Indo-China.

After he departed, I suddenly recalled an incident which had occurred at Grasse, on the French Riviera, when I was undergoing medical attention there. I was invited to lunch by General Nhiek Tioulong.[1] As we walked towards the restaurant past people enjoying an early apéritif, I heard someone say: 'Look, there goes Bao Dai.[2] Look how fat and sleek he is. He lives like a grand seigneur and it's you and I who are paying for it.' (A case of mistaken identity but a warning as to the sort of attitude I could expect in accepting such offers!) In Peking when I took a walk, people recognized me for who I was and said: 'You are rendering a great service to our country, to Asia and the world. You helped the Vietnamese resistance heroes. Now the Cambodian people have joined in the fight and you are their leader.' That felt much better than being dubbed a fat and sleek Bao Dai by rich vacationers on the French Riviera.

Among the diplomats who came to see me in Peking was the Cambodian Ambassador, May Valentin.[3] I asked him to send some equipment for my secretariat, a duplicator and typewriters. This he did but a few days later he sent someone to collect them, and at the same time informed me that he had a long and important cabled message from Lon Nol.

This was no less than an order to cease all activities and to stop making public announcements! Or else . . . I immediately convoked the Cambodian community in the presence of the ambassador and read out the message.

'What is your reply to Lon Nol?' asked Valentin.

'This,' I said and, tearing the cable into pieces, I flung it down and ground it under my heel. 'Send him this for my reply.' He picked up the scraps and withdrew. (He later confiscated two cases of diplomatic gifts which, as Head of State, I normally distribute on such official visits!)

Between 5 and 7 April, Chou En Lai was on an official visit to the Democratic People's Republic of Korea. In his speeches

1. At various times Minister of Defence or Commander-in-Chief of the Cambodian armed forces.
2. The 'ex-emperor' of Vietnam under the French and Japanese. Deposed in 1955 by Ngo Dinh Diem, he retired to the French Riviera.
3. Later sent by Lon Nol as ambassador to Australia.

and those of Marshal Kim Il Sung, as well as in the joint communiqué, the strongest support was expressed for the Khmer National United Front (set up as the result of my Appeal) and for myself as Head of State. I again met with the Soviet Chargé d'Affaires and pointed out to him that China's support was now open and official and that I would appreciate a similar statement by his government.

'But the statement of support was not made on Chinese soil,' he replied.

'I have no objection if Premier Kosygin would make a similar statement on Polish or Czech soil,' I riposted.

A month later, we set up the Royal Cambodian Government of National Union in Peking, with the three key ministeries of Defence, Internal Affairs and Information, on free Cambodian soil. This government was immediately recognized by over twenty states, but not by the Soviet Union, nor – with the notable exceptions of Albania, Rumania and Yugoslavia – by any of the European socialist states.

Many people have criticized me for being too dependent on China because part of our government is located on Chinese soil. But, in fact, a very substantial half of our government is deeply rooted in Cambodian soil. My original idea was to pay a short visit to Peking to secure concrete terms of support from China. I admired the way the North Vietnamese had achieved a balance in their relations with Peking and Moscow. They had China in one pan, the Soviet Union in the other, so the scales were balanced. We now have China in one pan – but the other is empty! (China is not, incidentally, opposed to the Soviet Union helping my cause. In fact, Chou En Lai has assured me that this could be a factor leading to some slight improvement in Sino-Soviet relations.) But what can we do? We are very satisfied that China respects our sovereignty and our way of thinking. But we would like to have both the major socialist countries with us. We would then have all the others as well.

Premier Kosygin was very emphatic that I prevent Lon Nol and Sirik Matak from stabbing the N L F in the back. We in fact had done our best by tackling the Lon Nol–Sirik

Matak coalition, the Saigon forces and the American air force without outside help. What more could he ask? And who is stabbing who in the back now Lon Nol and Sirik Matak never stopped their betrayal of the NLF but, nonetheless, the Soviet Union rewards them. Not only do the Soviets keep an embassy in Phnom Penh and maintain diplomatic relations with the traitor régime, but they send medical and surgical equipment to patch up the troops of Lon Nol whom we have put out of action, so they can attack us again. In October 1971, the Soviet Union renewed a financial agreement with that same Lon Nol régime which Premier Kosygin assured me he would 'never forgive'. I am now, in 1972, with the NLF; our troops fight side by side.

I reminded Premier Kosygin of his words to me at our last meeting, in a message I sent him on 15 January 1971. Recalling the warning of the Soviet government to the Lon Nol régime on 24 May 1970, two months after the coup, to the effect that Cambodia should return to the path of 'peace and neutrality' and reject that of uniting 'with the forces of aggression and transforming itself into a base for war against neighbouring peoples'. In my message I pointed out that Lon Nol was doing just the opposite to the course advised by the Soviet government. Among other things, I said it was 'not refraining from stabbing in the back the Vietnamese people who are fighting in very difficult conditions against US imperialism for the liberation of South Vietnam as your Excellency textually expressed it during our last interview at the Kremlin'.

Furthermore, in the same message, I appealed to Premier Kosygin 'to completely break off diplomatic relations with the anti-constitutional, anti-national, anti-popular, anti-communist, fascist and pro-imperialist republic . . . and to accord official recognition to the Royal Government of National Union'. I pleaded further that if it was 'still impossible' to recognize our government that, in 'awaiting that happy day', the Soviet government should put pressure on the United States to halt its armed intervention and that of the Saigon régime and 'grant, as speedily as possible military and other aid to the Cambodian People's Armed Forces'. Nothing came of this.

We were happy with the example set by Raoul Roa, the Foreign Minister of Cuba. Shortly after the coup, the Cambodian Ambassador asked to see him – and was greeted as a friend.

'You're going to fight on the side of Prince Sihanouk?' asked the Foreign Minister.

'No. He's been kicked out and everyone is for Lon Nol.'

'Get out of my office,' said Roa. 'Don't soil my chair any longer. I give you twenty-four hours to quit Havana. You are not only a traitor to Sihanouk but a disgrace to your people. No – I won't shake your hand. I'm only sorry that I shook it when you came in here.'

Soviet officials in Pyongyang told the North Korean Foreign Ministry that it was a mistake to withdraw their diplomats from Phnom Penh.

'Once you withdraw it will be difficult to get back,' they said.

This was reported to Premier Kim Il Sung and his reaction was:

'Better to leave a Cambodia without Sihanouk than to remain in a Cambodia with Lon Nol.'

The question which interested everyone – not the least, myself – was how this coup could have been organized, and what were the essential elements involved? A full and accurate reply would be of far-reaching importance, not only to Cambodia but in pointing a warning finger to the future for leaders who would dare defend their country's independence and national dignity against internal and external foes, whatever their origin.

Chapter 2

Organizing Treachery

In early September 1969, I left by plane for Hanoi to attend funeral ceremonies for the revered founder and leader of the Vietnamese independence struggle, the late President Ho Chi Minh. I had deeply admired 'Uncle' Ho. He belonged not only to Vietnam, but to Indo-China, to Asia, and even to the world, for he stood for the rights of oppressed people everywhere; in the former colonies, and for the blacks of the United States as well. For me, an Asian, he was above all a fellow Asian.

He had sent me affectionate notes. I had wanted very much to see him, especially during recent years, and had requested permission to see him in Hanoi. But when the bombings started, my North Vietnamese friends said it would be too dangerous.

'This is just the time to show my solidarity,' I argued.

'But you are the Head of State, and also our great friend,' they replied. 'We cannot accept the responsibility, before your people, of risking your life because of the air raids.' So we had never met.

As the plane took off, I thought how ironic and sad it was that my first visit should be occasioned by the death of my friend. I learned later that hardly had my plane left – right at the airport – than Sirik Matak turned to his friends, of whom Lon Nol was one, and said that now was the perfect time to depose me. At the very moment that Vietminh and Vietcong troops are illegally occupying Cambodian soil, the 'traitor' Sihanouk is flying to the funeral of their chief and has had the audacity to order official ceremonies of mourning for him in Phnom Penh. What better occasion could arise?

Sirik Matak predicted that, if it were done immediately, I would never dare to return. However Lon Nol was not prepared to act just then. His wife had died and he was still more occupied with the Buddhist ceremonies. He wanted to wait for a more propitious moment. (Lon Nol is extremely superstitious and he knew that no oracle would recommend interrupting his wife's funeral to stage a *coup d'état*.)

From sources in the United States I learned later that the CIA had drawn up a directive a month earlier recommending support for such a coup which a CIA contact on Lon Nol's staff had promised would take place in the 'near future'. By the time I flew off to Hanoi, the CIA had already assured Lon Nol of their support. It remained only for Lon Nol and Sirik Matak to work out the details and agree on the timing. As part of this scenario, I was to be assassinated if I happened to be in the country at the time.

Confirmation of what was going on at that time is contained in an interview given to an Australian professor and Asian expert, Milton Osborne, published in the *Age* of Melbourne on 12 January 1971. Son Thai Nguyen, who gave the interview, is a Vietnamese of Cambodian ethnic origin, a member of the South Vietnamese Senate. More importantly for this narrative, he is the brother of Son Ngoc Thanh, my life-long enemy, a puppet premier under the Japanese and head of the CIA-subsidized Khmer Serei (Free Khmer) traitor group. Son Thai Ngyuen is quoted as saying that his brother 'was guided throughout his long years of exile by a burning desire to bring down Sihanouk' and Osborne continues: 'According to Son Thai Nguyen, Lon Nol made clandestine contact with Son Ngoc Thanh in September 1969 . . . and began tentative discussions about overthrowing Sihanouk. Despite this step Lon Nol was still unready to act and the matter lapsed temporarily when Lon Nol went to France for medical treatment.'

The scene now shifts to the American Hospital at Neuilly-sur-Seine, on the outskirts of Paris. After the funeral ceremonies for his late wife were completed, Lon Nol suddenly found it necessary to go to France for treatment of a shoulder injury received when a jeep, driven by his fellow-officer and rival, General Nhiek Tioulong, overturned in a ditch, pinning Lon Nol underneath.

By a strange coincidence, some American 'patients' were admitted to the hospital at the same time as Lon Nol. These 'patients' showed no visible signs of injury or evidence of malady. They were, in fact, American CIA 'advisers', experts on coup-making. I was later to receive descriptions of these individuals from Cambodian students, because word had quickly spread around the student community in Paris that the easiest way to raise some 'quick money' was to call on the 'ailing' Prime Minister, Lon Nol, and listen sympathetically to whatever he had to say. Five hundred francs (about a hundred dollars) was the usual payment for a first visit. Lon Nol's aide, Colonel Kang Keng, always made it clear to the students that they should show their gratitude in the future for Lon Nol's bounty.

From this well-camouflaged headquarters Lon Nol telephoned instructions daily to Sirik Matak and other co-plotters. This was the period of advanced planning. The journalist, T. D. Allman, in the *Guardian*[1] after having interviewed some of the ringleaders, including Son Ngoc Thanh, wrote that some observers believed that Lon Nol, unlike Sirik Matak, was not wholeheartedly behind the plot. This of course was incorrect and the impression was doubtless created by Lon Nol's reluctance to act (a) at the moment of the funeral ceremonies and (b) until he was absolutely certain that he had the necessary US support to succeed. Allman correctly reports that 'my sources agreed that Lon Nol all along had manipulated events from afar; we always acted with his approval, on his instructions. He ran the government – and our plans – by telephone from Paris'; this was how Allman's sources expressed it. The missing element in his account was that the 'instructions . . . by telephone' came directly from a gang of conspirators in pyjamas working out of the Lon Nol–CIA operational headquarters at the American Hospital

For months prior to Lon Nol's departure for Paris in October 1969, there had been large-scale 'desertions' among

1. On 14 and 18 August and 18 September 1971.

the Thailand-based Khmer Serei troops, mentioned earlier as being wholly created, owned, armed, financed by and dependent on, the CIA. At first, individuals crossed over, then squads and finally company-sized and even bigger units. As early as January 1969, there had been one group of just over two hundred which crossed into Cambodia from Thailand and immediately 'deserted'. In May of the same year, a unit of over three hundred men who had come from the Khmer Serei base at Phnom Malai 'rallied' to our forces. Lon Nol, the Commander-in-Chief, gave himself the credit for all this as a triumph for his propaganda efforts to win over the traitors. He advised that they should be permitted to settle down in Battambang province – close to Thailand – more or less in units. He even incorporated some of them into the Phnom Penh garrison as well as into the Military Police.

There was a curious sequel to one such mass 'desertion'. I had set aside one million riels[1] from our National Mutual Aid work fund to give the 'deserters' a new start in life, and to encourage others to follow them. They returned the money, stating that, as they had 'deserted for patriotic reasons', they could not accept it. Strange words from people who were supposed to have arrived with nothing but their weapons! It later became clear that a million riels was small stuff compared to what they were getting from the CIA. I was perplexed by the reports that, although they had refused my money, they were spending freely. These men had remained true to the code of the mercenary and were loyal to the far richer hand that was feeding them. They had been instructed to refuse my money to convince me of their 'patriotism'.

Another curious matter: during my visit to Hanoi, Premier Pham Van Dong, a most intelligent and sensitive person, whose burning patriotism and honesty I appreciated the more I got to know him, brought to my notice something of which I had had no knowledge. The Chinese had been in the habit of buying our rice for dollars. The rice was then delivered to the National Front of Liberation of South Vietnam. It was sent in army lorries to agreed pick-up points near the

1. The official rate was thirty-five riels to the dollar at that time.

frontier, then carted off by the NLF. Lon Nol had been advanced an important sum of dollars for rice to be delivered in the latter half of 1969. But, according to Pham Van Dong, none had been delivered. The same thing had occurred with badly needed medicines. I promised to look into the matter. These were perfectly straightforward, commercial transactions that had been going on for years, and I could not understand what the difficulty was.

Our Vietnamese friends were justifiably astonished over the missing shipments for, in May 1969, we had elevated the status of the NLF representation in Phnom Penh to that of an embassy and now we seemed to be cheating. We had been one of the first states to recognize the Provisional Revolutionary Government immediately after its formation in June 1969. Shortly thereafter we had been the first country to receive an official visit from Huynh Tan Phat, Prime Minister of the new government, and had signed a trade treaty.

Lon Nol had become Prime Minister in August 1969, and had demanded as the condition of heading the government, that he have full powers. I received only evasive replies on the subject of the rice deliveries, and soon after I returned to Peking from the Ho Chi Minh funeral, Lon Nol left for Peking to represent our country at the National Day ceremonies marking the twentieth anniversary of the founding of the People's Republic of China. Normally I would have gone, but Princess Margaret of England was visiting Cambodia at the time. Lon Nol was accorded every mark of attention throughout his stay, being given the place of honour alongside Chairman Mao Tse-tung on the Tien An Men tribune for the October First parade.

Pham Van Dong was also in Peking and, through the intermediary of Chou En Lai, he was able to raise the question of the non-deliveries of rice and medicines. Lon Nol refused point-blank to give any assurances of delivery, giving as a pretext the presence of North Vietnamese and Vietcong troops in the frontier areas. I had a full report on this by the time he returned and told him either to resume the shipments immediately or return the money. Up to the time he left for Paris, Lon Nol had done neither.

By this time, Sirik Matak, whom Lon Nol had chosen as his deputy – acting Premier once Lon Nol left for abroad – had circularized all ministers and heads of departments, forbidding them to send any dossiers direct to the Head of State, as had been the custom till then. Everything had to be sent to the Prime Minister's office and I was to receive only what Sirik Matak thought fit for me to see. Anyone disobeying this instruction was threatened with 'severe punishment'. In retrospect it is clear that Lon Nol and Sirik Matak, once they had received CIA backing for their intended coup, had begun to act as though it was already a *fait accompli*.

The Lon Nol–Sirik Matak cabinet, set up in August 1969, represented the local compradores, feudal elements and their foreign backers. After the cabinet was formed, Lon Nol announced there was to be no more nationalization of private industries and that some state enterprises would be restored to the private sector. Thus on 15 November 1969, the ministers for the Economy and Commerce, Op Kim Ang and Prom Thos respectively, introduced measures to denationalize the import-export trade, to end the state monopoly on the production of alcoholic drinks, pharmaceuticals and other goods and to permit the operation of private and foreign banks.

At a session of the National Congress[1] from 27 to 29 December, I left it to delegates to decide for or against these retrograde measures, but I warned of the evil consequences 'when the swindlers will infiltrate Cambodia with the foreign banks in order to corrupt the elite, sap our economy and try to change the régime'. I cautioned against the role of 'foreign banks which serve interests other than those of Cambodia, and transfer abroad huge amounts of currency leaving an absurdly small amount to the state'.

Sirik Matak, as I learned later, thought that this period of denationalization might be the propitious moment to strike. T. D. Allman, in the articles referred to earlier, writes that, according to his sources,

the anti-Sihanouk faction was ready to oust Sihanouk in December

1. The National Congress of the Popular Socialist Community was held twice a year, its decisions binding on the National Assembly.

1969, during a national congress held in Phnom Penh. The sources said that 4,000 military police and soldiers under the command of Lon Nol were ordered to pack the meeting which Sihanouk used as a sounding board for his programme. Seeing he was outgunned, Sihanouk let the Congress vote for Sirik Matak's policies rather than dissolve the government and call for new elections.

Although much that T. D. Allman relates is correct, this passage is not. Lon Nol was already in France. The 'toughs' were all the Khmer Serei infiltrated into the Phnom Penh garrison by Lon Nol and directed by his brother, Colonel Lon Non, a fascist with political ambitions of his own. My police had informed me of the strong-arm infiltrators. The Khmers Rouges had also mobilized large numbers of their men, in defence of my previous economic policies which were supported by the vast majority of delegates and the public.

When the time neared for a vote, it became clear that the public would vehemently oppose the new measures. The Khmers Serei were afraid to expose themselves, and went with the majority, so the result was a unanimous vote against Sirik Matak's measures.

Much has been written about that National Congress, fated to be the last, for this form of democratic public action was quickly suppressed by the Lon Nol–Sirik Matak régime. This was the beginning of an onslaught against all democratic practices which had been built up since independence.

A few days after the Congress ended, I entered a hospital in Phnom Penh for medical treatment, and on 7 January, I left with my wife and a small suite, including Samdech Penn Nouth, for further treatment at Dr Pathé's clinic at Grasse. I normally took a cure there every two years. I needed complete rest, and treatment for certain chronic ailments, and I thought it would be a salutary lesson for Sirik Matak and his supporters to have a free hand and let them see how well they could solve our economic ills by scrapping my policies. After the cure I intended to pay political visits to Paris, Moscow and Peking. I would seek economic, financial and military aid during those visits and return home strengthened for a renewed effort to put our economy in order by our own means and the help of our real friends. I was convinced that, within a few months, Sirik Matak would have so compromised himself through shady financial deals that the nation would be glad to go back to the lines laid down during the first years of independence.

I had no idea of what had gone on, and was still going on, at the American Military Hospital at Neuilly, nor of Lon Nol's treacherous meeting with Son Ngoc Thanh while I was in Hanoi! My Minister of Security was Colonel Sosthène Fernandez, who later won notoriety at Saan, a town south-east of Phnom Penh, by utilizing Vietnamese Catholic men, women and children as a shield to protect his troops advancing on our resistance forces. Fernandez, supposedly a devout Catholic himself, knew of the plot to depose me, but never informed me.

T. D. Allman writes that his sources 'all of whom still hold high posts in Phnom Penh' (or did at the time he was writing), assured him that Lon Nol, Sirik Matak 'and important members of the High Command and Parliament, conspired to overthrow Sihanouk by force of arms and to assassinate him if necessary, as early as six months before the coup actually occurred'. This is further confirmation of the conversation overheard at the airport early in September.

On 18 February 1970, Lon Nol returned to Phnom Penh with the completed plans for what he was to do exactly a month later. He immediately toured the garrisons in the frontier areas, exhorting officers and men to prepare for the great confrontation with the 'hereditary Vietnamese enemy'. This was not his only activity. Allman reports that

the final steps in Sihanouk's removal were planned in a series of high-level clandestine meetings held in Phnom Penh in the early months of 1970. Several of them were held in the homes of Lon Nol and Sirik Matak; others occurred in moving cars to avoid detection by Sihanouk's secret police ... The results of the meetings, I was told, were personal orders issued by Lon Nol and Sirik Matak instructing the Minister of Education, Chan Sokhum, to arrange anti-Vietcong demonstrations in the communist-infiltrated province of Svay Rieng, and later in Phnom Penh itself.

This is exact. Leaflets and posters were prepared in advance in the printing plant of the Ministry of Information and Education on the orders of Chan Sokhum, to be distributed at the 'spontaneous' demonstrations. Because of Sirik Matak's orders censoring the dossiers before they reached me and because of the treachery of Sosthène Fernandez, I was cleverly and totally cut off from just the sort of information that would have enabled me to sense what was coming. On 9 March by order of Chan Sokhum, there were small anti-Vietcong demonstrations, mainly by school-teachers, students and pupils in the town of Svay Rieng and in five or six other small towns in the 'Parrot's Beak' area of Svay Rieng province. These were small dress-rehearsals for the 'main attraction' to be staged in Phnom Penh on 11 March. Loyal students had been artfully fooled into believing the demonstrations were to 'strengthen Sihanouk's hand' in my forthcoming talks in Moscow and Peking. The demonstrations were fully reported in the Phnom Penh press (Lon Nol had already taken over the Ministry of Information and had the press and radio under his control) as 'spontaneous patriotic outbursts of popular wrath'.

The T. D. Allman version of what happened next is worth quoting and correcting, firstly because it is the nearest authentic account published to date, second, because it has acquired something of an official aspect. Senator Mike Mansfield, a staunch friend of Cambodia, felt impelled to record the three Allman articles in the US Congressional (Senate) Record,[1] accompanied by a highly indignant commentary of his own.

After the small demonstrations on 8 March for students and teachers in Svay Rieng, larger demonstrations were ordered for Phnom Penh. Government sound trucks urged the students to demonstrate, and officers of the Government-created Assembly of Youth arranged for students to assemble at the two communist embassies.

However, the actual sackings of the embassies which, together with Sihanouk's fall and a Cambodian ultimatum to the communists, provided a *casus belli*, was arranged through the Cambodian

1. US Congressional (Senate) Record of 13 October 1971, pages S16252–4.

44

High Command and actually carried out by squads of military police in plain clothes under the command of Lon Non.

Here one must note that these squads were not just military police, but there were also CIA-trained commandos recruited from the Cambodian minority in South Vietnam and brought into Phnom Pehn a month before the coup to serve as storm-troopers for the plotters. Allman continues:

The demonstrations of 11 March were just one part of a planned two-part effort to oust the prince. 'We planned two demonstrations,' one of my sources said. 'One for the 11th to create the crisis, the other on 16 March to provide the pretext for ousting Sihanouk.'

(This sounds like a technique the CIA have taught Lon Nol at the cost of much effort, for he was not known among us for his quick grasp of political affairs!)

However, the anti-Sihanouk demonstrations on 16 March failed, when pro-Sihanouk students surrounded the National Assembly. The Phnom Penh police, also pro-Sihanouk, that day arrested 20 hand-picked demonstrators carrying anti-Sihanouk tracts as they moved towards the Assembly. As a result, I was told, 'it appeared for the moment we were foiled'.

Inside the National Assembly that day, anti-Sihanouk deputies, including the acting president of the Assembly, In Tam,[1] were waiting for the demonstration to materialize in the hope that they would stampede Parliament into ousting Sihanouk. Instead, 'we began to be attacked for our anti-Sihanouk statements. The Assembly adjourned in confusion'.

1. At the time Allman was writing, In Tam was still Minister of the Interior. He was sacked later by Lon Nol for his failure to implement the latter's plan for 'pacification' of the provinces. As 'President' of the Assembly, it was In Tam who gave Lon Nol the six stars of a 'marshal'. In return, Lon Nol gave him one star as 'brigadier-general'. But he took it away again when, in March 1971, 'General' In Tam proved incapable of following after the Saigon puppet troops in their ill-fated attempt to try to recapture Kratié, on the Mekong River. Named as one of America's 'white hopes' for the future following Lon Nol's disastrous defeats in the 'Chenla 2' operation in November–December 1971, In Tam tried to make a come-back as chairman of the 'constituent' Assembly after Lon Nol dissolved the existing National Assembly. In Tam opposed Lon Nol in the farcical 'presidential elections' in June 1972 and was predictably beaten.

One detail needs to be added. The main order of business for the 16 March meeting of the National Assembly was to remove the Secretary of State for Defence, Oum Manncrine and the Secretary of State for Security, Colonel Sosthène Fernandez, from their posts, ostensibly for corruption. In reality this was to decapitate the forces which the plotters feared might be mobilized in my defence at the first sign of a military coup. 'Corruption' had as little to do with the matter as the 'Vietcong sanctuaries'. Due to the well-known opportunist character of Fernandez, the plotters did not want to take a chance. However, because the demonstration had taken a different turn, Lon Nol and the others hesitated to go any further on the 16th.

As at the National Congress three months earlier, the real sentiments of the people prevailed. The strength of their support for me scared the plotters, not to mention the National Assembly deputies. (Two deputies were later beaten to death in Kompong Cham Province when they tried to explain why they had voted to depose me on 18 March. One of Lon Nol's brothers was also killed there at that time.)

It must be explained why the deputies at that time were less representative of public opinion than at any time since we adopted the parliamentary system.

In a later chapter I explain at length why I did not think it necessary for Cambodia to ape Western-style democracy with its multi-party system, 'loyal opposition', and so on. The results, even in the West where the system has been operating for centuries, were not convincing enough for it to be introduced into Cambodia, where there were no such traditions to support it. Our brief experiment with multi-party 'democracy' had proved disappointing to say the least. The Sangkum,[1] which I founded, was a fusion of political parties. In order to ensure a fair representation of left, right, and centre tendencies in the National Assembly, candidates for election were pre-selected by the Sangkum leadership. This method provided a measure of balance and stability, something very rare in South-East Asia, and did much to preserve national unity.

1. Sangkum Reastr Niyum (Popular Socialist Community).

46

Prior to the September 1966 elections which resulted in the 6th National Assembly (the one that deposed me) the CIA had financed an all-out press campaign against my so-called dictatorship. I was accused of having adopted the Marxist 'single-party system', of having 'massacred Cambodian democracy'. Tirades to this effect also poured out of the Khmer Serei transmitters which the CIA had put at Son Ngoc Thanh's disposal in Thailand and, quite simply, I fell into a CIA trap. In response to the press campaign at home and abroad, I decided to allow a completely free choice of candidates, with no pre-selection from above. The result was chaos. There were as many as twenty or thirty candidates for a single seat. The richest of the bourgeoisie, natural allies of the Americans, spent money like water, financing electoral campaigns for candidates who, for the most part, were merely their stooges. Voters received clothing, medicine, free cinema and theatre tickets and toys and sweets for their children from the sponsors of candidates. There was no way for the voters to distinguish between demagogues and honest candidates between truth and lies. The result was that only three candidates, of any merit were elected for the ninety-one seats. The three were from the 'left' and were chosen by overwhelming majorities. A campaign was soon whipped up against them as 'communists' and they left for embryo resistance bases – as a means of surviving, and to be ready for the worst. (They are now key ministers in the Royal Government of National Union, directing the struggle from the spot.)

Regarding that crucial 1966 election, it is interesting to note the views of a Frenchman, Daniel Roy, who lived many years in Cambodia, and who gives this version in *Le Monde Diplomatique* of April 1970:

In 1966, the electors found themselves disorientated because Sihanouk, wishing undoubtedly to escape accusations of personal power, permitted several candidates of the Sangkum to contest each other in each electoral district. Thus, one saw the curious spectacle of several candidates calling for votes offering the same programme under the same label. These candidates, in order to compete, resorted to demagogic methods, and made wide use of arguments which had only far-fetched relationships with ideologies. They outbid one another making promises which were impossible to keep, in an expensive debauchery of publications and leaflets, and in the distribution of advantages of all kinds; positions, honour and money. In this game, it was, with few exceptions, the most wealthy, and the feudalists, who triumphed.

This was by far the worst legislature elected since independence. The deputies, elected by bribes and corruption, were only awaiting the day when the dollars would start to pour in – as Lon Nol and Sirik Matak had promised. In anticipation of a massive return of US personnel – spearheaded by bankers and aid missions – there was a rush to build blocks of apartments to be let at exorbitant rents.

Small wonder that, on 16 March 1970, faced with hostile demonstrations outside the National Assembly, the deputies were torn by conflicting emotions: fear of the wrath of the people if they took the irrevocable step demanded by Lon Nol and Sirik Matak; fear of the loss of the long-promised dollar dividends if they did not act now. The day passed, as Allman reports, 'in confusion', without the decisive blow anticipated by the plotters.

Chapter Three

The Road to 18 March

Lon Nol and Sirik Matak were determined to repair the weakness in their position revealed on 16 March. Allman tells of another 'high-ranking meeting' at the home of Sirik Matak on the night of 16 March at which the plotter is quoted as saying: 'We have gone too far now to turn back.' So there may still have been some doubts in the minds of the conspirators. Lon Nol seems to have been plagued with doubts throughout – not because of pangs of conscience at his treachery, but misgivings if he could pull it off. Despite the assurances he had from his CIA experts in France, he was not completely convinced and was still afraid of hitches when he returned. In Milton Osborne's interview with Son Ngoc Thanh's brother, referred to earlier, Son Thai Nguyen is quoted as saying that:

When Lon Nol returned in February 1970, he again made contact with Son Ngoc Thanh, on some occasions travelling secretly to the Cambodian–South Vietnamese border himself, on other occasions working through intermediaries.

Osborne then quotes Son Thai Ngyen regarding his brother's fears that his own armed forces were not strong, or loyal enough, to defeat armed opposition to the coup:

He therefore sought a promise of material aid from Son Ngoc Thanh and this, his brother states, Thanh readily gave. Son Ngoc Thanh assured Lon Nol that Khmer Serei and ethnic Cambodian troops fighting with the American and South Vietnamese special forces in Vietnam would aid Lon Nol.

It was at this point, only shortly before the actual deposition took place, that Lon Nol, with Prince Sirik Matak very much a secondary figure, took the decision to overthrow Sihanouk.

49

As both the Khmer Serei and the 'Special Forces' were CIA units, Son Ngoc Thanh obviously could not have given such assurances unless the CIA was backing the whole enterprise.

After the 16 March meeting, Lon Nol agreed to go ahead and use the army to arrest key security personnel known to be loyal to me. That night, Major Buor Horl, head of the Phnom Penh police, together with officers loyal to Colonel Oum Mannorine, tried to avert the coup by striking first and arresting Lon Nol and Sirik Matak. But it was too late, and Mannorine was placed under house arrest. Lon Nol had the strong cards in his hands and Khmer Serei storm-troops at his disposal.

That night and the next day, he used selected units to arrest not only Colonel Mannorine and Major Horl, but also Colonel Huor Truok, governor of the strategic mountain resort of Kirirom; Colonel Pheng Phang Y of the Royal Army Staff Headquarters; Colonel Krauch Samrach, Commander of the Parachute Units; the governor of Kandal Province, adjoining Phnom Penh; and about fifteen other high-ranking officers. The head of the Army Signal Corps was killed during this action. I had originally set 18 March as the day for my return to Phnom Penh from Paris, after the initial news of the sacking of the Vietnamese embassies. By that morning the airport was sealed off; there were barbed-wire barricades along the road from the airport to Phnom Penh; machine-gun nests were located at all principal street corners and tanks and armoured cars patrolled the streets. In other words, sufficient force had been deployed to intimidate the citizens of Phnom Penh not to repeat their demonstrations of two days earlier, and to inject a little courage into the timid hearts of the National Assembly politicians.

'Only after Lon Nol's troops had taken over the civilian government of Phnom Pehn,' reports Allman, 'and tanks had surrounded the building [of the National Assembly, N.S.], did the actual vote ousting Sihanouk take place.'

The National Assembly, as its first act in ushering in a 'new era of freedom, democracy and republicanism' voted to suspend constitutional liberties for six months! After they had rubber-stamped the installation of this military dictatorship, the deputies proceeded to depose me by a 'secret vote' in which they had to sign the ballots before dropping them into the urn! Considering the show of force outside, and the arrests of the previous day, it was hardly a surprise that the vote to depose me was unanimous.

In my place they selected Cheng Heng, a rich landowner, President of the General Assembly, and a man whose chief claim to administrative experience till then had been running Phnom Penh's central prison. He was an insignificant puppet, not likely to give his masters at home or abroad any trouble.

A straw in the wind to which I had paid little attention at the time but which assumed its full significance later, was the following: a wealthy rubber-plantation owner, le Comte de Beaumont, who had big holdings in the Chup area near the South Vietnamese frontier, had been especially assiduous in courting my friendship. Because my father, on his deathbed, had recommended him to me, I entertained cordial relations with him, and no sojourn in France was complete without his invitation. But when I was in France in 1970, and heard nothing from him, I took the initiative and tried to contact him. Perhaps he was ill? 'Out of France' was the reply I received. As chance would have it, I learned that he was, in fact, in France – a revelation which merited little more than raised eyebrows at the time. Later I understood the reason for this little evasion.

In the first half of 1969, when Samdech Penn Nouth was Prime Minister, in order to protect our foreign-exchange holdings, he had limited the amount of foreign-exchange profits that could be transferred back to France. A proportion of plantation profits had to remain in the country and could be reinvested in the economy of the plantations. Le Comte de Beaumont had protested to Sirik Matak, who assured him that within a short time Sihanouk would be eliminated and he, Sirik Matak, would be at the helm. Monsieur le Comte could then be assured that all of his profits would be exported. Why, then, continue to be polite to a Sihanouk doomed to oblivion? But within two months after the coup, le Comte de Beaumont's rubber plantations and installations had been reduced to ashes and rubble – destroyed by the new allies of Lon Nol and Sirik Matak. For the Saigon régime did not brook the competition of Cambodian rubber and Chup was one of the very first targets of its air force. It was for the interests of men such as le Comte de Beaumont that Lon Nol and Sirik Matak and their co-plotters assassinated Cambodian neutrality and independence!

The rationalization for the putsch – the existence of the so-called sanctuaries, bases and supply lines of the NLF – was a sham. It was Lon Nol himself who signed many of the agreements with the NLF, agreements which the NLF had scrupulously respected. Lon Nol knew that, at one period, when we were under pressure from Thailand, it was the fact that the NLF occupied virtually the whole of the South Vietnamese side of our frontier that permitted him to transfer troops to the frontier with Thailand. The sudden noise about 'Vietcong implantation' was a smokescreen which I recognized as such immediately. T. D. Allman also came to this conclusion in a series of articles referred to earlier:

Interestingly enough, my informants, in the course of half a dozen interviews, never named Sihanouk's foreign policy of maintaining good relations with the Vietnamese Communists as a reason for ousting him.

'Frankly,' said one of the informants, 'Sihanouk was as anti-Communist as we were.' Another said: 'He had been in power too long. We wanted it. The only way we could get at him was by attacking the Vietcong.'

The former statement was only partly correct. I was not as 'anti-communist' as were those plotters. A very concrete illustration of this could be seen within a few days after the coup. Lon Nol began to collaborate with the American and Saigon forces immediately, first by exchanging intelligence information, then by combining operations against the NLF in the frontier areas. For years the Americans and the Saigon régime had been pressuring me to fight the NLF and my refusal to do so was a major bone of contention between Phnom Penh and Washington. To cover up their battlefield defeats in South Vietnam, American commanders – especially Westmoreland and Creighton Abrams, maintained that the only thing preventing 'complete victory' was the 'Cambodian sanctuaries'.

I refused to submit to Washington for two reasons. First, it would have meant surrendering neutrality. Second, I, together with the vast majority of the Cambodian people, genuinely sympathized with the Vietnamese resistance fighters who were clearly waging a bitter struggle against U S aggression. The more I met with the leaders of the N L F and the D R V in Hanoi, the more I appreciated their patriotism, self-sacrificing spirit, and warm, human qualities. I testified to this admiration by decreeing three days of national mourning when President Ho Chi Minh died. Although this was the moment when Lon Nol was shouting loudest about the Khmers Rouges and 'Vietcong implantation', I ordered the same ceremonies for Ho Chi Minh as I would have for the death of a leader of our own people. There were prayers by a hundred religious dignitaries in the throne room of the Royal Palace, in the presence of the highest officials of the Kingdom, and special memorial music diffused by Radio Phnom Penh. Incidentally, I was the only Head of State to attend the funeral ceremonies in Hanoi. (Premier Pham Van Dong recalled all this with gratitude when we met in Peking a few days after I had been deposed.)

It is true that I did not want communism in Cambodia. Under the influence of Lon Nol who – as I clearly understood when it was too late – wanted me to concentrate my gaze on an enemy on the left to conceal his own plotting with the extreme right, I was sometimes too harsh with my Khmers Rouges, especially when I reasoned that their activities could endanger our neutrality and independence.

What was perfectly accurate in the testimony of Allman's high-level informants was their trying 'to get at Sihanouk by attacking the Vietcong', just as Lon Nol had consciously sabotaged national unity and covered up his own subversion by faking evidence of Khmers Rouges plots. Proof that the Khmers Rouges understood my motives and never questioned my patriotism – even when they suffered from measures taken by me to limit their activities – is that they immediately rallied to my call for armed resistance. Moreover they insist with the greatest vehemence that, against my own inclinations, I continue to be Head of State after we have crushed the plotters and driven the invaders out of Cambodia.

The greatest fear of Lon Nol and Sirik Matak was that I would return immediately after the coup and win over the people and the armed forces to my side. Had there been the slightest chance of returning I would have done so. But the Lon Nol government was thorough and ruthless. For instance, they threatened to confiscate the plane and intern the crew of any foreign airline which dared fly me and my suite back into Cambodia – a threat in violation of international law which is probably without precedent in the annals of civil aviation. But in case any airline or pilot thought to call their bluff, even more drastic measures were ready. Allman reports:

Military orders, signed by Lon Nol, directed Government troops to assassinate the Chief of State if he returned to Cambodia. The main fear of the moment was that Sihanouk would return, rally the country around him and hold elections, which he would win 'because he was so popular with the peasants'.

In making extensive use of Allman's reports, I have quoted till now only from the three articles which became part of recorded history when Senator Mansfield read them into the US Congressional Record. With few exceptions, the facts contained in the reports tally with my own information received from the steady stream of defectors from the Lon Nol–Sirik Matak régime, including former Lon Nol staff officers in Phnom Penh at the time of the coup. Some of them succeeded in getting out and joining me in Peking, via Paris or Moscow; others sent me reports after reaching the Liberated Zone.

Allman, having got his teeth deep into the subject, proceeded in professional manner to cling to it like a terrier and dug out vital facts of which I could have had no knowledge, because I had no access to his 'impeccably non-communist source' – none other than Son Ngoc Thanh himself, whom

Allman incorrectly describes as the 'father of the Cambodian independence movement'. Allman, in revealing that one of his main sources was Son Ngoc Thanh, refers to the latter as 'a prime candidate to become the first President of the fledgling Khmer Republic'. From my own sources I know this was true and that, at the time Allman saw him, he was bitter because, after twenty years of treachery, he was not rewarded by being installed at the fountainhead of power in Phnom Penh. For he considered the coup to be his own handiwork. But when the great moment arrived, he was shunned by Lon Nol and Sirik Matak who temporarily managed to bury their own differences in a solid front against this potentially dangerous competitor. To the chagrin of Son Ngoc Thanh, he did not enter Phnom Penh mounted on a white charger (perhaps a 'white elephant' would have been more appropriate) and met no cheering crowds when, five months after the coup, the best his CIA patrons could do was to appoint him 'First Counsellor' to Lon Nol. Son Ngoc Thanh had never fooled the people, who had long known him to be a traitor. Even after Lon Nol was stricken with paralysis (a 'sign from heaven' as he himself commented), Son Ngoc Thanh was not called in to take over. It was certainly from a sense of frustration that he decided to unburden himself to Allman:

In early 1969, the US government, working through agents attached to Son Ngoc Thanh's staff of exiled anti-Sihanouk partisans, had assurances of US support for anti-Sihanouk moves in Cambodia, including a two-pronged invasion of the country.

This was simply a re-vamped version of the 'Dap Chhuon Plot' of early 1959, described in Chapter 7. A comment is necessary to clarify the phrase 'exiled anti-Sihanouk partisans'. Apart from sullying the honourable word 'partisan', with its overtones of patriotism and resistance to foreign invaders, Son Ngoc Thanh's mercenaries were recruited from the Cambodian minority in South Vietnam, trained at a CIA commando centre at Nha Trang on the South Vietnamese coast and then flown to CIA-run bases in Thailand. Others were conscripted into 'Special Forces' units and operated under CIA officers in South Vietnam itself. The majority of these 'partisans' never saw Cambodia until the day they crossed our frontiers to raid the countryside.

Thanh told Allman that the original plan was for him to direct a two-pronged invasion with eight battalions of US-trained troops (meaning the CIA-instructed and financed Khmer Serei based in Thailand, and the KKK[1] commandos from South Vietnam). Plans for this attack had been drawn up in early 1969, and it appears they were independent of the Lon Nol–Sirik Matak conspiracy. Son Ngoc Thanh hoped that once his forces had crossed the frontier, the Cambodian army would rally to him. 'The plan', he explained to Allman, 'received the approval of a US agent', whom he would only identify as 'Fred'. At that time Lon Nol and the 'Cambodian army' could not have been in touch with the arch-traitor without my having known about it. It was no coincidence, however, that the massive 'desertions' from the Khmer Serei started early in 1969, as part of the strategy of the Son Ngoc Thanh invasion.

The CIA, which was master-minding the affair, at some point decided to pin their main hopes on the Lon Nol–Sirik Matak plot to seize power from within, instead of an overt act of aggression. After the scandals in Laos, not to mention the 'Bay of Pigs' fiasco and the events in the Dominican Republic the Agency perhaps needed something more 'constitutional', more 'legal' – especially for a country which was so much in the world's eye as Cambodia. Probably unbeknown to Son Ngoc Thanh, he was to be relegated to second place, and his soldiers, including the 'deserters', were to be placed at the disposal of Lon Nol and Sirik Matak. Suddenly, Son Ngoc Thanh found himself without a considerable part of 'his' army. His original plan, he lamented to Allman, had been

1. Khmers du Kampucheau Krom, sometimes referred to as Khmer Krom, the 'president' and immediate military commander of which is a bloodthirsty, cannibalistic bandit, former chauffeur of the US Embassy in Phnom Penh, who boasts to Western journalists – Jean-Claude Pomonti of *Le Monde* for instance – that he and his fellow-bandits enjoy eating Vietnamese flesh, 'especially the liver'. A worthy servant of Son Ngoc Thanh, Lon Nol and Sirik Matak!

'overtaken by events' and he had now to play a support role for his new chiefs.

Lon Nol's contact with Thanh, after returning from France in February was, as Allman relates it, to discover

if the Vietcong attacked Phnom Penh the way they had attacked Saigon in 1968, could Lon Nol expect the help of Son Ngoc Thanh's forces in defending the capital? Thanh, after checking 'with my American friends' both at the end of February and in early March answered affirmatively.

By the end of February 1970, several weeks before Sihanouk was deposed, a dozen Cambodian army officers, as well as several US agents, were assigned to Son Ngoc Thanh's headquarters, where they apparently exchanged information and promises of mutual support. Lon Nol, at that time still Sihanouk's Prime Minister, in February accepted in principle to meet Son Ngoc Thanh at a rendezvous point on the Vietnamese–Cambodian border.

To have accepted such a rendezvous with a convicted traitor was in itself high treason. By that time, Son Ngoc Thanh told Allman, he had set up his 'field headquarters' at the village of Tinh Bien, near the Cambodian border on the South Vietnamese side of Route 2.[1] At first, Lon Nol sent some of his agents, and the account states that 'several meetings were held on Route 2 on the Cambodian side of the frontier'.

It was after these preliminary meetings, following which Lon Nol installed his own officers inside Son Ngoc Thanh's headquarters, that the two traitors met and worked out the next phase. Allman comments:

Cambodian [Lon Nolian, N.S.] official spokesmen have denied American pledges of support preceding their decision to oust Sihanouk. But after Sihanouk's ouster, a total of ten of Son Ngoc Thanh's Kampucheau Khmer Krom battalions, equipped and paid for by the US, were sent to guard Phnom Penh. 'We moved four battalions to Phnom Penh in April 1970,' Thanh recalls, 'and a total of ten into Cambodia by the end of July.'

By this time, Western newspapers were carrying photos of decapitated, disembowelled Vietnamese with KKK youngsters holding human livers in their hands 'to cook with vegetables'. KKK troops were in fact moved into Phnom

1. Which leads from Phnom Penh south through Takeo to the coast.

Penh before the coup and were among those who attacked the embassies and later massacred the Vietnamese.

Son Ngoc Thanh's revelations to Allman have all the ear-marks of coming from a disgruntled office-seeker who felt he had been badly treated in spite of all his contributions. The rewards had proven to be meagre compared with his 'meritorious' services and even when he later became 'Prime Minister', the office was a sinecure. Son Ngoc Thanh's folly was to believe that a puppet can ever rise above his status, for it is always the puppet-master, in this case the CIA, which pulls the strings. Soon the three ringleaders were to become the puppets when Saigon took over.

The above represents the essential facts, as I know them today, of the elaborate conspiracy to bring about my down-fall and end the oasis of peace which Cambodia had once been. No doubt there were all sorts of plots within plots, as these creatures of the CIA jostled each other for the lead roles. But the main lines and the identities of the culprits are now revealed for all to see. That they knew the outcome would bring war and devastation to my land is clear from the last paragraph of Allman's 12 October article (written for Dispatch News International) based on the Son Ngoc Thanh interview.

The interviews with Son Ngoc Thanh suggest that the Lon Nol–Sirik Matak régime not only planned to remove Sihanouk as early as January, but that it fully realized that the consequences might be war with a much stronger adversary. The United States, according to Thanh, pledged support in case the war occurred.

Senator Mike Gravel (Democrat, Alaska), after studying the Allman articles, remarked that it was

incredible, to take the position — as the White House has done — that the US conducted clandestine incursions into Cambodia, hired and trained members of a sect avowedly dedicated to Sihanouk's overthrow, and did not know that a coup was being planned.

One other element in the plot is worthy of mention. There was the mysterious case of the *Columbia Eagle*, in which just

1. As quoted by Dispatch News International, 4 April 1972.

two US sailors 'mutinied' and imprisoned the whole crew. Shades of Captain Bligh and the *Bounty*! Ostensibly these men were war protestors who sailed the *Columbia Eagle* into Sihanoukville harbour because they objected to carrying napalm bombs to Bangkok. It so happened that some French secondary-school teachers at Sihanoukville took photos of the 'hijacked' ship when it arrived, and again when it left. They noted that it had been very low in the water on arrival, and very high on departure.

And, after dark on the day when the *Columbia Eagle* dropped anchor, the Sihanoukville–Phnom Penh road was suddenly closed to civilian traffic – something without precedent – and convoys of GMC military trucks from the Sihanoukville docks passed along the road to Phnom Penh until the next morning. On the day of the coup, Western correspondents noted that the troops massed outside the national Assembly were armed with brand-new, M16 rifles, weapons our army did not possess. It seems the *Columbia Eagle* was one of the CIA's responses to Lon Nol's request, delivered via Son Ngoc Thanh, to help in case of a 'Vietcong' counter-attack. What they really feared was the response of the Cambodian people.

While it is conceivable that Lon Nol and Sirik Matak were too dense to foresee the dire consequences of their actions (their main concern being to get their hands on as many dollars as possible), the United States, consciously and deliberately, exported the war in South Vietnam to Cambodia. They made their usual miscalculations, however, as to the long-term effects.

Chapter Four

Resistance Starts

The Proclamation which I drafted on the way from Moscow to Peking, and broadcast over Peking radio on 23 March 1970, had an immediate impact on my countrymen. I formally demanded the dissolution of the Lon Nol régime as illegal and unconstitutional, and called for the creation of a broad front of national union, and a national liberation army:

A Government of National Union will be formed. Pending Cambodia's return to a normal situation, a Consultative Assembly will be established. Its members will be qualified representatives of the Buddhist clergy, the army, the police, the provincial guards, youth, intellectuals, peasants, workers and others who live by their labour, industrialists, business people, civil servants, women, etc. belonging to all patriotic, progressive and anti-imperialist tendencies.

A National Liberation Army will be created to free the country from the dictatorship and oppression of the clique of traitorous and pro-imperialist reactionaries headed by Lon Nol, Sirik Matak and Cheng Heng and for the struggle against the US imperialists – their masters.

The Government of National Union, the Consultative Assembly and the National Liberation Army will unite with the rest of the people to form a united front to be known as the National United Front of Cambodia which will have the double task of liberating the country and reconstructing it after victory.

I knew from the experience of our Vietnamese friends that the road to victory would be long and hard, but shorter for us because of the experiences and successes of the Vietnamese.

On 24 March, I issued an appeal to my supporters inside

the country to go underground and await arms and training, and asked those abroad to try and make their way to Peking. There were ferociously repressed uprisings and seizures of power all over the country in the days that followed; the Western press unfortunately reported only those in the eastern provinces close to the capital, where journalists had easy access. In vast areas, Lon Nol's administration simply evaporated before he could get it organized, and it has not been reconstituted since. He tried to pass off the uprisings as the work of the Vietcong, but Western journalists said otherwise. The *Financial Times* accurately described them as 'an almost spontaneous outburst of rural dismay at the departure of a ruler who made every effort to win the sympathy of the countryside'.

Between 26 and 30 March, hundreds of my compatriots – unarmed – were shot down in cold blood for demonstrating in my favour. At least thirty were killed on 27 March at the Neak Luong ferry, some forty miles from Phnom Penh on Highway 1, leading from Saigon. Another fifty were killed in the town of Kompong Cham on the same day when Lon Nol's troops fired into a crowd point-blank with anti-aircraft, heavy machine-guns. About fifty more were shot down at Suong and Memot, both near the South Vietnamese border. Journalists reported counting about eighty corpses at Takeo and twenty to thirty each in the towns of Prey Veng and Angtassom. The dead were indisputably Cambodians. I have photos of long lines of our peasants, hands tied behind their backs, awaiting their turn for the firing squad; of students executed by being beaten to death in front of their fellow-students. We were able to identify some of the executioners, at least, as the CIA-suborned 'deserters' from the Khmer Serei, whom Lon Nol had infiltrated into the Phnom Penh garrison and the military police.

In a broadcast on 4 April, I reported that over three hundred patriots had been massacred, and again advised my supporters to go underground, 'to go into the jungle and join the resistance forces already there', and where by now arms were available.

One of the developments which pleased me most was

receiving a message, dated 26 May, three days after the broadcast Proclamation, from three leading Khmers Rouges – the leftist deputies mentioned earlier as the only honest men elected in the 1966 elections – who had chosen to flee to embryo resistance bases in the jungle. These were three of our outstanding intellectuals: Khieu Samphan and Hou Youn, French-trained economists with PhDs, and Hu Nim, a lawyer. In view of our rather strained relations in the past, I thought they might pose questions or demand conditions, or that there might have to be negotiations before they committed themselves. Nothing of the sort happened. They had monitored the Proclamation and replied in effect: 'That's marvellous. If you, the traditional leader of the Cambodian people, decide to fight with us – we demand nothing better.'

Lon Nol had secretly and systematically worked to separate me from the left. But the Khmer Rouges later told me: 'We never suspected your patriotism and devotion to the people. We always distinguished between you and creatures like Lon Nol and Sirik Matak.' That there was no need for negotiations between us struck me very much. I had launched an appeal, and they had responded wholeheartedly. When, later, we formed the Royal Government of National Union, Khieu Samphan was appointed Minister of Defence (later deputy Premier as well), Hou Youn became Minister of the Interior, Communal Reforms and Cooperatives; Hu Nim, Minister of Information and Propaganda.

As the question of the previous hostile relations between the government and Khmers Rouges is intimately linked with the speedy takeoff of the resistance movement in March 1970, it is worthwhile looking into the origins of these bad feelings. Lon Nol became Prime Minister of the right-wing assembly that emerged from the 1966 elections. In early 1967, he deliberately provoked what became known as the 'Samlaut affair'.

In Cambodia, the land traditionally belongs to him who clears and cultivates it. Lon Nol's troops arrived in the Samlaut area of Battambang province and started evicting peasants who had cleared the land years before and had been cultivating it since. His officers produced documents to show the land 'legally' belonged to this or that local official, and ordered the peasants to pack up and leave, for he wanted the land to settle the Khmer Serei, the so-called deserters, as a reserve force of shock troops for what he was planning. (Even as early as 1967, one of my ministers, Chau Seng, had warned me that Lon Nol was plotting my overthrow. It seemed so improbable that I disbelieved him. Chau Seng later went into voluntary exile in Paris, and, after the March coup, became one of the first to rally to the National United Front. He is now Minister of Special Missions.)

The Samlaut peasants acted as peasants have done throughout history. They resisted. And they were supported by the people. There were mass demonstrations in Battambang city in their favour. There are many Chinese and Vietnamese residents in Battambang, and they joined the protest. This gave Lon Nol the pretext he wanted in order to claim there was a Chinese–Vietminh plot to take over the country. The left-wing deputies were denounced as Maoists and had to flee Phnom Penh. Open warfare began between the peasants and the Lon Nol forces. I was out of the country at the time, but the reports sent me by Lon Nol genuinely sounded as though the whole thing were a revolt directed from Peking and Hanoi.

The situation was all the more embroiled because this occurred during the height of the ultra-leftist deviation of the Great Proletarian Cultural Revolution in China. Chinese residents in Phnom Penh and elsewhere were being incited to undertake all sorts of activities amounting to interference in our affairs. There were portraits of Chairman Mao all over Phnom Penh and other cities, an unprecedented display of Chinese nationalism. So I returned from abroad to find a peasants' revolt in Battambang province and the Chinese minority turned against my régime and against myself personally. (One of the reasons for the ultra-leftist criticism levelled against the Chinese Foreign Minister, Chen Yi, at the time was that of his friendship with the monarchist Sihanouk!) There was an anti-government demonstration in Phnom Penh within a few days of my arrival home. Lon Nol had already instituted a witch-hunt against the left, and many young people had followed the example of the three deputies and fled Phnom Penh for the security of the jungle.

The CIA was not slow to take advantage of the situation. They started a campaign of rumours and distributed false tracts in the name of the Khmers Rouges – tracts which I denounced at the time as lies. The armchair experts who accuse me of having turned to the right in 1967, should take into account the extremely tense and complex situation. For the first time, there seemed to be substantial evidence that our independence was being threatened from the left, a possibility I had always resisted admitting.

As for the long arm of the CIA, there was a fascinating revelation by a CIA 'Green Beret', Captain John J. Mc-Carthy, Jr, one of the accused in the case of the murder of Inchin Hai Lam, an alleged 'double agent' of Cambodian origin in the pay of the CIA. McCarthy resigned his commission in May 1971, disgusted at what he had had to do – not to mention the way in which he had been treated by the US army for having obeyed CIA orders. He revealed at the time that he had headed a CIA team in an 'Operation Cherry', which involved leading a Khmer Serei unit deep into Cambodia. This much was revealed in the *Norfolk Virginia Pilot* on 25 May 1971.

At my initiative, further inquiries were made in the USA, and the following facts were unearthed, and forwarded to me by Richard A. Fineberg, reporter for Dispatch International News Service:

John J. McCarthy, Jr, formerly a Captain with the US Army's Fifth Special Forces and commanding officer of a top-secret Cambodian operation known as 'Operation Cherry', says Son Ngoc Thanh was a key figure in his 1968 court-martial. McCarthy was accused of killing a Cambodian interpreter, who was also a member of the Khmer Serei, a secret, right-wing rebel sect, headed by Thanh and reportedly financed by the CIA.

The ex-Special Forces Officer was convicted of murder and served two years of a 20-year sentence before his conviction was overturned on appeal in 1970.

McCarthy says that his attorneys requested Thanh's appearance at the two-day trial at Long Binh, South Vietnam, in January, 1968, but the Army said it could not compel foreign nationals to testify. At that time Thanh was living in Vietnam, where he was a powerful figure among the Cambodian minority of that country.

Thanh did not testify, but the trial record reveals that US military officers met with members of the Khmer Serei – and possibly with Thanh himself – at a pagoda in Saigon shortly after the agent's death. At that meeting, the US paid an indemnity, reportedly 25,000 dollars, to the Khmer Serei for the death of their member.

The transcript also indicates that Project Cherry was set up to conduct incursions into Cambodia from across the South Vietnam border. For this covert mission, the US hired Cambodian guides and interpreters, at least some of whom were members of the Khmer Serei. During the trial, McCarthy identified the Khmer Serei as an 'organization which in effect plans the political overthrow of the Cambodian government'.

Although the heavily-censored unclassified version of the transcript makes no direct reference to Thanh, the record refers to a man named Tan Son Hai, who was identified by one member of the Cherry team as 'the leader or high priest of the Khmer Serei'. McCarthy told this reporter he believes that Thanh and Ton San Hai are 'one and the same person'.

Prior to the trial, the Khmer Serei presented McCarthy with a gold medallion for his 'revolutionary act' on the assumption that he had killed the agent, whom the Khmer Serei believed to be a Communist-trained double agent. The citation accompanying the award was signed by (Son Ngoc) Thanh as 'leader of the Khmer Serei'.

Excerpts from the unclassified part of the transcript which have come into my hands are most revealing. For instance, the testimony of Sgt Ben W. Hancock, a member of McCarthy's team, testifies under oath regarding a meeting he arranged between 'Tan Son Hai' and a Special Forces officer following the killing of the agent. This verbatim account is from page 138 of the trial proceedings:

Hancock:	Because Special Forces was involved in the . . . (classified) he asked me if I would go to the pagoda to see if I could make an arrangement for him to meet with Tan Son Hai.
Q:	Who is Tan Son Hai?
A:	He is the leader of the . . . (classified) in South Vietnam.

Q: Did anything occur with reference to this proposed meeting?

A: I made a meeting for 6.00 that evening. And Col. Grover, myself and Maj. Adams met with Tan Son Hai, and the interpreter. And Col. Grover told them exactly what happened; they thought he had been killed by an American captain.

Q: What, if anything, was their reaction?

A: Well, he didn't seem bitter or anything, so first he asked how much money the American government would pay for Inchin Hai Lam's death. So a price was agreed on; we made an arrangement, or he made an arrangement with me to deliver the body the following morning to the pagoda in Saigon.

On page 141 of the same verbatim record, Hancock further identifies 'Tan Son Hai' as 'the high priest or leader of the Khmer Serei' so there can be little doubt that it was the arch-traitor, Son Ngoc Thanh, which explains why the US army was so accommodating in protecting him from appearing at the court-martial. McCarthy subsequently informed journalist Fineberg that the compensation paid was 25,000 dollars. The Fineberg report continues:

Although Project Cherry ended prior to McCarthy's trial, Green Berets continued to conduct covert intelligence operations in Cambodia for the CIA.

The 1969 death of another suspected double-agent employed on a secret Cambodian intelligence project caused a sensation in the press when the Army attempted to court-martial eight Green Berets, including Col. Robert Rheault, the commanding officer of the Fifth Special Forces in Vietnam. The Army dropped the charges when the CIA refused to testify.

Captain Robert F. Marasco, one of the Green Berets involved in the latter case, ran two intelligence nets in Cambodia during 1968 and 1969. His mission, he told this reporter, ranged from 'pin-pointing targets' and gathering information in Cambodia, to 'keeping tabs' on the whereabouts of Sihanouk when the Cambodian ruler visited the countryside. Marasco said he hired and trained Khmer Serei agents, as well as other Cambodians for his missions.

On 2 June 1970, Marasco revealed in an interview with the National Broadcasting Company that the code name of his

Cambodian mission was 'B 57', that it was divided into two groups with a network of agents 'in all of the Parrot's Beak and sometimes as far as Phnom Penh'. Among the tasks of the twenty South Vietnamese and Cambodian agents employed by Marasco was that 'of keeping watch on Prince Norodom Sihanouk',[1] which meant, among other things, deciding on propitious moments for assassination attempts.

What 'Operation Cherry' and the 'B 57' groups were really up to may never be known. Journalists have informed me that it is unprecedented that the full transcripts of the McCarthy trial were put on the 'top secret' list. Not the least of CIA activities in 1967, at the time of the Samlaut affair, was the distribution of inflammatory leaflets in the name of the Khmers Rouges aimed at giving Lon Nol the pretext he needed to step up his persecution of the left and to drive a wedge between the Khmers Rouges and myself.

Fortunately the jeep accident in which Lon Nol was injured removed him from the scene at a critical moment, and I was able to look into the Samlaut affair myself as soon as I returned. I found the peasants did indeed have justifiable grievances, and I immediately dismissed the governor of Battambang. I publicly announced the responsibility of the authorities in the unhappy affair, rebuilt villages that had been destroyed by Lon Nol's troops and settled the peasants back on their lands. Lon Nol's accident made it easy for me to reshuffle the cabinet to bring back Penn Nouth as Prime Minister. In an article written in *Études Cambodgiennes* it was made clear that

the rebellion was a strictly internal affair without any foreign support or encouragement, and the Royal Government will settle the problem by its own means and as it thinks best. However, hostile propaganda and CIA agents carried out a frenzied campaign of false information aimed at splitting the nation in two irreconcilable and hostile parts in order to prepare a pretext for direct intervention.[2]

1. The Fineberg account was published by Dispatch International News Service, Washington, 5 April 1972. Marasco's ABC interview was published in *International Herald Tribune*, Paris, 3 June 1970.

2. *Études Cambodgiennes*, official organ of the Royal Cambodian Government, No. 10, April–June 1967.

I did not know anything about 'Operation Cherry' at that time, but I clearly recognized the long arm of the CIA in the forged leaflets and in the phrasing of certain slogans that were launched against me.

Sensational stories began to appear in the Western press, picturing the oppressed Battambang peasants as being in bloody rebellion against Sihanouk and demonstrating the hand of Peking and Hanoi in this uprising. Worth noting is the opinion of a French journalist, Gérard Brissé, who lived for many years in Cambodia, and who investigated the Samlaut affair:

> Contrary to what was written at the time, it was not directed against Norodom Sihanouk ... but against certain local petty despots ... The popularity of Norodom Sihanouk among the peasant masses remained intact, as was proven by the extent of the resistance organized over virtually the entire Cambodian country-side.[1] (Brissé was referring to the resistance after the 1970 coup.)

However, Lon Nol's witch-hunt against leftist intellectuals, and the military campaign against the Battambang peasants, combined to drive both groups into an attitude of open, armed defiance which died down after I intervened in the Samlaut affair, then blossomed forth after the 18 March 1970 coup.

In connection with the cloud which passed over my relations with Peking (but never with Chou En Lai, with whom I remained on the best of terms) there occurred a regrettable incident in August 1967. The Chinese-Cambodian Friendship Association in Peking had addressed a message to the Chinese-Cambodian Friendship in Phnom Penh, implicitly advocating my overthrow. This obviously amounted to direct intervention in Cambodian affairs and I had no choice but to dissolve the Phnom Penh association, together with all such bodies, and to replace them with official organizations. My critics jumped on this as conclusive evidence that I had turned to the right. But when I went to China in 1970, Premier Chou En Lai told me that I, in fact, had acted correctly in thus assuring Cambodia's integrity, for all this had taken place at a time when extremist elements had

1. From *L'Année Politique et Economique*, Paris, July 1970.

68

gained control of China's foreign policy, and were issuing all sorts of provocative instructions through their embassies abroad. Not only Cambodia suffered from this, but in our case it did, unfortunately, happen at a particularly crucial moment in our postwar history. Chou En Lai told me that the leaders of the association in Peking had been punished. In general, the 'ultras' who emerged at the height of the Cultural Revolution were later thoroughly discredited, but not before much harm had been done to China's relations abroad.

To throw my own dissenters – rightists such as Lon Nol – off the track, I occasionally made speeches attacking the Vietminh, Vietcong and Khmers Rouges. The first two realized that the main thing was my unswerving political, diplomatic and material support of their resistance struggle. But I did not know at the time that the Khmers Rouges had also understood this. The proof was their immediate acceptance of the alliance for resistance in 1970.

What had depressed me in 1967, when I saw so many hundreds of Cambodian young people deserting home, studies and professions to march off to jungle and mountain guerrilla bases, turned out to be a blessing when I sounded the call for armed defiance in March 1970. The bases were there; the arms came soon after. The NLF, which had been very reluctant to give arms to the Khmers Rouges in 1967, thus risking a Cambodian civil war which might bring about US intervention, had no such misgivings in March of 1970. Immediately after the coup they started distributing weapons stocked in the frontier regions. When the Americans attacked six weeks later they were dismayed to find the storage areas almost empty. A high proportion of these arms went directly into the hands of the first units of our Peoples Liberation Armed Forces.

The very rapid development of our armed resistance – something which astonished even our Vietnamese friends – was due to the fact that we had veteran cadres which had learned irregular warfare in protecting their own lives and their bases from Lon Nol's raiding expeditions. There were bases in Ratanakiri Province in the north-east, in the Elephant Mountains in the south, and in the Cardamome

Mountains in the west. The Khmers Rouges were quickly joined by tens of thousands of what some journalists called 'Sihanoukists'. These were peasants and townspeople, soldiers, including entire army units which had remained loyal to me, and Vietnamese and Chinese residents who joined us for ideological reasons, or because they saw no alternative if they wanted to remain alive – and free.

By mid April, most of Cambodia was liberated, and our forces were knocking at the gates of Phnom Penh, eager to join our supporters inside the city. This, despite the importation of the 'Mike Force' (KKK commandos) for the defence of the capital. The Lon Nol–Sirik Matak régime was sagging at the knees, knocked on to the ropes, and awaiting the final count, when the United States invaded Cambodia with its own and Saigon forces on 30 April 1970, in one of the most flagrant acts of unprovoked aggression in modern history. No word but 'aggression' can be applied to this act. Lon Nol, to cover up his own involvement, claimed that he had neither invited the Americans in, nor had received any warning of the invasion. It is hard to believe, but this is the official, on-the-record position of the Lon Nol–Sirik Matak government. On 2 May, in the first days of the invasion, Lon Nol was reported by Western journalists as 'pondering' whether or not to lodge an official 'protest'. In the end he decided to 'approve' the invasion!

The best he could do to justify himself was to address a gathering of Buddhists on 11 May, by which time scores of towns and villages had been reduced to rubble and ashes by US air power, and hundreds of innocent civilians had been bombed, burned and machine-gunned to death by American and Saigon troops. With this inept and hypocritical disquisition, he tried to vindicate the slaughter of thousands of Vietnamese civilians in an officially decreed rampage of racism and terror without precedent in our country's history. That he should seek to justify butchery and treason in the name of Buddhism, the most humane and tolerant of religious philosophies, provides a measure of the man's degeneracy. In a broadcast over Radio Phnom Penh, he said:

I address this appeal to my fellow countrymen who are Buddhist believers. It is believed that our religion will last 5,000 years. We are now at 2,500 years, right in the middle of the Buddhist era. It is also believed that the Buddhist religion will prosper during the next 500 years. According to an oracle, the current war in Cambodia is a *religious war*. Our religion is Buddhism. We have our bonzes, our prayers, our disciplines, and belief that good will be rewarded and evil will be punished. The communists do not believe in religion because they do not believe in the existence of Buddha.

I wish to inform my fellow countrymen who are Buddhists that an oracle has predicted everybody will enjoy equal rights. Everybody will be happy and good when this *religious war* ends. But while the war is still going on, you must respect your religion and pray. Those who follow this advice will be spared all misfortune and will be rewarded with security and prosperity. The oracle who predicted a *religious war* in the middle of this era said that gold and silver palaces will be erected in the middle of the four branches of the Mekong, and that there will be killing in the middle of the four branches of the Mekong. This means the enemy of Buddha will kill the religious people. Then the King will flee, and a comet will appear.

When the Khmer people refused to abandon their Buddhist morality and to aid the Vietcong aggressors, the war broke out in accordance with plans mapped out by the Chinese and North Vietnamese communists. China does not love Sihanouk; it is using him as a tool to help the Vietcong wage war in our country with a view to transforming it into a communist base in South-East Asia.

To make it easy to understand, according to the Buddhist religion, there must be war – a war against the Vietnamese communists who consider religion their enemy. In this *religious war* against the Vietnamese communists, who are the enemies of Buddha, there are many Buddhists who will come and help us. Our country will win final victory on the battlefield as predicted by the oracle. Therefore, we Buddhist believers must rise up together to struggle against the enemy who is committing the war of aggression in our country.[1]

One could possibly deduce from the last sentence that Lon Nol was appealing to his Buddhist compatriots to rise up against the Americans, but his intentions were anything but that. I have italicized the repeated use of the expression 'religious war' in Lon Nol's ravings. This, together with the

1. *Cambodia: The Widening War In Indo-China*, pp. 109–12, Washington Square Press, New York, February 1971.

reference to the 'four branches of the Mekong', seems to be an attempt to explain the massacre of over a thousand Vietnamese civilians, men, women and children, whose bodies, arms tied behind their backs, were found drifting down the Mekong in mid April. This terrible stain on Cambodian honour was well reported in the world press at the time, but a 15 April dispatch from Jeff Williams of the Associated Press, is especially worth recalling. Writing from the Neak Luong ferry crossing, he says:

Hundreds of executed Vietnamese bodies floated down the Mekong River Wednesday morning, many of them with hands tied behind them. It appeared to be the greatest mass killing yet disclosed in Cambodia. The stench swept across the broad waters, and ferry passengers gagged as the ferry churned through bodies floating in the river.

A police official at this ferry, sixty kilometres south-east of Phnom Penh, said he had counted four hundred bodies during the morning. Still the bodies came and the bodies could be seen stretching for more than one mile up the river until they disappeared behind a bend.

A religious killing! Many of the Vietnamese were also Buddhists. And those who were Catholics? Buddhism preaches religious tolerance. Who are 'the many Buddhists who will come and help us'? Since when have Americans been considered Buddhists? I would urge all members of the US Congress and the American public at large to read Lon Nol's speech and then to assess the sort of leaders to whom they have entrusted so many hundreds of millions of dollars, and the political and moral philosophy being endorsed with American treasure and military might – not to mention prestige.

Americans might also meditate on the following passages from the conservative *Far Eastern Economic Review*:[1]

Foreign officials in Phnom Penh who brood over Cambodia's problem and vie for Lon Nol's ear may be a bit disconcerted to learn that the premier gets some of his most intimate advice from a clique of Buddhist monks who often see him for hours at a stretch.

1. Published in Hong Kong, 16 January 1971.

High among these well-placed advisers is Mam Prom Moni, a crafty-looking 20 year-old bonze whose confident air and haughty demeanor befit his title: 'Grand Intellectual of Glorious Purity'. He belongs to the Mohanikay sect. He describes himself as an astrologer, mineralogist and historian! He sees Lon Nol each week but will not divulge the content of their discussions beyond saying that they range from personal problems to affairs of state. To provide some sense of the wisdom he shares with the Cambodian leader, Mam Prom Moni offers the following predictions:

'Peace will come to Cambodia this spring, but will not endure until several requirements are met: all Vietnamese, from north and south, must leave the country ... US businessmen must help Cambodia recover through heavy investment – and they must act before their Japanese counterparts do!

Perhaps rumours of CIA-manipulated soothsayers are not so far-fetched after all!

One can readily understand why so many of my compatriots, faced with a choice of listening either to the obscurantist ravings of this turncoat or to logical, intelligent appeals to patriotism, national unity, and militant solidarity with comrades-in-arms across our borders in Vietnam and Laos, did not hesitate to choose the latter. With the invasion of 30 April, Nixon's military strategists hoped to crush our resistance forces before they could get organized, and to smash the NLF in a vice between Lon Nol's forces and their own. The western jaw of the vice did not close because Lon Nol's forces had no stomach for the fight. Our embryo resistance forces, on the other hand, gave a good account of themselves. The 'Vietcong Pentagon' proved non-existent; the overwhelming bulk of supplies in the frontier bases have been transported elsewhere – as the Americans were to find out in the spring of 1972 – or are in our hands; the 'sanctuaries' now spread westwards to include most of Cambodia. Nixon's Cambodian adventure resulted in the destruction of many Cambodian towns and villages, the loss of thousands of Cambodian – almost exclusively civilian – lives. But from a military viewpoint it was a disaster for the United States and its puppets – a disaster the extent of which Nixon has never dared reveal to the American people.

The invasion of April-May 1970 was the first baptism of fire for our PNLAFC (People's National Liberation Armed Forces of Cambodia). Within a very short time, Khieu Samphan and his comrades set up three types of forces; local guerrillas and regional guerrillas and a regular army. If, in the beginning, these branches lacked equipment, they more than made up for it by their superb morale. How could it be otherwise when they had seen their homes looted and burned; their parents massacred; their mothers, wives, sisters and daughters raped? If there were Cambodians who still had no clear idea of the difference between a Lon Nol and a Sihanouk after the coup of 18 March 1970, there were none after the aggression committed – by invitation or not – on 30 April. The seeds of our defiance fell on soil fertilized by the blood of our people. Sihanouk propaganda? One need only follow the tragic course of events since 18 March 1970.

Chapter Five

Manila Interlude

My first reactions to the events immediately preceding the 18 March coup – and to the coup itself – was to see the hand of the CIA at work. In a TV interview in Paris on 14 March and again immediately after my arrival in Peking, I made declarations to this effect. Obviously I did not have the type of documented evidence which I later obtained. But so much had happened that was indisputably the work of the CIA that I was justified in entertaining well-informed suspicions that what took place on 18 March was the logical conclusion of all that had gone on before. Everything that I have been able to collect since as evidence has only confirmed those suspicions.

My first experience with CIA intervention in Cambodian affairs dates back to late 1955, when Allen Dulles, then head of the CIA, visited me in Phnom Penh. Prior to this, his brother, the late John Foster Dulles, had called on me in his capacity as Secretary of State, and he had exhausted every argument to persuade me to place Cambodia under the protection of the South-East Asia Treaty Organization. I refused, because such an arrangement was contrary to the pledge of neutrality accepted by Cambodia at the 1954 Geneva Conference, and which I was to reaffirm at the Bandung Conference in April 1955.

I considered SEATO an aggressive military alliance directed against neighbours whose ideology I did not share but with whom Cambodia had no quarrel. I had made all this quite clear to John Foster, an acidy, arrogant man, but his brother soon turned up with a briefcase full of documents 'proving' that Cambodia was about to fall victim to 'communist aggression' and that the only way to save the country, the monarchy and myself was to accept the protection of SEATO. The 'proofs' did not coincide with my own information, and I replied to Allen Dulles as I had replied to John Foster: Cambodia wanted no part of SEATO. We would look after ourselves as neutrals and Buddhists. There was nothing for the secret service chief to do but pack up his dubious documents and leave.

Pressure continued to be applied against me, and also against my mother and father by the US Ambassador, Robert McClintock, known to my intelligence staff as an experienced agent of the CIA. McClintock harped on the same stale themes as had the brothers Dulles: the Chinese intended to gobble us up . . . The US Congress would withhold economic aid from countries steering a neutral course . . . No nation could conceivably remain neutral in the struggle against world communism . . . Not to be with the US in this crusade was to be against her. Many variants of the John Foster Dulles notion that neutralism was 'dangerous and immoral' were presented. (He never abandoned this theme. When I saw him in 1958, he glowered at me and said: 'Cambodia cannot be a Switzerland in Asia. You cannot be neutral. You have to choose between the free world and the communist camp.')

At the invitation of the Philippine government, I went to Manila, arriving there on 31 January 1956. I was given a tremendous reception. It was 'flowers, flowers, all the way'. Cheering crowds lined the streets – a New York ticker-tape welcome, with confetti floating down like coloured snowflakes from the buildings lining the street. The most gorgeous TV and cinema stars had been mobilized to emphasize Philippine hospitality. Although my office was that of Prime Minister, I was received with something of extravaganza – including massed bands – that my former status of King might have justified. (I had abdicated some ten months earlier.) But who would not have been delighted by all of this beauty and enthusiasm?

I was somewhat less than enthralled next morning when I picked up my newspapers. An obviously government-inspired editorial in the *Manila Chronicle* stated that 'the arrival of Prince Norodom Sihanouk should end in Cambodia signing with SEATO' and that 'careful preparations for the visit of Sihanouk are part of a campaign to push the neutral state into the East-West fight'.

The disagreeable thought crossed my mind that the flowers, the music – even the film stars – were part of a charming but insidious psychological ploy; an extension, by much more pleasant means, of the political pressures the Dulles brothers and McClintock had been using on me and my parents.

In my first speech before the Philippines parliament I firmly defended Cambodia's neutral position, without attacking SEATO, and received an ovation. Some senators and deputies even got up and said that Philippine policies should be re-examined in the light of non-alignment.

Prior to the speech I had accepted an invitation by a Senator Manglapus, with whom I had become friendly during the Bandung Conference, to spend the evening at his home. Like myself, he was a musician. The party was intended to be a celebration of the fact that he had been partly instrumental in bringing me to the Philippines, where he was sure that I was to officially accept the SEATO 'umbrella'. We spent rather a glum evening together!

My next engagement was to be a visit to the Philippine army headquarters at Camp Murphy, where there was to be a ceremonial welcoming parade, and I was to make another speech. Something quite extraordinary happened before I went there. I had rendered a favour to a certain François Baroukh, a 'businessman' of Lebanese origin – or so he said – who had passed several months in Phnom Penh. The authorities pointed out to me that he seemed interested in all sorts of curious things in addition to commercial affairs. Mr Baroukh had asked me if he could take advantage of my voyage to the Philippines to travel in the same plane, as he had business there also. In fact, he said, he had originally come to Cambodia from the Philippines.

To my great surprise he came to see me in Manila, and asked me to make a speech at Camp Murphy which would 'soften' the toughness of my speech to parliament. He explained that the tone of my discourse had put him, as a friend of the Philippine government, in a very difficult situation and begged me 'as a personal gesture' to smooth matters over. With the aid of close contacts in government circles, he had drafted a version which he knew would be acceptable. There it was – written out by hand on the stationery of the Manila Hotel! (Later, members of my suite informed me that they had witnessed a secretary of the US Embassy in Manila dictating 'my' Camp Murphy speech to Mr François Baroukh in the bar of the hotel.)

I at first accepted his text, thinking perhaps I could use it as a convenient outline. But when I read it, I saw that he had me saying almost the opposite of what I had told the parliament. I had not come to the Philippines with the intention of offending my hosts; neither had I come to barter away the very foundations of Cambodia's foreign policy. I sat up that night preparing a new text, which I took the precaution of distributing at the Press Club in order to forestall any attempts to 'plant' the Baroukh version. I made a photocopy of the embassy official's handiwork – also as a precaution. Mr Baroukh had me saying that:

I am sure that the preparations undertaken by the Philippines government in cooperation with other free countries *against communist aggression or subversion* will benefit all free people in South Asia. The Cambodian people, which only recently had to defend itself *against communist aggression* considers with interest and sympathy measures taken by President Magysaysay and those of other free nations to prevent *a new communist advance* in this part of the world. All the sacrifices and sufferings of the Asian people, because of their love for independence, will be in vain *unless we cooperate to preserve our liberty* . . . It is urgent that *we defend Asia* against all forms of conquest or new colonialism.

I have italicized phrases which were drawn from the tiresome stock terminology of the brothers Dulles, and McClintock. My amended text, doubtless to the consternation of the US Embassy, stressed:

Although we cannot take part in any military blocs because of the agreements we freely signed at Geneva, our Khmer army is at one with the forces of countries, such as the Philippines, whose only ambition is to defend the ideals of peace, justice, and democracy . . . I express the wish that a better understanding desired by all peoples will, one day, enable countries exhausted by the recent war to reduce their crippling military expenditures and to maintain, despite ideological differences, correct relations with all other powers on the basis of non-interference in each other's affairs, the only solid basis for lasting peace.

This obviously smacked too much of peaceful coexistence to please the USA, but it was not to make propaganda for SEATO that I had been invited to the Philippines. I saw nothing more of Mr Baroukh after I had distributed the text of my speech to the press. The visit to Camp Murphy was cancelled – there was no ceremonial parade. The *Philippines Herald* commented that by my declaration I had 'thrown cold water on the hopes of the Philippines government to bring Cambodia into SEATO'. I later discovered that Baroukh was a CIA agent, and that the Philippines government was merely acting as spokesman for US policies. I would enjoy no more music, flowers, or glamorous TV stars!

President Magysaysay invited me to a farewell dinner to which he had also asked the director of the National Library. After the meal was over, he asked the director to produce a famous historical document which showed that during the seventeenth century, when an ancestor of mine was about to lose his throne, he was saved by Filipino mercenary troops. 'You see,' said Magysaysay, 'we did not remain neutral when your throne was imperilled. We will soon all be in danger of Chinese aggression – but you want to remain neutral.'

'Mr President,' I replied, 'if ever the day comes that your independence is threatened, we will not remain neutral. The Cambodian people, the Cambodian government, and I, personally, would not remain neutral. We will repay our debt if you become the victim of aggression, and this applies also to communist aggression.' I do not know whether the President was happy with my reply. He died in a plane crash a few months later, and my people, to whom I had related in detail what had happened in Manila, saw the hand of fate in his death. After the failure of the 'Manila Mission', Baroukh was recalled by the CIA. Later I heard that he too was dead.

I was soon obliged to reveal in a communiqué what I could only regard as a plot against our neutrality. John Foster Dulles had taken exception to some articles and radio commentaries written outside Cambodia by a journalist who had visited our country and had described some of the pressures exerted by the US on Cambodia to accept SEATO 'protection'. Dulles had taken the diplomatically unusual course – something which I could not overlook – of sending a letter of protest to the Cambodian foreign ministry, claiming that the offending journalist had made intolerable

allegations according to which the US tried to force Cambodia to join the SEATO pact by threatening to withdraw US economic aid ... I regret that these allegations have been made, as they are completely false and could damage the friendly relations existing between our two states. I am certain this letter will end these false allegations regarding our policy which, I repeat, has no aim other than to help free nations preserve their liberty and independence.

He included some phrases from a communiqué issued following a visit by Ambassador McClintock to the King and Queen, wherein it was stated that the USA had 'never made any official observations concerning Cambodian neutrality'.

My riposte was a communiqué which contained the details of the Manila incident, photo-copies of the Baroukh text, copies of my amended speech (never delivered), and a preface which stated: 'It is a fact that officially and publicly the US has never made observations about Cambodian neutrality. However, private American "advice" and un-official "criticism" have not been lacking.' As the Dulles brothers had been the most active in their pointed observations concerning our neutrality, John Foster would have no problem in comprehending my meaning.

My departure from Manila was in marked contrast to my arrival. The US Ambassador was absent from the frigid airport leavetaking ceremony. The sight of a nation which had fallen so completely under the domination of a foreign power strengthened me in my vow to defend Cambodian independence to the end. At the time, I could not guess the terrible cost in maintaining such a stand. Even had I known, however, I do not think I could have acted otherwise.

Public disclosure of the scandalous events in Manila had their consequences. Vice-President Garcia complained rather picturesquely that I had not even shown 'gut gratitude' for I had eaten Philippine food, then had 'bitten the hand that fed me'!

In an ironic turn of fortune's wheel, in early 1964 – eight years after the events described – the then President of the Philippines, Macapagal, asked whether, in view of my good relations with President Soekarno of Indonesia, I could not play some role in easing tensions between Indonesia, Malaysia, and the Philippines. It was the time of Soekarno's 'confrontation policy' with Malaysia. The Philippines also had territorial claims on Malaysia. I invited Tengku Abdul Rahman of Malaysia and President Macapagal to Cambodia. First of all we met at Angkor – the calm of which I always found useful for cooling tempers – later in Phnom Penh, where I arranged a tremendous reception for the President of the Philippines – a hundred thousand people lining the streets from the airport. The next step was for me to visit Kuala Lumpur, Djakarta, and Manila. No welcoming crowds at the Manila airport – just President Macapagal and his wife, bravely clapping as I stepped down the gangway. He had arranged for schoolchildren to line the streets with Cambodian flags. But, seemingly unbeknown to the President, National Assembly deputies had sent out trucks to pick up the children: 'Go home!' they were told. 'Don't wave those Cambodian flags!' So I was met with banners reading: 'Sihanouk Slandered Us in 1956', 'Sabotage His Visit', 'Sihanouk – Enemy Of The Philippine People!' We drove through empty streets. It was one of the worst moments of my life – worse even than being deposed, because then I knew that even in exile I had my people with me and that we would fight back and win. But to be humiliated in this way in a so-called friendship visit was galling in the extreme, and further embittered me toward the U S and its satellites.

After the fiasco of the 1956 Manila visit, I went to Peking

to renew with Premier Chou En Lai a friendship that had begun a year earlier at the Bandung Conference. What a difference in the dignity and bearing of a country which stood on its own feet! In China, although I was a prince and a Buddhist, and Chou En Lai a communist revolutionary, and despite the enormous disparity in the size of our countries, I was treated as an equal. There was a total absence of pressures of any sort, and a genuine interest in Cambodia's problems.

In travelling around the country, I noted that China's agricultural implements, and many of her consumer goods, were better suited to the needs of Cambodians than many Western products. I quickly acquired the conviction that here was a powerful friend who would stand by us through thick and thin; one who was threatened by the same forces that threatened us, and thus fully understood and sympathized with our problems. My visit to Peking lasted from 13 to 21 February, and the concrete result was the signing of a Sino-Cambodian Declaration of Friendship, which reaffirmed Cambodian neutrality, and our mutual agreement for basing relations on the Five Principles of Peaceful Coexistence adopted at Bandung.

As a result of this visit, on my return to Phnom Penh, I became the subject of attacks by the press of two satellites even more completely under the US heel than the Philippines: South Vietnam and Thailand. I was accused of preparing the way for a Chinese invasion of these two countries by permitting 'outflanking manoeuvres' through Cambodian territory. If South Vietnam and Thailand had to take defensive measures' then only Sihanouk would be to blame! Ambassador McClintock echoed the same arguments and threats. Across the border, in Bangkok, the CIA was strongly entrenched, agents having been installed there by William Donovan, US Ambassador to Bangkok until 1954, and former director of the Office of Strategic Services, the forerunner of the CIA. Donovan's successor in Bangkok was none other than John F. Peurifoy, another CIA operative who, eight months previous to the Manila incident, had masterminded the coup in Guatemala which overthrew the Arbenz government because it had dared defy the USA. Hardly a good omen for me, considering the propaganda calling for my overthrow which poured out of Thailand! Almost immediately after my return from Manila, Thailand and South Vietnam clamped an economic blockade on Cambodia. This was serious, for our communications with the outside world passed either along the Mekong River through South Vietnam or by railway through Thailand.

To buttress the effects of the economic blockade, there were daily military provocations. Deep intrusions were made into our air space by planes based in South Vietnam and Thailand, and CIA-financed irregulars began to make commando raids into the frontier areas. These were more than just threats. They looked more and more like preliminary softening-up probes for a Guatemala-type coup.

In order to be independent of our two hostile neighbours in maintaining contact with the outside world, we had asked US aid in building a road or railway to a deep-water port which the French had promised to build for us at Kompong Som (later Sihanoukville) on the Gulf of Siam. Washington had promised to build us a road, proclaiming that a railway would not be economically viable. But after my defiant stand at Manila, it was clear that the road would not be built unless I became more 'cooperative'. Why build a road along which Cambodian rubber would be shipped to Red China? This was one of the unofficial arguments used.

In April 1955, the SEATO members, meeting in Bangkok, had decided to place our country, along with Laos and South Vietnam, under their 'protection' – without consulting Cambodia or, as far as I know, Laos or South Vietnam. Cambodia wanted no such 'protection'. We all understood only too well what it would entail, and I told Ambassador McClintock this. The question was whether or not we would be 'protected' against our will! In March 1956, I received two visiting journalists, Yuri Grishchenko of the Soviet Union and Wilfred Burchett of Australia. I explained to them that the US, as a professed democratic country, should accept my position. As Prime Minister, I was bound to interpret the will of the people and the people wanted to remain independent and not to be pushed around by everybody. At our National Congresses, I had asked those who thought we should accept S E A T O to raise their hands. Not a hand was raised. I asked those who thought we should refrain from being involved in military pacts to put up their hands. Every hand was lifted. Grishchenko was from *Pravda*. I assured him that Cambodia would be glad to establish diplomatic relations with the Soviet Union. At the time, the only non-S E A T O countries represented in Phnom Penh were Japan and India so I felt that representation from the socialist camp would be normal and useful, especially in view of mounting military pressures from the United States.

In March 1956, I resigned as Prime Minister and Foreign Minister. Thus I was released from the odious, almost daily visits of Ambassador McClintock, an arrogant and most offensive person. I also wanted to have my hands free in order to fight better. Just a year earlier I had abdicated the throne for similar reasons. Then it was because of internal dissensions; this time it was to face up to external perils.

Shortly after resigning, I justified my action at a press conference held at Kampot on the southern coast. 'I realize', I said, 'that my resignation will be considered a moral victory by the Americans, and I hope they will now be satisfied. They, who have so often promised to defend the liberties of small countries, have just shown their real face in Cambodia. It is not edifying. Let our compatriots rest assured of one thing, however: we will not permit anyone to trample on our neutrality or on our sovereignty. We will not retreat a single step. We have victoriously rebuffed threats of this sort before – we shall do so again.' I was, of course, referring to the continuing military intrusions and open threats of 'defensive measures' by South Vietnam and Thailand, with scarcely veiled support from the US. I decided to take my case to the people and, at the Kampot press conference, I announced the date – 21 April 1956 – of the Third National Congress of the Sangkum.

During the weeks preceding that Congress, pressures were stepped up almost to flashpoint. Thai troops invaded our territory and seized the historic Ankorian temple of Preah

Vihear. The frontiers with Thailand and South Vietnam remained closed.

The agenda for the National Congress was to include 'Cambodia's attitude towards foreign powers in relation to the attitude of these foreign powers towards our country', and the question of 'Foreign aid granted or proposed to our country'. Announcement of the agenda caused a flurry in diplomatic circles. Washington in particular understood that I meant business. Not only was I determined to reject any form of cooperation with SEATO, but I planned to end once and for all the monopoly of US influence in our country. I would turn to the socialist world for help. The Third National Congress was shaping up as an historical turning point in Cambodia's relations with the outside world. Washington would have to eat the bitter fruits of trying to push a small country too brutally in a direction which it did not want to take.

What could have been a pro-Western neutrality would be a purer form of neutrality as between East and West. My trip to China; my discussions with Chou En Lai and Mao Tse-tung in Peking; my experience at the Bandung Conference – not to mention the Manila visit – all combined to point the way to the future. The Chinese were already inquiring as to what forms of economic aid from them would be suitable. Contact had been made with the Soviet Union. Just when economic and military pressures were reaching their climax, on the eve of the Congress, McClintock made it known that he had an important message. But by that time, neither the new Prime Minister, Khim Tit, nor any other minister, would receive him. He was informed that if there were any communications to be made, they should be sent through the Indian Chargé d'Affaires, Mr Mitra. But personal relations were so bad between McClintock and Mitra – a strong supporter of my anti-SEATO line – that communications between the US Embassy and the Indian Legation had to pass through the Australian Legation. This was the sort of situation created by that infamous non-diplomat, Robert McClintock! Through this roundabout channel, an appointment was made for the US Ambassador to see the

King and Queen and thus deliver the urgent message from the State Department.

The message was to announce an American diplomatic retreat. Economic aid would be continued; the famous road to Sihanoukville would be built, and the State Department gave its assurances that US aid would contain 'no conditions prejudicial to Cambodia's neutrality and independence'. Before long we were to appreciate the real meaning of this phrase! My father and mother were perfectly aware of what had been going on, and, in addition, had personally suffered from the humiliating discourtesies of McClintock. The diplomatic corps in Phnom Penh well understood the background to the passage of the communiqué following the visit which stated:

As was thus recognized jointly between their Majesties and Ambassador McClintock, their Majesties and the Ambassador have reaffirmed once more the principle that the foreign policy of Cambodia can be fixed only by the Royal Government itself, in accordance with its sovereignty and free from any foreign influence. The only aim of American policy to Cambodia is to help her strengthen and defend her independence.

(It was this communiqué that John Foster Dulles later quoted in attempting to refute the allegations of economic blackmail.)

My strategy of bringing things out into the open before the eyes of the people had succeeded. For the blustering McClintock to have toned down his language to normal diplomatic prose was a measure of the defeat he had suffered. No country could have been worse served by an ambassador than was the US by McClintock.

In keeping with Washington's sudden *volte-face*, its two satellites followed suit. Two days before the National Congress opened, Thailand and South Vietnam opened their frontiers. Thus the economic blockade ended. Thailand stated it was ready to submit the question of the Preah Vihear temple to international arbitration. While I welcomed these moves, they represented more proof of the total subservience of these two countries to US policies. The *volte-face* came too late and was too transparent to affect the mood of the Congress delegates, however. On the opening day, an incident occurred which was like a punctuation mark to everything I was about to reveal.

In those days the National Congress was held in a courtyard of the Royal Palace. It had always been a colourful affair. The diplomats, in white, gathered on the tribune. As President of the Sangkum, I delivered the main report, and then answered the delegates' questions. The delegates, and a public drawn from all walks of life, gathered in open-air pavilions decorated with the national colours and with green branches. Behind me on the tribune was ranged the whole cabinet, and ministers had to be be ready to reply to any questions or criticisms concerning their functions.

On this occasion, 21 April 1956, as I went up to the microphone to make my opening report, Ambassador McClintock stood up and, making a curt gesture with his head to the rest of the diplomatic corps to follow him, strode off the tribune, together with other members of the US Embassy. As dean of the diplomatic corps, he obviously expected the others to follow. Some did half-rise from their seats, but the French High Commissioner, Pierre Gorce, who outranked McClintock, remained stolidly in his chair, and the rest followed his example. This public display of bad manners, in front of our government and of delegates from every corner of the country, had the opposite effect to that intended by McClintock. Whether it was because of this *faux pas* – perhaps too blatant, even for the US State Department – I do not know, but he was withdrawn soon afterwards.

In my report to the Congress I dealt with the harm caused by the blockade of our frontiers to our modest initial two-year economic plan. I also spoke of the possibilities of economic aid from China, the Soviet Union and other socialist states. I mentioned the very recent *détente* with the US and our two neighbours, and the moves towards establishing formal diplomatic ties with the Soviet Union, Poland and, later on, with other socialist states. I described the attempt to force Cambodia to accept SEATO 'protection', and how and why I had resisted these pressures in Manila and elsewhere. To one of the first questions, 'How real and solid is our neutrality?', I replied: 'Did you not just see the American Ambassador stalk off the platform?'

After thorough discussion, it was decided without a single dissenting voice, that Cambodia should remain strictly neutral, and not get involved with SEATO or any other military blocs. The question of establishing diplomatic relations with the Soviet Union and Poland was unanimously approved. As to accepting economic aid from the Soviet Union and China, I pointed out that if we did this the US might cut off its aid. I was asked if the socialist countries had threatened to refuse aid if we continued to receive US assistance. My answer had to be 'No'. But I did not try to influence the decision and carefully restricted myself to giving factual answers. Opinions were voiced that, if we offended the USA by accepting aid from the socialist countries and thus US aid was cut off, we would wind up by accepting assistance only from the socialist countries – and thus lose our neutrality! But in the end delegates voted without dissent to accept aid from the socialist world – as long as the aid was unconditional – and the USA could do as it pleased.

Next morning, one of the Phnom Penh papers described the result as a 'slight slide to the left' – and this was correct. Better said, it was a push to the left by the USA and its two satellites. Their bullying tactics had contributed to my own education and to that of the entire Cambodian people. The National Congress debates went on for three days and nights, and were in themselves an important forum of political education. Anyone who wished to speak could do so – not only to me and to the other delegates, but to the nation as a whole, as everything was broadcast live from the tribune. Delegates, opposition party members, only had to identify themselves, and the tribune was at their disposal. It was a place where everyone with responsibility, including myself, had to defend his activities and his ideas.

I had hoped that the result of the Congress – the clearly expressed opinions of the majority of our people – would give the Americans reason to reflect, but they continued in the old ways. McClintock's behaviour, which I thought was due only to his warped personality, symbolized official US policies right up to the 18 March 1970 coup and the outright aggression six weeks later. After the Congress adjourned, pressures on us to accept SEATO or to abandon our neutrality seemed to ease somewhat. We later discovered that the pressures had only gone underground, and that the CIA had changed its strategy to concentrating on building up the Khmer Serei in South Vietnam to prepare for a coup.

Late in 1956, I left for a tour of Europe which included stops in the Soviet Union, Yugoslavia, Czechoslovakia and Poland – my first visits to the European socialist countries. After I returned, the Fourth National Congress was held (at the beginning of 1957) – this time with a Soviet Ambassador and delegates of a Chinese Economic Mission seated on the tribune. McClintock had been replaced by Carl Strom, who did not get up and leave when I rose to give the opening report.

Despite dollar bribes to some of the delegates, the Fourth Congress approved a formal and permanent Neutrality Act. The debate was very long, for there were those who questioned the advisability of writing it into our constitution. At one point, when near-unanimity had been reached, I put the question: 'What if the US Congress does not like our Neutrality Act, and votes to cut off economic aid?' The reply came from Hou Youn, of the Committee in Defence Of Neutrality.

'If we are sincere in our neutrality,' he said, 'other powers should respect this. But if the US does not, and stops its aid, we have powerful friends to whom we can turn for help.' Hou Youn's words were heartily applauded, and it was unanimously decreed that the National Assembly draft a law which would include the following points:

1. Cambodia is a neutral country.
2. Cambodia abstains from military or ideological alliances with other countries.
3. Cambodia will not commit aggression against other countries, but in case she is the victim of aggression, she reserves the right:
   Firstly, to take up arms in self-defence.
   Secondly, to appeal to the United Nations for help.

Thirdly, to appeal for aid to a friendly power capable of crushing the aggressor.

This act was later incorporated into our constitution. The United States never respected our decision, and worked day and night to render it meaningless – with results which the world now knows. But the Fourth National Congress was another milestone in Cambodia's development, and the Neutrality Act will form a cornerstone of our foreign policy after victory.

Chapter 6

What Price Dollar Aid?

In 1956, just after I resigned as Premier and Foreign Minister, and thus no longer encountered officially the objectionable Ambassador McClintock, I accompanied the Queen Mother to a new maternity clinic, fitted out with recently arrived American material. To my consternation, McClintock turned up to officiate at the handing-over ceremony. Oozing with the self-satisfaction of a socialite patron of the charities handing out gifts to the poor, McClintock strutted about, remarking on the excellent quality of the equipment. At one point, he turned to me in front of the assembled diplomats and said: 'Ah, Prince Sihanouk ... this should particularly interest you – as a great one-man manufacturer of babies!'[1]

I replied: 'No, Mr Ambassador. There will be no more babies. Those that might have come have smelled the bad odour of equipment from US imperialism. They prefer to remain where they are for ever rather than to be born under such conditions. They don't like the odour.' The diplomats tittered; McClintock reddened and removed himself to the far side of the Queen Mother. This was the last such gaffe he ever made in my presence.

This is a trifling anecdote, but it illustrates the endless series of affronts to our national pride entailed by the acceptance of gifts from the USA. For they obviously expected us to forget our dignity, swallow their clumsy insults and grovel with gratitude. Paradoxically, the genius of American

1. In keeping with the tradition of the Cambodian royal family, Sihanouk had half a dozen wives – his grandfather had had sixty – and thirteen children (editor's note).

diplomats for verbally treading on our toes, though sometimes the most hurtful, was the least harmful of their traits.

What I soon discovered was that in accepting their 'aid',
we were infecting ourselves with a virus which poisoned the
national bloodstream. I tried to resist their 'dollar diplomacy', but it was like an insidious, paralysis-type illness – and
by the time the symptoms appeared it was too late to do much
about it. Even after I cut off aid altogether, the poison continued its work. Top level 'dollar addicts' in our government
were prepared to commit treason and maybe to undermine
my stop-gap measures, in order to get the dollars flowing in
again.

With hindsight, it is now clear that dollar 'aid' was used
to purchase treachery. The modest twenty-five million dollars
Cambodia received annually during a decade to patch up a
war-shattered and colonialist-plundered economy, and, as I
naively thought, to improve the lives of my compatriots,
suddenly spiralled up to about 400 million annually when it
became a question of massacring them.

Hire Asian traitors to kill Asian patriots: that is the essence
of the Nixon doctrine, in the name of which Cambodia has
been laid waste. If American taxpayers could see the use to
which their money has been put in my country, they would
be revolted.

Why did I accept dollar 'aid' in the first place? By the
time the 1954 Geneva Conference put an end to the shooting
war in Indo-China, the US was footing eighty per cent of the
bill through credits made available directly to Paris. France
allotted a portion of this money to pay the Cambodian army
and administration, as well as the costs of waging war there.
With the granting of independence – and, later, the end of
the war – the Americans halted the payments to France, and
proposed making them directly to Cambodia. The French
objected, but were in no position to dispute the matter. The
first US overtures to us were based on the theme of expanding
and modernizing our army in order to play our appointed
role in the defence of the 'free world'. John Foster Dulles
portrayed to us the spectre of imminent 'communist aggression', and demonstrated the need for a strong army – for

which the US would be prepared to pay – and offered financial help in other fields.

We had to have an army, but we were more interested in repairing the war-damaged infrastructures, building up independent communications with the outside world, repairing roads and bridges and, in general, doing something to give our long-suffering people some of the necessities of life. We wanted especially to improve education and health facilities. So I gratefully agreed to accept financial aid. But it proved a source of corruption from the beginning.

Apart from the purely military side, dollar aid was used largely to finance consumer-goods imports. The importers paid riels into a 'counterpart fund' at the official rate of thirty-five riels to the dollar, and the administration could then withdraw these riels from the 'counterpart fund' to pay the army and finance economic projects. This soon developed into a frantic scramble by importers to get their hands on the largest possible share of dollar loot for ends which had nothing to do with the economic development of the country. At the top level, it was the Americans who decided who got how much! Dollar allocations were often in proportion to the degree of political cooperation of the recipients. Such cooperation, as time went on, meant the undermining of our Cambodian concepts of neutrality and independence.

There was a premium on corruption for those who handed out the import licences, and the dollar allocations which went with them. There was a premium on corruption for customs inspectors who closed their eyes to the fact that the goods actually imported often bore no relation to the invoices for which dollar allocations had been made. We later found that a high proportion of these dollars were salted away in Hong Kong banks, and the goods for which they had been allocated were either never imported, or were imported in miniscule quantities compared to the dollars granted. A whole new breed of 'importers' sprang up, getting dollars for badly needed imports at the official rate, selling them off on the black market again at two or more times that rate, reinvesting the proceeds in more dollars at the official rate, and so on *ad infinitum*.

Those who fattened on this system were the loudest in praise of US 'aid'. As Americans sat in on the organs that controlled both the 'allotting' and the 'counterpart fund', they were involved in the corruption from the start. As a means of penetrating the economy and the politics of the country, one American cynic was heard to boast that the 'counterpart fund' was the 'greatest invention since the wheel'! Fund administrators consciously developed a sort of compradore class with a vested interest in pushing US policies; a class which had no interest in building up our economy. Trafficking would come to an end if we started producing, from our own factories, the goods they were supposed to be importing. These new compradores were against my policies, and they sabotaged them. Their champion from the beginning was Sirik Matak.

The rightists sneered, many of the leftists scoffed, when I spoke of 'Buddhist Socialism', and when I stressed the term 'socialist' in the Sangkum, the Popular Socialist Community. But I knew, and I repeated many times in those first postwar years, that there could be no political independence without economic and financial independence. We had no industrial or manufacturing class to speak of, so I favoured setting up a certain number of state-owned industries, while helping to develop artisan-type small industries in the private sector.

I had announced plans to set up, with Chinese help, plants to produce cement, textiles, paper, plywood, agricultural implements and other goods. We had no capitalists with the money or the will to develop such projects. If we were to have such factories at all they had to be built and run by the state. Not to have them was to condemn the country to perpetual underdevelopment or non-development, and to living off American handouts. Chinese aid was completely free, without conditions, and aimed specifically at developing the economy. There was nothing paternalistic or charitable in the spirit with which it was given.

In a report to the Third Sangkum cabinet in February 1956, I made my position clear when I said we did not want a 'capitalism, which in our country is one of the major obstacles to social progress. Our capitalists', I said, 'are only interested in enriching themselves and shamelessly exploiting their employees and the country's resources without giving the least return either to the state or to the employees.'

The scramble for bigger shares of dollar aid had nothing in common either with national dignity or Buddhist concepts. The US would not make dollars available to state-owned industries, nor for anything connected with servicing them. And there was soon developed a vested interest among the compradores against industrial development. They used their dollar earnings moreover to buy supporters in the National Assembly, and to set up powerful lobbies there against our economic policies. Needless to say, these individuals later on were amongst the ringleaders of the Lon Nol–Sirik Matak régime.

Utilization of aid from China was sabotaged, because the factories China was prepared to build would have produced just those goods that the compradores were making fortunes in pretending to import. It suited US economic and, above all, political interests, to keep Chinese and Soviet aid out. In this the interests of the US and the compradores were identical – but for the latter this represented treachery. US economic 'aid' was designed to thrust our economy irreversibly into the so-called liberal system which, as one could see in Thailand and South Vietnam, only accentuated social injustice and in no way corresponded to the needs of an underdeveloped country – not to mention the disastrous political effects in terms of lost independence.

Within a couple of years, and exclusively through manipulations of dollar 'aid', the US had created a powerful internal lobby in our country, a political fifth column working to scrap neutrality and place Cambodia under the SEATO umbrella. If this came to pass, the dollar rewards would be boundless. The sky was the limit. True – except that from the sky rained down tens of thousands of tons of bombs from B 52s, bringing death and destruction. But there was a boundless flow of dollars!

It was impossible for me to keep track of all that was going on in the economic sphere, and there were groups who made it their business to keep me from knowing. But in December

1956, a cabinet crisis occurred – ostensibly over failure to prosecute corruption, but in fact because of measures taken to halt currency-swindling and black-marketeering. This was the first open political move by the compradores who included former cabinet ministers and heads of government departments. The government fell despite my efforts to save it. I had evidence that the US Embassy and the wealthier of the compradores had bought up enough deputies in the National Assembly to override my recommendations.

When the cabinet fell, there were strong rumours of an impending coup, but it appears the Americans had not yet found a strong man capable of pulling it off. My reply to the new crisis was to convoke the Fourth National Congress of the Sangkum, as described in the previous chapter. But it was not only the Neutrality Act that was to be discussed. Above all it was the question of defining the role and relations of the National Congress *vis-a-vis* the National Assembly. I was worried about the implications of the buying up of National Assembly deputies – the immediate cause of the crisis. But, even if a majority of the ninety-one deputies in the Assembly could be bought up, it would be impossible to do the same with the thousands of grassroot delegates to the National Congress, not only because of their numbers, but because of their high morality.

In my opening report, looking the newly arrived US Ambassador, Carl Strom, squarely in the eyes, I referred to the fact that, according to information from our police, 'an insurrection financed from abroad is now being prepared'. I spoke of 'politicians and ambitious individuals grouped together in clans, ready to tear each other apart to seize power in the interests of a foreign state'. The foreigner, I warned, does not give something for nothing, especially when his bounty is directed towards individuals whose ambitions have made them turn their backs on the higher interests of the nation. 'It is clear,' I said, 'that myself or the Sangkum are the constant targets of one or another of these forces, because they will never forgive us for having practised policies with a courage and an energy disproportionate to our size as a nation.' Reading that speech sixteen years later, it does not seem an inapt description of what happened from 18 March 1970 onwards!

Referring to the various gifts offered to Cambodia during my travels in the socialist countries – including a 500-bed, completely-equipped and staffed hospital from the Soviet Union, and specific promises of economic aid from China, Poland, and Czechoslovakia – I pointed out that the acceptance of these gifts was being sabotaged by internal and external enemies opposed to our independent development.

During the discussion, there were barbed references to various personalities within the National Assembly and the Sangkum who had been bought up with foreign money. At that point I dropped a bombshell: I proposed that the National Congress should become the nation's supreme policy-making body. Its decisions should be binding on the National Assembly. This would block any possibility of a majority of Assembly delegates being bought up to block or reverse fundamental national policies. The National Congress would continue to meet twice a year to define major policies. The role of the National Assembly would be to discuss, ratify, and implement decisions of the Congress. It was a bold, far-reaching move, which would temporarily block efforts to subvert the National Assembly – and thus national policies – with dollar bribes. My enemies had brought about the downfall of the government on the pretext of 'lack of democracy'. I threw democracy back at them in a much purer form, and they were dumbfounded. I think I gained many years of life – specifically thirteen years – for Cambodian peace and neutrality by that one move.

Only thus can the will of the people really be imposed. The opinion of our peasants and working people is a very precious thing to us. The voice of the people must be heard, and it is through the National Congress that it can be most effective. It is not enough for National Assembly deputies and ministers to meet the people only every four years when they want to get themselves re-elected. They should come here and give an account of their activities every six months. They should answer people's questions; listen to their advice; explain their own activities.

My opponents were so taken aback that no one dared to step

to the microphone. To oppose this wider form of democratic decision-making, in the ancient Greek pattern of democracy, would have been to identify themselves with the bribe-takers and corrupters. So the guilty were tongue-tied and found no advocates. The Pracheachon (People's or Communist) Party immediately supported my proposal, as I knew was certain they would, for they had once proposed something similar. Delegate after delegate rose to affirm his support. With a few minor changes, the proposal was accepted with hardly a dissenting voice. In the future the National Congress would be supreme and indeed it remained so until its final session in December 1969. After the 18 March coup, it entirely ceased to function.

The National Assembly's powers were thus severely restricted. If it refused to ratify a decision of Congress, the most it could do was refer it back to the next National Congress session, where the decision taken would be final. In case delegates of Congress could not reach agreement on an issue, this could be submitted to a nationwide referendum.

My most inveterate adversaries, including those who were later to depose me, sat on the tribune and could do nothing but hide their fury, smiles frozen on their faces, politely applauding with the rest when the measure was adopted. I was later accused of manipulating the National Congress for my own ends. My reply is: In how many countries is such a direct form of democracy permitted? And what better way could be found to seek a true expression of the people's will? Certainly, the size of Cambodia – like Greece in the past and Switzerland today – facilitated such direct confrontations between people and legislators. But whereas my enemies worked with their money and their subterfuges in the shadows, I brought shafts of sunlight to focus on the problems of the day. I was always prepared to discuss with the representatives of the people for as long as necessary. I fully realized, of course, that my prestige as former King, and leader of the royal crusade for independence, gave me an advantage over my opponents. But had the cause I was espousing been unjust, or contrary to the people's interests, I would neither have wanted – nor dared –

to advocate it. Had I spoken for the cause of my opponents, I firmly believe the people would have rejected me.

'Of the people, for the people, by the people' – although never so precisely formulated – had been the motto of my royal ancestors for centuries in their conduct of public affairs. Perhaps it was for that reason that our monarchy is one of the oldest in the world, and I was the eighty-fourth King to be crowned.

The dollar offensive, protean-like, was to assume other forms, as will be seen in the following two chapters. But those who hoped to take over power 'constitutionally' through a hireling National Assembly had to wait another thirteen years. Then they struck like cowards, during my absence, and violated the popular decision to place the National Congress above the National Assembly. By that time, however, the political consciousness of the Cambodian people had moved to a much higher level, partly because of their direct participation in the National Congress debates.

At that fateful Fourth National Congress, as a deterrent to those who would make a career out of pocketing US dollars, a number of corrupt people in high places had to explain their activities to the delegates. The result was that dossiers were handed over to the courts for further action. In my opening report, I said that we had 'arrived at a turning point in our history' and that the welfare of the country depended henceforth 'on the consciousness of the outstanding personalities of the elite and on our people as a whole. May this consciousness regain once more its purely national character, and our country its freedom and peace.' This was the case for more than a decade of relative peace and prosperity. It abruptly came to an end in March 1970, but valuable time had been gained in forging national unity.

Looking back, one could say we got along well enough when American bounty was limited to about twenty-five million dollars a year, and better still when we finally renounced all US military and economic aid for reasons which I will explain in detail in later chapters. But what did Lon Nol and his followers do with their official, annual 341 million-dollar reward for treachery?[1] Within the first few months after the coup, they were using it to destroy what we had built up during the previous sixteen years. Universities, schools, hospitals, factories, dams, hydro-electric projects, rubber plantations, clinics, playgrounds, scores of towns, hundreds of villages, tens of thousands of homes were bombed and napalmed off the face of our motherland. No funds for construction; no limits for destruction – this was the precept for US 'aid' in Cambodia!

There is no better illustration of the depths to which the dollar-seekers sank than the fact that 'Marshal' Lon Nol and 'General' Sirik Matak turned their howitzers on Angkor Wat, the unique and irreplaceable monument to the glories of our past. Irreparable damage has been done to it by shells, fired by Lon Nol's troops which exploded in the upper portion of the southern gate, but above all by those that landed in the ground floor gallery, reducing to powder the exquisite bas-relief frescoes which portrayed in the form of allegory the history of our people. The French, in their colonial wars of conquest and reconquest, the Japanese, during the years of their occupation, respected Angkor Wat. It required renegades of our own race to commit this atrocity. They will be cursed for a thousand and more years. So will those who corrupted them, fattening them with dollars. Nothing could be more symbolic of their treachery than that they dared turn their cannon on the Angkor temples.

President Nixon has explained that the 341 million dollars spent annually in the officially-approved slaughter of Cambodians is 'the best investment in foreign assistance that the United States has made in my political life'.[2] Because of the 'success' of the Cambodian operation, 'US casualties have been cut by two thirds, a hundred thousand Americans have come home and more are doing so'.[3] In other words, Lon Nol and Sirik Matak, by allowing Nixon to export the fighting from South Vietnam to Cambodia – to substitute Cambodian

1. I quote the official figure for 1971, but others, including Senator Mansfield, have quoted up to one billion dollars as the total annual sum for the destruction of Cambodia.

2. As reported by UPI, 10 October 1970.

3. In a press statement, 16 February 1971.

for American and South Vietnamese corpses – have rendered valuable service, for which 341 million dollars is a reasonable annual reimbursement!

If this bargain was not sufficiently clear from the start, it was spelled out by Sirik Matak in an interview with Christian Hovelacque of *Le Monde*, published on 3 December 1971. 'After all,' asked Hovelacque, 'was not the war in Vietnam exported to Cambodia?'

'Yes, exactly,' replied Sirik Matak, 'and this is the real key to the Indo-China war. We've known this from the first day. If the communists cannot succeed in breaking down our resistance, they will not be able to succeed in South Vietnam, faced with an army of 1,300,000 men.'

'Our problem is not how to get out of Asia but the proper way to stay in Asia,' said Marshall Green, US Under-Secretary of State for Asian Affairs.[1] And he claimed that the Cambodian operation had reduced war costs in Indo-China from twenty-nine billions to between eleven and fourteen billions per year. 'We pay them for killing each other while we reduce our own forces,' said Senator George McGovern,[2] referring to the extension of the war in Indo-China and the Nixon Doctrine.

Perhaps the essence of the real dividends of American 'aid' in financing Asians to fight Asians, Indo-Chinese to fight Indo-Chinese, and Cambodians to fight Cambodians, was summed up by Green when he said that 'a reduced American presence in South-East Asia should not mean a reduction in the overseas activities of our private sector, or of the presence of our commercial and investment interests'.[3] In other words, Indo-China will be safe for US investments as long as the Lon Nols, the Sirik Mataks and the Son Ngoc Thanhs are around.

Because I was not prepared to accept this prostitution of my country, and was prepared to fight anyone who was, I became the object of innumerable plots and assassination attempts, some of which are described in the chapters that follow.

1. Reported by AP, 25 December 1970.
2. Reported by UPI, 22 February 1971.
3. As reported by UPI, 13 January 1971.

Chapter 7

The Dap Chhuon Plot

In June 1958, I received a shock: Saigon troops had invaded our north-east province of Stung Treng. They had penetrated to a depth of about nine miles, and showed every sign of staying indefinitely – they were even putting up new boundary markers. But, although bad enough, it was not this that affected me the most; it was the revelation that, because I was receiving US military aid, I was refused the authority to expel the invaders. At least, this was how US Ambassador Carl Strom explained matters: US military aid was provided exclusively for the purpose of repelling communist aggressors, and in no case could it be used against America's SEATO allies.

I started by asking Strom to use his influence to persuade Ngo Dinh Diem to withdraw his troops. The ambassador's reply was that the United States could not interfere in a dispute between neighbouring states, both friends of the USA. Dispute! There was no dispute – just a case of flagrant invasion.

I replied that he left me no alternative but to alert our troops for combat. The ambassador's reaction was worthy of McClintock at his worst. US military aid would be suspended, he said, if a single bullet were fired in anger at one of America's protégés. Not only that, but even the use of a single US-supplied truck to transport Cambodian troops for a military confrontation with a SEATO member would constitute grounds for cancelling aid. In vain did I argue that no communist aggressors threatened us, and that the only menace to our frontiers came from South Vietnam and Thailand. Strom's third edict capped the other two. When I intimated that I would then have to consider alternative sources of military aid (meaning China), Strom countered that US military assistance was granted only under conditions that precluded recipients from accepting military aid from any socialist country!

To put it in plain language as I explained in a speech at the time, we accepted aid for one reason: to defend our territorial integrity. But, by the terms under which it is granted, we must sit back with folded arms while our frontiers are violated, our territory occupied. And where would it all stop? We urgently needed to become masters in our own house, at least as far as national defence was concerned. We had to adopt policies which 'are more in keeping with logic and reason, and the necessities of survival as a race, a nation, and a free and independent country'.

In August of that year, I visited Peking for a second time. The Saigon troops were still entrenched in our territory. I had several long talks with Chairman Mao Tse-tung about the recent crisis. As a result of that visit diplomatic relations were established between our two nations and China agreed to build a number of industrial enterprises for us. As was to be expected, the setting-up of diplomatic relations soon stirred the fires of CIA wrath. This time it assumed a more concrete form than it had after my 1956 visit to China.

The man they were grooming to overthrow me, Son Ngoc Thanh, was building up his Khmer Serei bases in South Vietnam and Thailand by that time. A few words are necessary to explain the character of this life-long intriguer. He is a former *guru*; a sort of spiritual adviser to the Democratic Party; a one-time puppet Premier and Foreign Minister under the Japanese occupation forces, who was condemned to death as a traitor by the French. I had interceded with the French to have the death penalty commuted, and later to have his exile annulled so he could return to his homeland. He has been at my throat ever since! To serve the CIA was a logical step in his sinister career. They set him up as leader of the Khmer Serei and took over the financing, training and arming of the commando bands in bases and training camps in the South Vietnam and Thai frontier regions. By the end of 1957, Son Ngoc Thanh adopted as deputy leader of the Khmer Serei, Sam Sary, a former vice-Premier, and our ambassador in London until I dismissed him in 1957 because of a scandalous incident.[1]

In September 1958, about a month after my return from Peking, the SEATO council met in Bangkok. There were two main items on the agenda. One was a US plan to extend the scope of SEATO operations to include Taiwan. Despite the efforts of Admiral Harry Felt, who headed US naval forces in the Pacific, this was rejected. (The 'off-shore islands crisis' was at its height. But after the Korean experience, America's European allies were not eager to burn their fingers again on American chestnuts.) The second item was how to deal with Sihanouk's 'crime' of having established diplomatic relations with Peking. A majority opinion did me the honour of deciding that 'something' should be done. It was left to the Thai government and its CIA advisers to decide what. As the experienced plotter, John Peurifoy, was on the spot, still crowned with the laurels won in triumphs of subterfuge in Greece and Guatemala, there was little doubt that action would follow.

Three months after the SEATO council meeting, there was a less publicized conspiratorial get-together in Bangkok, presided over by Field-Marshal Sarit Thanarat, who had seized power as military dictator in traditional Thai fashion.[2]

1. Sam Sary had used an embassy servant as his concubine. When she became pregnant, he beat her and otherwise ill-used her to the extent that she ran out into the street one day and was rescued by the London police. Sam Sary had the effrontery to claim that he was only acting according to established Cambodian customs. His subsequent association with Son Ngoc Thanh was short-lived. He disappeared mysteriously in Laos – liquidated, it was rumoured by Son Ngoc Thanh, who never brooked rivals.

2. Sarit Thanarat, after ten months abroad, mostly in the US for 'health reasons', secretly returned to Bangkok on 19 October 1958 and carried out a military coup the following day. To show his 'devotion to the free world', he banned all political parties the following day, declaring martial law, and arresting political leaders, editors and journalists. The parallel between Thanarat's putsch in 1958 and Lon Nol's in 1970 (after Lon Nol's prolonged political grooming for 'health reasons' abroad) needs no comment. Nor the fact that to have régimes

There were other generals at this meeting, also Son Ngoc Thanh, Ngo Trong Hieu, Saigon's Consul-General in Phnom Penh and a relative of Ngo Dinh Diem, and of course some CIA operatives from Peurifoy's staff.

Three decisions were taken:

1. To finance an opposition party in Cambodia aimed at undermining my neutralist régime.
2. To create an atmosphere of insecurity by kidnappings, armed holdups, and false rumours of an imminent communist takeover.
3. To form armed groups inside Cambodia, ready for H-hour, D-day.

Son Ngoc Thanh would concentrate his Khmer Serei forces on the Thai-Cambodian frontier, with two Thai officers and over a million CIA-supplied dollars at his disposal. Ngo Trong Hieu promised that a similar quantity of Khmer Krom commandos would be concentrated on the South-Vietnamese-Cambodian frontier. General Dap Chhuon, commander of our armed forces in Siem Reap and Kompong Thom provinces (an officer whose loyalty I never doubted at the time) and Sam Sary were to prepare an armed uprising in Cambodia itself. To coordinate contacts, arrange supplies and finance, there was a CIA agent stationed in the US Embassy in Phnom Penh – an American of Japanese descent, Victor Masao Matsui – a dangerous fellow who was expelled from Karachi in 1966 for subversive activities. He worked hand-in-glove with Ngo Trong Hieu.

In the autumn of 1958, I headed the Cambodian delegation to the United Nations, following which I went on official business to Washington. I met with President Eisenhower who gave me some paternalistic advice, following which I laid a wreath at the Arlington National Cemetery. When I returned to the UN, members of my delegation informed me that, in my absence, Slat Peou had spent almost all his time with Americans. He had numerous conferences with them – even in his hotel room – but had never

---

ready to carry out their policies, the US, in the end, had to install military dictatorships in Saigon, Bangkok and Phnom Penh.

mentioned this to anyone. Slat Peou had been a very close friend of Matsui in Phnom Penh. Slat Peou's brother, General Dap Chhuon, had used his influence to get him elected to the National Assembly as member for Siem Reap, and thus launched him in a political career. It was Dap Chhuon also who arranged for his brother to go to India to study English. He was probably first recruited by the CIA in that country, joined my delegation and became a natural link between Matsui, Ngo Trong Hieu, and Dap Chhuon.

Everything seemed to be going according to the Bangkok plan. In January 1959, Sam Sary sent me an open letter asking permission to form a new political party. Tens of thousands of leaflets, distributed at the same time as the letter, made it clear that this new party was to push for a more pro-Western 'neutralism' and seek to turn our country away from its stand of unyielding independence necessitated by US meddling in our affairs. There were demagogic appeals against the monarchy and our traditional institutions. One could see the hand of Son Ngoc Thanh everywhere. The real aim was obviously not to form a political party but to sow confusion.

There were outbreaks of banditry and kidnappings – especially of children of prominent political personalities – in widely separated parts of the country. Son Ngoc Thanh massed three battalions of Khmer Serei troops aimed at Battambang province (seized by Thailand during the Second World War) and Khmer Krom commando units started infiltrating into our territory from the South Vietnam provinces of Tay Ninh and Kien Tuong. Dap Chhuon quietly concentrated his forces in strategic points of Siem Reap and Kompong Thom provinces and even placed some of his men inside the Royal Palace at Phnom Penh. This was easy, for I was not suspicious of him, even when I began to catch wind of the plot.

Generally speaking, we had a good intelligence network, and were fortunate in enjoying the friendship of persons in other diplomatic services. Together with reports of our own, we received warnings from the Embassies of the People's

Republic of China and France, that something nasty was afoot. There was now evidence enough to act. On 13 January 1959, when the situation seemed to be reaching flashpoint, I revealed in a speech at Kompong Cham that we had uncovered a plot aimed at liquidating me, seizing power at the top, setting up a pro-US puppet régime and ending our neutrality.

This plan was drawn up by a marshal, head of the government of a neighbouring kingdom, by the envoys of a neighbouring state, and by Son Ngoc Thanh. Like nocturnal birds of prey blinded by the hunter's torch, dark schemes hatched in secret will come to nothing once they are dragged out into the light.

As it turned out, there was still quite a lot to be dragged out into the light inside Cambodia itself, although my revelations dampened the ardour of the Saigon-Bangkok plotters at the top level. It was not easy to get to the bottom of the plot inside the country. A week after my Kompong Cham speech, I had enough evidence to strike at Sam Sary. In a sudden move, I arrested most of his henchmen. But, due to some fast work by Matsui and Ngo Trong Hieu – and, as I discovered years later, treachery by Lon Nol and some of his top aides – Sam Sary escaped. Precautionary movements by our troops along the borders foiled the main part of the plan.

In early February, I received reports of unusual happenings at Siem Reap. A brief visit by Ngo Trong Hieu to Dap Chhuon preceded Ngo's abrupt departure for Saigon. On 7 February, two Chinese from the 'Kam-Wah Film Company' arrived from Hong Kong with huge cases of equipment – all installed in Dap Chhuon's villa. Later that day, a more distinguished visitor arrived at Siem Reap airport, also on his way to see Dap Chhuon: Admiral Harry Felt.

Siem Reap, at the site of the Angkor temples, is used to receiving visitors of mark, but the interest displayed in Cambodian antiquities in the couple of weeks that followed was unprecedented. Ten days after Admiral Felt, General Lawton Collins arrived. He had rather brusquely taken over from the French the problem of training the South Vietnamese army. Next to sign the visitors' book was none other than Colonel Edward Lansdale, the renowned CIA specialist in cloak-

and-dagger operations. It was he who had established Ngo
Dinh Diem in power in Saigon, and had helped kick out the
French. Finally, Admiral Hopwood, Commander-in-Chief
of the Pacific Fleet, dropped in for a look at the temples and
a whisky-soda with Dap Chhuon.

Other details came to my ears. The two 'Chinese' were in
fact South Vietnamese; their 'film equipment', when
assembled, turned out to be powerful radio transmitters
which they started to set up in the jungle surrounding the
temples. Dap Chhuon had established a network of posts
along all roads leading to Siem Reap from Phnom Penh to
warn him of any movement of troops from the capital. But,
when I decided on 21 February (1959) to send troops to arrest
him, it was the sentries from these key posts who guided our
forces to the key spots, enabling them to enter Siem Reap
without a shot being fired, or Dap Chhuon being warned.
He was strolling in the garden of his villa when he first
realized the game was up. He fled and managed to reach a
nearby village before he was wounded and captured.

There followed a curious incident, the details of which have
become known to me only since the 18 March coup. I had
entrusted General Lon Nol, then Chief-of-Staff of the armed
forces, with the task of arresting Dap Chhuon. In order to
unravel the whole plot, I wanted him alive. Lon Nol reported
to me at the time that Dap Chhuon had been mortally
wounded trying to flee. In fact, he was only slightly wounded,
and, when captured, insisted on being brought before a
senior officer. Lon Nol's response was to have him shot. Dap
Chhuon was demanding permission to make a statement.
Available evidence later established that this would have
implicated Lon Nol in the plot – so Dap Chhuon was silenced.
It had crossed my mind at the time that it was odd that my
information as to what was going on at Siem Reap came from
low level sources contacting me directly and not through
reports from Lon Nol's channels; but in the euphoria of having
thwarted a plot of such dimensions, that detail was over-
looked.

The two radio operators were arrested in Dap Chhuon's
villa. They had South Vietnamese passports, but no visas or

stamps showing they had entered Cambodia. Their radio equipment was seized, as were the logbooks of communications between Dap Chhuon and Saigon and Bangkok. Seized also were 270 kilograms of gold in small ingots for paying agents and commando groups. There was ample evidence of the roles of Matsui, Ngo Trong Hieu, and Slat Peou. Matsui and Ngo Trong Hieu were expelled; Slat Peou was shot as a traitor; the Saigon radio operators were shot as spies. All the evidence was shown to Ambassador Strom.

On 26 March 1959, I conducted a group of some twenty diplomats – including those from the United States, Soviet Union, People's Republic of China, Britain, and France – on a personal tour of the Dap Chhuon villa, so they could see for themselves. The exhibits included all sorts of American arms – not supplied within the framework of US military 'aid'.

The Dap Chhuon conspiracy was based on two possibilities; a maximum and a minimum with subordinate alternatives based on circumstances. The maximum, thwarted by the exposure and flight of Sam Sary, was simply to seize power at the top in a military coup. There was also to have been a link-up of forces moving in from Thailand and South Vietnam with those of Dap Chhuon, thus opening a corridor joining Vietnam and Thailand through Cambodia. The minimum possibility, the success of which the plotters seemed to have had no doubts at all, was the separation of the northern provinces from the rest of Cambodia, and their merger with the southern provinces of Laos, to form a new secessionist state which would have been immediately recognized by the USA. The right-wing Laotian, Prince Boun Oum of Champassac, is said to have agreed to this. This was to be a starting-point from which to take over the whole of Cambodia. All of these potential threats were foiled by timely warnings from foreign friends, by the vigilance and loyalty of my troops at ground level, and especially by the local militia in Siem Reap, who first alerted me as to what was going on in the Dap Chhuon villa.

The Dap Chhuon plot was only one of the sinister events to occur in our country in 1959. Just six months later, on 31

August, I was preparing to join my mother and father in the throne room of the Royal Palace, as was my custom when we were together in Phnom Penh. Normally we went through the morning mail together. On this occasion I was slightly delayed because Son Sann, our Prime Minister, was about to leave to head our delegation to the United Nations and we had some matters to discuss. He expressed the wish to take leave of my parents. Part of the mail had already been brought in, including a packaged gift for my mother. She usually opened such gifts herself but to save time and because Son Sann was waiting to leave for the airport, she sent it into the anteroom to be opened. Hardly had the Prime Minister entered the throne room, when there was a tremendous, shattering explosion. Prince Vakrivan, the Chief of Protocol who opened the parcel, was killed immediately. A hole was blown through the thick concrete floor, killing King Norodom Suramarit's personal valet, and wounding two more. A bomb of exceptional explosive force had been concealed in a small lacquer box, and set to go off when the wrappings were removed. The palace was cordoned off immediately, and the identities of all present were checked. My guards turned up some relatives of Sam Sary's who admitted that the latter had asked them to be at the palace that morning, and to report on any unusual events. At that time Sam Sary was with Son Ngoc Thanh in Saigon. We were able to trace the origin of the deadly gift, and established that it had been sent from an American military base in South Vietnam.

My parents were unharmed, but I am convinced that the shock hastened the death of my father, the kindly, universally-loved King, seven months later, at the age of sixty-four. In this connection it is worth noting that, in January 1960, an Indian newspaper published a photostat of a letter written by Sam Sary to Edmund Kellog, CIA political counsellor attached to the US Embassy in Phnom Penh. Dated 3 September 1959, the letter expressed 'regret' for the failure of 31 August and said that 'only the most effective measures can help us attain our common goals'. According to the photostat, Sam Sary expressed 'complete agreement with the opinion of your Ambassador, His Excellency Mr William

Trimble . . . and I can count upon his help and cooperation'. Trimble, meanwhile, had replaced Carl Strom as US Ambassador in Phnom Penh.

Later, the Dap Chhuon plot was used as the theme for a film I produced, *Shadow Over Angkor*. Many Westerners thought it was the product of an overly active imagination. Alas, I did not at that time possess an imagination sufficiently fertile to foresee the grotesque and fantastic schemes which the CIA was dreaming up.

The CIA was in the forefront (except, when it suited their purposes, to remain concealed) of every plot directed against my life and my country's integrity. From 1954, until diplomatic relations were broken in 1965, my intelligence services listed twenty-seven known CIA agents registered as 'diplomats' at the Phnom Penh embassy, and the list was certainly incomplete. They were backed up by scores of others in the Saigon and Bangkok embassies, working hand-in-glove with them. For those who still question whether the USA, through the CIA, was involved in the 18 March coup, I can do no better than urge them to study the details of the Dap Chhuon plot and the lacquer-box attentat.

Chapter 8

The Survival Miracle

In the flurry of commentaries after the 18 March coup, some of which read like premature political obituaries of myself, a constant theme was the 'miracle' that my neutralist régime had been able to survive so long; that the oasis of peace had not been submerged by the shifting sands of war swirling about our frontiers. There was much talk of the miraculous balancing act I had performed *vis-à-vis* the great powers and my war-bedevilled neighbours, to preserve the peace, independence and neutrality of my country.

Even those who, while I was engaged in a desperate diplomatic game, had dismissed me as the 'playboy prince' or the 'royal saxophonist', now that I was out of circulation, found a few kind words for the tight-rope act that had preserved Cambodian integrity for so long. Now that I was 'finished', they could afford to be charitable. It was not only the international political commentators who promptly interred me when I could no longer perform miracles, but diplomats as well.

I was informed, for example, that the ambassador of one Anglo-Saxon state told his colleagues immediately after the coup (and even sent a cable saying the same thing to his government): 'You will soon see Sihanouk looking for a job as a film director of some French studio.' In fact, I remain Head of State. I trust that the subsequent demotion of that ambassador was not due to my failure to fulfil his prophecy! I include this anecdote because it demonstrated the general inability of Western diplomats to comprehend either Cambodian mentality – or myself.

It is no exaggeration to say that my physical survival – let alone that of my policies – was something of a miracle, considering that the CIA never stopped working behind the scenes to bring about my death.

The National United Front leadership expressed this opinion in a published document:

The United States arrived at the conclusion that, in order to destroy the peace and neutrality of Cambodia and to transform it into a neo-colony and a base of aggression against Vietnam and Laos, it would be necessary to kill, or at least to set aside, Prince Norodom Sihanouk, who was the incarnation of the policies of peace, national independence, and neutrality, unanimously supported by the Khmer people.

It was a question of finding the occasion and a reliable murderer – someone who was prepared to exchange his life for mine. But hired killers want to live and enjoy their wages, and few others wanted the job. Phnom Penh is not Vientiane, where assassination of political personalities is commonplace, killers can be whisked across the Mekong River at night into Thailand before the blood has ceased to flow from the victims. It is much more difficult to escape from Phnom Penh – hence the technique of the lacquer-bomb, mailed from abroad. And what did they care if the King and Queen died, as long as they got me?

Another attempt was made at the end of 1959 by a certain Rat Vat, in the pay of the CIA. But he was arrested and put out of harm's way before he could strike. He was just a young fanatic, who had been worked on by Son Ngoc Thanh to the point where he agreed to assassinate me. He was infiltrated into the country from Saigon with the help of the CIA, and instructed to mingle with the crowd during one of my frequent visits to the provinces, where I had the habit of mixing in a completely informal way with the people. His nervous behaviour attracted the attention of the police. He was detained, and found to be armed with a hand grenade and a pistol. He was to make up for the failure of the Dap Chhuon and the lacquer-box attentats. The CIA came close to succeeding in that fateful year of 1959.

1963 was also full of tensions. It was the year in which

South Vietnam and Thailand built up a big propaganda campaign for a 'preventive war' against Cambodia, and in which I broke off diplomatic relations with both countries. In Laos, too, tensions ran high. There were numerous political assassinations. The rightists were trying to sabotage the agreements concluded the previous year at a conference held at my initiative. (The Western powers had, for years, ignored my proposals for a Geneva Conference on Laos, until a military debacle of the rightists sent them hastening to the conference table.) Events reached a high point in Laos on the night of 1 April 1963, when the staunchly neutralist Foreign Minister, Quinim Pholsena, was gunned down and killed on the steps of his home in Vientiane, and his wife gravely wounded at his side. This was the signal for an all-out assault against the pro-Pathet Lao neutralist forces, on the Plain of Jars. Shock waves from these events were clearly felt in Cambodia, and the left became increasingly nervous.

Exactly one month after Quinim Pholsena's murder, Liu Shao Chi, then President of the People's Republic of China, arrived on a state visit to Cambodia. Following the warmest possible reception at the airport, he joined me in an open car and we drove through cheering, flag-waving crowds of Cambodians and Cambodian-Chinese residents lining the road from the airport to the capital. Close behind was a cavalcade of cars with other members of President Liu's suite, members of my government, and other leading dignatories.

Had all gone well for the CIA, at a point about three miles from Phnom Penh, there would have been a tremendous explosion under my car, and a hundred yards of roadway, cavalcade, bystanders and all would have been blown to smithereens. But when I invited the President to step into my car, I knew that the CIA-hired criminals were secure behind bars in a Phnom Penh jail.

A week or so before the scheduled visit, two strangers rented a house alongside the airport road, at a point quite close to what was then Phnom Penh's best-known Vietnamese restaurant, the Nakry Bopha. The senior of the two was a high-ranking Kuomintang army officer from Taiwan. From their residence, the newcomers started digging a tunnel towards the centre of the road. In this tunnel they proposed to place a bomb – a 'CIA special' like the lacquer box, with a super-explosive charge. President Liu's visit was a splendid occasion for them to kill two birds with one stone, and to satisfy two patrons at the same time: the Kuomintang and the CIA. Peking tipped off my security services when the two desperadoes departed from Taiwan and headed for Phnom Penh. So we had them under surveillance, and our police caught them *in flagrante delicto* – digging tools, bombs, false identity papers, and all. They could do nothing but make a complete confession, including details of their dealings with the CIA. They were duly tried and sentenced to death.

They were not executed. I did not pardon them nor did I sign the papers that would have sent them before a firing squad. Relations with my immediate neighbours were bad enough at the time, and I did not want to provide unnecessary pretexts for further complications. Lon Nol, incidentally, pleaded with me for their pardon, for reasons I did not understand at the time. He was usually the first to propose the firing squad! One of his first actions after the 18 March coup was to return the would-be assassins to the CIA.

It was also in 1963 that a customs inspector, who noticed something suspicious in a damaged crate, one of a number addressed to the US Embassy, asked permission to investigate. Normally anything addressed to an embassy was protected by diplomatic immunity but, as the inspector's suspicions seemed well-founded, permission was given. The crates were full of arms, almost certainly for the Khmer Serei, members of which our services knew were being infiltrated into Cambodia by the CIA. If Thailand and South Vietnam were to carry out their 'preventive war' threat, the CIA's job was to provide an effective fifth column at strategic points within the country. So the arms were smuggled in like the Kuomintang agent's bomb, under cover of US diplomatic immunity – an odd sort of military 'aid' for us.

Can any reasonable person wonder, after such episodes, why I ended US aid at the end of 1963 and kicked out some three hundred American military and economic officials who moved around our country as if they already owned it?

Towards the end of that year, Preap In, one of the right-hand men of Son Ngoc Thanh, swaggered across the frontier, confident in CIA claims that Cambodia was only awaiting the arrival of someone like himself to rise up and do away with Sihanouk. At that time, the Khmer Serei had their main bases in South Vietnam, so he entered Takeo province just across the Cambodian frontier, from one of these bases. He presented himself to In Tam, then governor of Takeo, as a conquering hero, and said he would be prepared to 'negotiate' with Sihanouk – presumably my surrender! The CIA had hypnotized him to that point.

At one of the Sangkum National Congresses, in replying to Son Ngoc Thanh's propaganda to the effect that everyone was against Sihanouk and for Son Ngoc Thanh, I dared Thanh to poke his nose inside our frontiers and see for himself. He and the CIA apparently persuaded Preap In that this was a surrender offer. Negotiate? Share power with traitors? Never. I called a special session of the National Congress to hear Preap In, and for him in turn to listen to the *vox populi*. Faced with reality as expressed by delegate after delegate, he admitted that he had been sadly misled by the CIA. But backing down was not enough: we had difficulty preventing the delegates from lynching him. For years he had plotted against us. Much innocent blood had been spilled by the Khmer Serei commandos. The unanimous opinion of the National Congress was that he should be handed over to a military tribunal. He was condemned to death and, in his case, I had no inhibitions in signing the death warrant. He was shot. Ironically enough, In Tam who arrested him, later made common cause with Preap In's chief, Son Ngoc Thanh.

From all points of view, 1963 was a year of trials and tensions with pressures applied on all fronts to try to make us crack. The Americans had already taken over the running of the war in Vietnam – although not yet with their own troops – and the big drive was on to force the rural population to accept life behind the barbed wire of 'strategic hamlets'. Large-scale rounding-up operations swept right up to our frontiers and spilled over in the form of air strikes against our frontier villages. Waves of refugees sought shelter in Cambodia from the planes and tanks, usually for a few days, until the troops withdrew and they could return to the ashes of their villages. The thrice-persecuted Khmer minority from the Mekong Delta preferred to stay in the haven of Cambodia. These were hundreds of families which had suffered, first as peasants who wanted to remain in their villages, secondly as a despised national minority whose culture the Saigon régime set out to destroy, thirdly as Buddhists at the hands of the racist and fanatically Catholic Ngo Dinh Diem. They did not want to return to the blessings of the 'free world', which in their case was expressed by bombs and napalm if they did not move quickly enough into the camps.

Because of my attacks on the irksome conditions of US aid, and the fact that the Americans realized that I knew much of it was being used to finance a network of CIA agents inside the country, plus the scandalous plots in which they had been engaged, the Americans began to feel their days with us might be numbered. I had already broken off relations with Bangkok and Saigon, which made Washington furious. Adding fuel to the fires of their wrath was the strengthening of the state sector in areas such as banking and the import-export trade. Sirik Matak, Yem Sambaur, Sim Var and others were also very unhappy. This I knew, but I did not know that, even then, Lon Nol was with them. We had a stable government then with the left represented by Khieu Samphan, as Secretary of State for Commerce, and Hou Youn, as State Secretary for Economic Planning.

It was at this time, in 1963, that Lon Nol began compiling dossiers with 'proof' that the left was plotting my overthrow. I cannot say that I have proof that the CIA was directly or indirectly involved in this attempt of Lon Nol to mislead me. It is reasonable to assume, however, that having been so thoroughly exposed in 1963, the Agency would not be averse to rigging something up against the left.

In any case, false accusations and fabricated evidence was the order of the day, and Lon Nol used this as a pretext for one of his periodic witch-hunts against the left, which included the summary execution of suspects at the moment of arrest. The result was that the first wave of intellectuals and others, including several hundred from Phnom Penh, left the cities for the former resistance bases (set up in the independence struggle against the French). Among those who left in 1963 was a college professor, Ieng Sary, followed by his wife, who had been a headmistress at a Phnom Penh secondary school. He immediately rallied to the resistance after the 18 March coup and became an assistant to Khieu Samphan. (Ieng Sary was the first resistance leader to be sent from the Cambodian National United Front's jungle headquarters to Peking, to present a report to government members on the situation inside the liberated areas.)

It was not only in Cambodia and Laos that 1963 was a year of plots and attentats. Indeed, I must consider myself more fortunate than some of those who worked for my destruction. On 1 November of that year, my two arch-enemies, Ngo Diem and Ngo Dihn Nhu, were assassinated with CIA help, and ten days later it was the President of United States himself who fell. Incidentally, I must correct an error which unfortunately was printed in the American press. I did, in fact, order three days of national celebrations when the detestable Saigon dictatorship ended. But, at the time of the assassination of President Kennedy, many of our shops displayed his portrait in their windows as a sign of respect. An unscrupulous American photographer asked a Cambodian passerby to pose and smile alongside one of the Kennedy portraits. This was published in the USA with captions to the effect that in Cambodia there was official rejoicing over President Kennedy's death – an absurd slander. Later I named a boulevard in Sihanoukville in his memory, and it was his widow, Jacqueline, who inaugurated the boulevard on 2 November 1967.

It was also in 1963 that Son Sakd, banker and top-level CIA agent, spent money like water to sabotage our economic reforms by buying up officials right and left with funds established by the CIA in his own Bank of Phnom Penh. Probably alarmed by the sudden dismantling of the American-staffed spy network, when I ordered all US military and economic 'aid' personnel out of the country at the end of the year, Son Sakd prepared his own plans accordingly. Perhaps he felt that he soon would be exposed, and that nobody would stand by him after the Americans departed.

In any case, Son Sann, then governor of the National Bank, came to see me one day to discuss Son Sakd. The latter was not a Cambodian but a Thailand-born Chinese. He had contacts with many rightists, including Sirik Matak, and had come to Phnom Penh from Bangkok with a very large sum of money, supposedly to set up business. It was at a time when I was encouraging foreign investment in the private sector of our economy, as long as the money genuinely contributed to our development. At the rate he threw his money around, Cambodians were convinced that he really was a flourishing businessman. He built some motels at Sihanoukville because I expressed interest in developing the tourist trade. He signed contracts to build more motels at the hillside resort of Kirirom, and also to construct a plant there for processing dairy products. This was the legitimate side of his activities.

He also founded the Bank of Phnom Penh with CIA capital, as we later discovered. Sirik Matak became an important shareholder in this bank, and subsequently became chief supporter and protector of Son Sakd.

'I am convinced this man is a swindler and not a banker,' said Son Sann, opening a dossier before me. 'How is it possible that the directors of a number of state enterprises have deposited their assets and working capital in his private Bank of Phnom Penh and not in one of our state banks?' Son Sann explained that he had been making some investigations, and had found that Son Sakd had spent large sums of money buying up directors of state enterprises, deputies, and even members of the government. He named, among others, Long Boreth, deputy in the National Assembly (who later became Lon Nol's Minister of Information). 'The official pretext given is that his bank pays a higher interest rate than the state banks,' continued Son Sann, 'but I have every reason to believe that Son Sakd has been pocketing this money and we are being robbed of the capital itself – not to mention the interest.'

I gave immediate instructions to send controllers to verify the accounts at the Bank of Phnom Penh and, if there were any irregularities, I ordered that Son Sakd should be detained for questioning.

When the controllers arrived, Son Sakd was not there – nor was there any money. From the vaults to the till, everything was empty. Not a single riel. Son Sakd had been tipped off – almost certainly by Sirik Matak. He had taken off for Saigon like a thief in the night, in a plane belonging to the Phnom Penh Aero-Club. From Saigon he went to Bangkok to join Son Ngoc Thanh, as the number three in the Khmer Serei triumvirate, after Sam Sary.

From the bank's ledgers, however, we learned that Sirik Matak, Long Boreth, Yem Sambaur, and others – the whole rightist coalition in the National Assembly – were involved. I wanted to have them all arrested, but they claimed parliamentary immunity. When the matter was referred to the National Assembly, enough deputies had been bought up – or were silenced by blackmail threats to reveal their own involvement – to vote against rescinding their parliamentary immunity. All the capitalists in the Assembly were involved, so quite understandably they rallied around their ring-leaders.

The ledgers enabled us to track down a number of Cambodians whose names were listed as having received 'loans' with no record of repayment or even provision for repayment. How much of this was straight CIA money and how much had been embezzled from our state enterprises, we had no way of knowing, but these people were made to pay back what they had received and a close watch was kept on their activities. We also seized a number of villas and other properties of Son Sakd, and in this way we recovered quite a good proportion of our loss. But the affair shook the government and the nation. With typical Phnom Penh humour people spoke of the 'battle of the two SSs' – Son Sann of the National Bank versus Son Sakd of the Bank of Phnom Penh. But there was little cause for joking, for the latter had taken with him about 400 million riels, the equivalent of over ten million dollars at the official rate of exchange.

This was the most telling counter-attack against our nationalization measures. How could state enterprises show profits when even working capital was being siphoned off to finance the Khmer Serei? It was this scandal that strongly influenced the decision to nationalize the banks and strengthen the state sector in general. With such plots against the economy to contend with, the 'miracle' of Cambodian economic survival has to be viewed with that of my personal survival and that of the policies which I defended.

Son Sakd was sentenced to death *in absentia*, but Lon Nol, towards the end of 1970, demanded – despite many protests from the students – that the sentence be annulled and he be allowed to return to Phnom Penh. This was done.

Chapter 9

Agonizing Decisions

From the end of 1963, there was a respite from the plots and attentats of that year and of 1959. But the CIA kept up its attacks on other fronts. There was no pause in the steady build-up of the Khmer Serei forces. In November 1963, NLF forces in South Vietnam overran one of their headquarters bases at Hiep Hoa, in Can Tho province, south-west of Saigon. Nguyen Huu Tho, President of the National Liberation Front, later sent me training manuals and operational plans captured in the attack. (Also captured were some American 'Special Forces' personnel, two of whom were later sent home through Cambodia.) These documents proved how far along were plans for setting up fifth column bases inside Cambodia under the cover of commando raids across our frontiers. The training manuals covered every method of assassination and sabotage, including the poisoning of wells. It was following the wiping out of this headquarters base, and the fact that the NLF had gained control of most of the South Vietnamese side of the frontier, that the Khmer Serei main base area was transferred to Thailand. In South Vietnam, the CIA concentrated in setting up the Khmer Krom commandos, the so-called 'Mike Force', which operated directly under American Green Beret officers. The Khmer Krom fought for the French during the first Indo-China war, then for the Americans, finally they were hired by Lon Nol.

From fixed and mobile transmitters in South Vietnam and Thailand – including one powerful station provided by the Australian government – Son Ngoc Thanh poured out invective against myself, the monarchy and our neutrality, and exhorted the people to rise up and overthrow me. He promised a bright future once this was done, conjuring up visions of an easy life for all if they would only get rid of the 'corrupt monarch' Sihanouk in favour of the 'republican patriot', Son Ngoc Thanh. For then, the treasure chest of US dollars would be at their disposal for all time.

Son Ngoc Thanh, as a Khmer Krom from the Mekong Delta, and not a native-born Cambodian, was as ignorant of the psychology of the Cambodian people as were American 'aid' officials. The lack of interest of Cambodian peasants and fishermen in material benefits caused the despair of the US aid officials, once they grasped the truth. In this connection, there is an anecdote which became a classic. It was in the early days of American economic assistance. One conscientious American – and there were such – after surveying economic possibilities, decided that with the application of modern techniques, Cambodia's rice production could be doubled. This would mean a big rice surplus for export – and rice equals hard currency, or did then. But how to get backward peasants to introduce new techniques? He asked and received permission to experiment in one pilot village. At a meeting with villagers, using simple diagrams to show how chemical fertilizers increased crop yield, he won their cooperation in the experiment. A plot of land, placed at his disposal, was divided in two equal parts. The fields were laboured, the rice seedlings planted by traditional methods. One part was sprayed with chemical fertilizer, the other not. Sure enough, at harvest time, the yield was doubled. Everyone was delighted. The peasants measured the lengths of the stalks, feeling the weight of the heads of grain and even pulling off sample heads from plants in the two plots, counting and comparing the number and size of the grains. They were completely won over.

They were even more enchanted when the aid official offered to provide, free of charge, fertilizer for the whole village next season, which he did. When he came back at harvest time, the results were the same: double the yield. But he was horrified to find that each peasant had cultivated just half of his land! 'Why', said the peasants, 'cultivate the entire area when you can get just as much by cultivating the half?' The unfortunate, well-meaning official, though steeped in Yankee 'know-how', was foiled by the total lack of interest in even the most primitive form of the profit motive.

In the first of a series of articles, begun in 1963, explaining why the decision had been taken to end all US military and economic 'aid', I referred to the venal and demagogic appeals made by Son Ngoc Thanh, and which were so out of harmony with our national concepts:

'In his ravings, he has solemnly promised our compatriots that the day he directs Cambodian affairs, every citizen will be clad, will have a house to live in and will be able to eat his fill.'[1] As if each citizen did not already enjoy all that, and far more, including education and public health facilities unequalled in South-East Asia. And what, in fact did the Cambodian people have once Son Ngoc Thanh had fulfilled part of his ambitions and became Prime Minister under Lon Nol? Scores of thousands of our compatriots who had houses prior to the 18 March coup, now have none. Hundreds of thousands who were then adequately fed and clad are now starving in refugee camps or concentration camp-style 'strategic hamlets'. Or they are beggars in Phnom Penh – driven there by US bombs and napalm. How many more thousands then, well-fed, well-clad and well-housed, are now dead – massacred by the planes, tanks, and artillery of Son Ngoc Thanh's sponsors?

Whether or not the CIA believed the propaganda absurdities it financed, I cannot know. Recent history shows the extent to which the CIA chiefs are either prisoners of their own wishful thinking, or use their propaganda inventions to force adventurist policies on their own government. As far as Son Ngoc Thanh, the prime CIA investment in destroying Cambodian neutrality, was concerned, there were plenty of qualified Anglo-Saxon observers in Phnom Penh who knew that Thanh had no credit inside the country. Even General Scherrer, who headed the MAAG (military aid) mission in Phnom Penh, shared this view. I was officially informed by President Kennedy that 'on his honour' his

1. *Neak Cheat Niyum* (the *Nationalist*), No. 196, 24 November 1963.

country had played absolutely no role in the affairs of the Khmer Serei. I considered President Kennedy to be an honourable man but, in that case, who really represented the American government? Almost at the same time as I received this assurance, traitors like Preap In were openly asserting that the CIA completely controlled the Khmer Serei – of which Preap In was a leading cadre. This was the equivalent of President Eisenhower firing a 21-gun salute in my honour when I visited Washington in 1958, even as Allen Dulles was drawing up a contract in New York with Slat Peou for his part in the Dap Chhuon plot! I am not the only one to ask who, and what is, the American government.

General Scherrer, when he was in Phnom Penh, assured me that he considered Cambodia to be truly neutral, while his opposite numbers in Saigon and Bangkok continued to work for my destruction. Were the latter influenced by the psychological warfare services of our neighbours, and believed them rather than Scherrer? Or was Scherrer just an ignoble hypocrite, worming his way into our confidence as part of the softening-up process? Did the CIA chiefs in Bangkok and Saigon really believe the propaganda they put out to the effect that I was on the point of 'handing over our Buddhist monks and peasants to foreign communists', and that it would be sufficient for Son Ngoc Thanh to appear for Sihanouk to be overthrown?

There was, in fact, a striking parallel between the inflammatory and wildly optimistic exhortations to which the Cuban mercenaries were subjected in Florida on the eve of the Bay of Pigs farce, and those to which the Khmer Serei received every day in their training camps. The moment the Cuban mercenaries set foot on Cuban soil, they were told Castro would be overthrown, and the 'liberators' carried shoulder-high in triumph to Havana. Did the CIA truly believe all this or did they only want others, including their own government, to believe it?

It was the same sort of nonsense that sent Preap In marching along the road to Takeo, his chest stuck out, ready to 'negotiate' my surrender – a road which in fact led him to a firing squad. Those who invaded Cambodia found themselves embroiled, too, in a 'Bay of Pigs' type situation in which they found not an iota of support from the local population.

To my protests over American sponsorship of the Khmer Serei commando raids into our territory, and propaganda activities, Washington always pretended to have no relations with this group and went so far as to say the Khmer Serei were based, radio stations and all, on Cambodian territory. After the decision was made to close down the 'aid' missions and send the personnel packing, I threw out the challenge that, if the Americans really believed what they said, 'then I solemnly invite them, before their numerous military and civilian personnel leave our country, to search where they will – in the towns, countryside, and jungle – unearth these Khmer Serei'. The offer was not accepted, for they could only have unearthed a few cells implanted by themselves, and whose activities were under our surveillance.

In an article, published in the *Nationalist* dealing with the rejection of further US military aid, I spelled out the details of what happened after the invasion of Stung Treng Province by Saigon troops in June 1958:

I found that the United States had outrageously abused the confidence we had placed in them, by according us a military aid which was not only conditional, but pernicious and humiliating. The Americans had already warned us that they would cut off supplies and munitions if we dared accept any gifts whatsoever of arms from socialist countries while accepting US military aid. We swallowed our pride in accepting this clause, incompatible as it was with our sovereignty, because of the assurance of our 'benefactors' that they would provide our armed forces with up-to-date equipment and weapons, adequate to defend the honour, peace and territorial integrity of Cambodia. The Stung Treng affair suddenly threw the real light on American aid.[1]

What I found was that even the transport equipment was utterly useless for the most elementary forms of defensive warfare. That we could not expand our transport facilities from the most readily available sources – China and the

1. 'L'Aide Militaire US et Nous', *Neak Cheat Niyum* (the *Nationalist*), No. 197, 1 December 1963.

Soviet Union – was scandalous. To move our troops to Stung Treng, for instance, we had to use old Chinese charabanc buses which broke down all along the road, for their wheezy, patched-up engines were not intended for military needs. Armaments were neither modern nor sufficient, especially in comparison with what our neighbours had. And of course we could not fire them, even in self-defence, at those neighbours. In the same article I pointed out:

Thus to neutralists like us, the Americans give arms only to kill communists, who never threaten us. As for the troops of Bangkok and Saigon, who then had occupied, by force of arms, the Preah Vihear temple and part of Stung Treng respectively, there was no question of harming them in the slightest way. In the military aid agreement, it was set forth that the United States was desirous of giving us the necessary and sufficient means to safeguard our sovereignty and freedom. In 1958, however, it was evident that this American aid could only be used against hypothetical communist invaders, not against the real aggressors – that is, the Thai–South Vietnamese 'free world' mercenaries . . . The United States is only interested in the preservation of our 'liberty' when this is threatened by communists. But this liberty, our independence, and our territorial integrity, could be light-heartedly sacrificed the moment the dear allies of Uncle Sam desired to trample it down under the jack-boots of their soldiery.

Today, I have no reason to change a word of this. The only thing I had not anticipated was that the United States would take part directly in trying to tear our country to pieces. The aims of Bangkok and Saigon were always clear. My country has had to cope with Siam for over a thousand years. We have suffered too much for too long from our eastern and western neighbours to have any illusions when we see them governed by aggressive, expansionist régimes such as those under US sponsorship. What was the real US policy towards Cambodia? To pin our arms behind our back, and egg on our traditional enemies to strike us when, and where, and as hard, as they could.

I had not been able to rid Stung Treng of the Diemist forces with US weapons given 'to defend the honour, peace and territorial integrity' of Cambodia, but rather because of

energetic warnings given by Premier Chou En Lai and Foreign Minister Chen Yi. The withdrawal of Thai troops from Preah Vihear was not due to US military aid but to the International Court of Justice in The Hague.

My adversaries, especially in the Anglo-Saxon world, like to charge me with being unpredictable. This accusation was made precisely because I did what I said I would do, but many diplomats chose to write off my warnings as 'Sihanouk's capriciousness'. I had solemnly informed the United States in 1958, immediately after the Stung Treng affair, that the day would come when I would prefer to reject their military aid, and even break US and Western ties, rather than put up with false friendship and even insults.

At the beginning, American military aid offered some relief to the national budget. Of total receipts of about 115 million dollars in 1954, the US contributed some 23 millions for military purposes. But by 1963, when our budget had risen to 170 million dollars, US military aid had dropped to 8.6 millions. As I expressed it at the time: 'This was really too small to compensate for humiliations that had lasted so long.' Worse than that: as military aid to Cambodia decreased, aid to South Vietnam increased proportionately to Saigon's threats against us. In the period under review – from 1954 to 1963 – it had grown from 180 million to 450 million dollars. (That was nothing, of course, compared to the cosmic heights it was eventually to attain.) Even in 1961, Laos, with about one third the population of Cambodia, was getting twice as much in military aid. Why the difference? The answer was very simple: Cambodia had refused to join in the business of trying to suppress by force of arms the political opposition within its own borders. In essence that was what was going on over our borders in South Vietnam and Laos.

All the efforts of the CIA were aimed at implanting an armed political opposition inside the country so that we would have to beg for American arms to keep order, and we refused to fall into this trap.

At a time when our air space was being violated by our neighbour's jet fighters, I managed to squeeze out of the

United States, after interminable negotiations, four minuscule, unarmed, propeller-driven planes, and two helicopters. At the same time, the right-wing Laotian leader, General Phoumi Nosavan, received thirty helicopters. Nosavan, incidentally, was in the habit of periodically abandoning huge quantities of arms on the battlefield – at Nam Tha in north-west Laos in May 1962, for instance – and of losing his planes and helicopters on the ground. The Americans smiled indulgently and replaced them. To cap it all, I was accused of having wasted and made ill-use of the dribble of US aid that I received. When I protested, the Thai dictator, Sarit Thanarat, described me as 'a pig trying to stand up to a lion'. This, incidentally, was the 'drop of water that caused the vase to overflow' as far as Thailand was concerned, and led me to break diplomatic relations.

In the article published in the December 1963 issue of the *Nationalist*, I wrote that

the mercenary armies of Diem and Sarit crushed us with contempt and sarcasm, carrying out murderous raids into our territory with impunity. Their naval craft systematically violated our territory, and their planes, our air space. We had to bow our heads in shame and frustration, bound hand and foot by our poverty, fettered by restrictions aimed at keeping us in a permanent state of inferiority and impotence. Even a child can understand that our Royal Cambodian Armed Forces have nothing to lose and everything to gain by rejecting once and for all everything connected with US military aid. We must face up to the fact that it is absolutely imperative to cut those ties which fettered us in such impotence and humiliation.

It was indeed an agonizing decision to make, and a turning point in our development. I really had no choice. Once again, the United States had pushed me into the arms of the socialist world by policies pursued in the name of friendship, but which in fact disarmed us in front of our declared enemies. Perhaps this could have been justified had we ever, by word or deed, threatened our neighbours, or had our armed forces violated their frontiers, or had we advanced territorial claims. History gave us every right to do this. But I had

decided at an early date to bury the past and accept the frontiers as they were.

We were being punished, humiliated, and prepared for the chopping-block because we had stood on our dignity. We refused to become US puppets, or join in the anti-communist crusade. We spurned the billion-dollar rewards for such a role. That was our crime in the eyes of successive US administrations. My article continued:

We will gratefully accept unconditional and spontaneous aid from friendly countries, but they must not think they can force humiliations of any sort on us because of this. No matter what happens, we prefer to live in poverty, because at least we will be free – in any case, we have more than enough to eat and clothe ourselves. It should be made clear that we will only accept aid in material goods and weaponry, and never again financial aid, which would place us in a humiliating position *vis-à-vis* the donor . . . Our army will be largely compensated for its material inferiority by moral and social superiority. Our soldiers who come from the ranks of the people know today that they depend on the people; whereas the Thai and Saigon forces, armed from abroad, are mercenaries paid to spill their own and others' blood in a cause which is not, and never will be, the cause of their motherlands.

This is the spirit I wanted installed in our troops. It is to the disgrace of Lon Nol, Sirik Matak, Son Ngoc Thanh, and the others, that they tried to turn our armed forces against their own people. They only partly succeeded, and thousands of troops from the regular army, including units of up to battalion size, rallied to the resistance forces in the first days following the coup. I have any amount of testimony, mainly from French residents, that it was not the Royal Army troops that took part in the massacres following the coup, but above all the CIA's Khmer Krom commandos. The proof of the reluctance of the Royal Army to massacre their own compatriots is that ten battalions of Khmer Krom troops had to be brought in before and immediately after the coup, and when they failed, the Americans had to invade with tens of thousand of their own and Saigon troops.

Those from our regular armed forces who deserted – and still continue to desert – prove themselves to be worthy sons

of the people, once they join the ranks of the resistance forces. The Saigon mercenaries behaved according to my most sombre predictions. A murderous rabble, demoralized on the battlefield, champions at murder of unarmed civilians, at rape, and above all at plunder. They proved totally devoid of any ideal, any belief in the cause for which they were fighting. Their main concern was to survive to enjoy the fruits of their plunder, but the lifeblood of many thousands of them mingled with the mud of our ricefields.

Without benefit of US aid, except for booty seized on the battlefield or paid for in cash from Saigon troops on the black-market, our resistance fighters have defended our national dignity and virtue, and our Buddhist ideals. They will be honoured forever. Lon Nol, Sirik Matak, Son Ngoc Thanh, and their hired scum will be cursed for generations, as will their American puppet-masters. The names of some of them will enter the Cambodian, indeed the Asian vocabulary, as the name of Quisling entered the European vocabulary after the Second World War. They will be remembered as very rare examples of national treachery in the history of our nation. Our resistance forces, on the contrary, uphold all that is most noble in our thousands of years of history. They represent not only the best of our past, but the present and the future. National in form, patriotic in content, officers and troops welded into perfect unity – this was the ideal I had in my mind's eye when I ended our dependence on US aid.

Some of my loyal supporters questioned my decision to end US military aid, and I must admit that this was one of my most difficult moments. Events since have proved that I did the right thing. The concept of preserving national dignity was approved by the people through the National Congress. It has now become a major factor in the resistance struggle. I feel, in looking back, that the decision was made in time – before our will had been sapped; entrapped in snares of false aid and false friendship – not to mention the economic and cultural fare with which such snares were baited. By our policy of economic independence we gained a valuable breathing space which prevented – among other things –

cultural aggression from making headway. The cultural bait which had such a corrupting influence in Thailand and South Vietnam never got a foothold among the peasantry, who make up eighty-five per cent of our people, and hardly succeeded even among the youth of the towns. It is the peasantry and youth who now form the backbone of the resistance.

If I have quoted from some articles written in 1963 to illustrate my feelings at the time, it is because I am often reproached for having 'turned left' since I took up residence in Peking. A glance at the record, however, shows that my ideas on independence have been constant for three decades – from the time I was called upon to become King, with total independence and the preservation of all that is good in our national heritage as my goal. I could not have acted otherwise. It is unfair to present this unswerving attitude as some 'leftist deviation' that I acquired by coming to Peking.

Chapter 10

Total Break

As with military, so with economic aid – I decided to make a clean break. I felt that the terms were so onerous that they amounted to national humiliation and that dollar aid actually retarded our development. The fact that it was being used to finance CIA-directed activities inside the country struck me as a little like solving the problem of the poor by paying them to dig their own graves. As with the restrictions on military aid, we were prohibited from using US financial 'aid' for projects aimed at promoting a real economic take-off.

To cite one example among many: a pretended industrialist of overseas Chinese origin received an allocation of dollars to import machinery for a match-manufacturing plant. I encouraged such projects in the private sector to reduce our dependence on imported goods. According to the documentation in which the allocation was made, the equipment was to be new and ultra-modern. What arrived was found to be useless except for scrap iron. The US economic mission demanded reimbursement for the dollars – not from the Chinese who had conveniently gone bankrupt and couldn't pay anyway – but from the royal government. I proposed that since they demanded reimbursement from the government in such cases, it was logical that in the future only the government should have the right to import such equipment. As had happened many times before, and would happen many times after this incident, the US authorities refused point-blank, stating that they absolutely could not give dollars to any state institution whatsoever. Dollar 'aid' was to be used exclusively to aid private enterprise.

There we had it – the basic, built-in flaw of American economic help – the economic equivalent of the shackling conditions of military 'aid'. It was being used as a lever to impose the implantation, consolidation, and development of exclusively capitalist enterprises in our country; not only that, but the enterprises were in no way connected with the legitimate policies of the government or the interests of the people. How could we remain masters in our own house if we accepted such limitations on our sovereignty?

We had tried to steer the aid into spheres where it would be useful, such as building roads and bridges. But if these were intended to serve state-owned plantations or industries, US aid could not be used. At an Extraordinary National Congress convened on 17 November 1963, to discuss ending US military and economic aid, I explained these matters in detail. I no longer have the texts of those speeches, but in the last of a series of articles in the *Nationalist*, referred[1] to earlier, I noted that the 300 million dollars we had received in about ten years was minuscule compared to the 400 or more millions that South Vietnam was receiving for 1963 alone. Certainly, this was to finance a war and, seven years later, we were to find the Americans spending about the same amount annually to finance a similar type of war on our own soil. Even the amount allocated by the US in 1963 to pay Ngo Dinh Nhu's secret police was reported by Western journalists to exceed the annual total granted to Cambodia for all types of aid. (Incidentally, the lavish subsidy for Nhu's police did not save him and his brother Ngo Dinh Diem from being liquidated in November of that year by Saigon forces also in US pay!)

By an overwhelming majority, the National Congress delegates, at the November 1963 session, decided to end all US aid forthwith. On 20 November, on the basis of the Congress decisions, our government informed Washington that 'it considers that the most elementary dignity forbids Cambodia to continue to accept any form of American aid, no matter how small', and that 'Cambodia demands the end of all aid granted by the United States in the military, economic, technical and cultural fields.' This was received as something of a bombshell in Washington, as it was almost without precedent that a country, once having decided to accept US aid, voluntarily repudiates it.

This was bound to cause us difficulties, and my critics predicted swift economic disaster. If, in the early years, aid had largely been used to import cars, air conditioners, refrigerators, and so forth, in later years, and at my insistence, it had been diverted to road and bridge construction, to small irrigation and other rural development projects. It had come to be accepted as a normal item in our national revenue. Why then end it?

The reason was that so many social and political evils had become associated with the dollar handout. The unhealthiest appetites had been stimulated. It had given rise to endless corruption, intrigues, and jealousies; to unprincipled criticisms of ministers and department heads, who were accused of having discriminated for or against this or that person in the distribution of dollar favours. Measures taken earlier to limit the risk of having the entire National Assembly bought up had been partially effective. The enhanced powers of the National Congress had acted at least as a brake on the vote-buyers. But dollar aid still remained as the single most corrupting and disruptive influence in our political, economic and social life. This was so patent, that even French importers confided to foreign journalists that 'without greasing the palms' of Cambodian ministers and high officials, it was impossible to remain in business. This sort of international discredit was an affront to our national prestige. It was true that the same criticisms of the handling of US 'aid' applied to a certain extent to the allocation of our own foreign currency holdings, earned from our exports. But as I wrote at the time:

I must stress, for those who have forgotten it, the US dollar aid during the first years of independence constituted the major source of our foreign currency, and the practices which I denounce today were born in 1955–6, when we were heavily dependent on American allocations ... Our present organization in handling foreign exchange, whether national or from foreign aid, has retained the *imprimateur* of procedures initiated for handling US economic aid ...

This is a major reason for the continuing unpopularity of successive governments. All ministers of the national economy, no matter what their academic qualifications, experience or background, 'break their teeth' on these problems.

Some French writers have pretended that under former French administrations there was no corruption. They would like to give Cambodians the 'credit' for having invented it. This is too much of an honour! I lived and worked with the French for a long time. Their functionaries were champions of venality. Some of our people were doubtless eager learners. I remember a case connected with the Royal family. An uncle of a certain princess sought a post in the French-run administration. In those days posts were gained by competitive examination, and a good knowledge of French was essential. The uncle in question knew not a word of any language other than his native Cambodian. But the examiner was a collector of antique Chinese porcelain, of which the princess had a fine collection. A choice specimen was sent to the examiner and the uncle, knowing no French, was among those who came out with top marks. Of course he got the post.

In the matter of currency black-marketeering, one only has to recall the 'piastres scandal' in Saigon in the latter days of the Indo-China War, involving officers all the way up to General Revers at the Defence Ministry, to appreciate French expertise in such matters. By and large, corruption in its contemporary dimensions was an imported, rather than a local, product. It increased qualitatively as American standards replaced those of the French.

In commenting on the episode of the Chinese 'industrialist' and his 'match factory', and its sequel, I wrote that the American 'practice of reserving dollars for the benefit of a certain class of traders and businessmen exposes the true face of American aid. It is not help for the Cambodian state which was trying to build up true economic dependence. This "aid" in fact only favours "certain Cambodians" who normally finish up by constituting a "clientèle" necessarily obedient to the demands of the lavish bestower of foreign funds.'

For all these reasons, the following conclusion has become obvious to me. We will never achieve our economic independence, the end aims of all our efforts, unless we free ourselves from this aid which denies the state the right to go ahead with the development of the nation's production potential, and seduces its citizens to engage in facile and profitable trading operations, destroying any spirit of real enterprise. Despite the assurances of our donors that they are only interested in helping us attain economic autonomy, it turns out more and more clearly that over the years they have only steered us into corruption and, in consequence, into remaining a dependent country. If we wish to avoid the fate of countries now prisoners of an 'aid' that has engulfed them – Thailand, South Vietnam, and Laos for example – then we have to carry out the essential surgery and amputate, without further hesitation.

I warned of possible difficulties ahead, but asserted that we had no choice if we wanted to attain and maintain real independence. 'If we have to die, we prefer to do it in a more courageous and honourable way than by suffocation and rotting to death through American aid.'

As a first measure to bring imports and exports under control, the November 1963 National Congress decided to establish mixed, state-private companies: SONEXIM to handle exports and imports, and SONAPRIM for distributing imported goods through state shops and engaging in wholesale and retail trade. At least part of the profits which formerly went into private bank accounts could now be diverted into national development projects, and the state would have control over foreign currency allocations for imports.

It is possible that it was from this moment that Lon Nol, Sirik Matak, Yem Sambaur, and others in the top hierarchy of the army and other government departments, turned against me. That their patriotism went no further than their bank accounts became clear only later. It was obvious that if we were going to pay our way, there must be a tightening of belts at all levels, and this was resented. Lon Nol cloaked his real feelings by being more than usually obsequious during this period. I was not aware at that time of his close ties with the compradore business community, leaders of which were already bemoaning the prospects of losing their ill-gotten gains from US 'aid' and the profits from the exorbitant rents they had been extracting from US military and 'aid' personnel. Critics were not lacking – behind my back at home, and openly abroad – predicting that bankruptcy would immediately overtake Cambodia for daring to renounce economic aid. Most of the critics abroad consistently showed themselves far more concerned with the 'dangers' to Cambodia's independence than with the fate of their own countries where, in many cases, US economic penetration had seduced them into a state of subservience to US foreign policy. As far as I was concerned, we had taken another of those essential steps in fixing our sights on the target of true national independence desired by the whole nation, excepting a handful of compradores and their protectors at home and abroad.

We did not go bankrupt. In fact for the next couple of years, the economy progressed very well. But it was also during that period that the CIA, working through Son Sakd, concentrated its efforts in subverting key personnel in the state enterprises, culminating in Son Sakd's flight with the entire assets of his bank, plus the assets of a number of state enterprises. My reply to that act – a reply enthusiastically endorsed by the National Congress – was to eliminate the private sector – with compensation – in the import-export trade, and to create two state trading banks which alone were empowered to handle all international banking transactions. As predicted, this created an uproar at home and abroad. But the Son Sakd affair had proved that it was unrealistic to take one step without the other, and impossible to maintain our state enterprises without both these steps. Foreign banking circles – especially the French – were highly indignant. The powerful Banque d'Indochine took the lead in appealing to President de Gaulle to intervene. That great statesman, whose patriotism was always an inspiration to me to defend Cambodian freedom to the last, rose to the occasion. 'Let them shut all their doors,' he said in effect, 'except one that can function exclusively to handle matters concerning our financial aid.' The mighty Banque d'Indochine, symbol of many decades of French colonialism, thus had to close its doors.

1965 was a trying year for several reasons. In February, the United States started the systematic bombing of North Vietnam and in March the first US combat troops disembarked in South Vietnam. I felt that, on the one hand, we had to be more vigilant than ever to avoid giving pretexts to extend the war to our territory. On the other hand, I felt that we had to make our position quite clear. We had to show where we stood: against direct US aggression of our neighbours, and against the operations of a US fifth column on our territory. (The new economic measures represented an aspect of our determination in this latter respect.) We unreservedly condemned US aggression against the Vietnamese people and took steps to strengthen our (at the time) unofficial relations with the resistance leadership in South Vietnam, the NLF.

I had few illusions as to what was in store for us: provocations in the border areas were bound to be stepped up. Bombings of frontier villages had steadily increased throughout 1964, to a point where it had become intolerable. One of the pretexts given by the US command in Saigon was that the frontiers were 'ill-defined'. This was another way of camouflaging Saigon's claims on some of our border areas. Drastic action was needed to make our position absolutely clear.

On 27 October 1964, a joint declaration of the Royal Cambodian Government and the National Assembly warned that 'in case of any new violation of Cambodian territory by US ground, air, or naval forces, Cambodia will immediately sever diplomatic relations with the United States'. Most diplomats and journalists in Phnom Penh thought we were bluffing. Small countries like Cambodia simply did not do such things! A mass demonstration outside the US Embassy some months earlier, in which tens of thousands of workers and students took part, ripping down the Stars and Stripes and burning embassy cars, should have warned the US Ambassador as to the state of public opinion.

At the beginning of May 1965, US planes bombarded

villages in the 'Parrot's Beak' area, killing and wounding several dozen of our peasants. I spent several sleepless nights before coming to the conclusion that there was no choice but to sever diplomatic relations with the US if any shred of our national dignity was to be preserved. After long discussions with Samdech Penn Nouth, who entirely agreed with me, the historic decision was taken on 3 May 1965.

A whole phase – and a most degrading one at that – of our relations with the United States had come to an end. Once it was done, and the last of the US Embassy personnel had packed their bags and left, taking their radio transmitters and other espionage equipment with them, I felt as if an enormous weight had rolled off my shoulders. It is often like that. The process of making decisions of such importance is difficult and painful, causing plenty of sleepless nights and passionate debate. For a small, underdeveloped country to throw out, bag and baggage, the mightiest of the world powers was no small thing and would almost inevitably lead to overt and covert reprisals. But if we were going to be put to the supreme test, it was better to have cleaned out beforehand the leadership of the fifth column, and to face our enemies with honour and prestige. These were not idle terms. It was politically imperative that I respond to the indignation and fury of our peasants in the frontier areas, subject to daily bombings and shellings. If I had not cut diplomatic relations, the rural population, under the influence of the Khmers Rouges, would have become disillusioned with me and would have accused me of having become a pro-imperialist traitor. I have been labelled 'dictatorial' by my critics, but in fact I was always sensitive to public opinion, like any other leader who wants to retain the support of his people. In this case, as so often, public opinion coincided precisely with my own views.

In a speech to the National Assembly two weeks after the break, I remarked that 'if a chain of anti-imperialist states throughout the world would follow our example and eliminate resolutely and totally American presence and influence, US imperialism would be uprooted like a tree, no matter how big, once it can no longer draw nourishment from the soil'. Later, at some international conferences, I tried without success to persuade third world countries to follow our example, and found that many of them had become too addicted to dollars to break the habit.

There is an eloquent commentary on what happened after Lon Nol and Sirik Matak, seven years later, reversed all that had been done to safeguard political and economic independence, in a book written by two Frenchmen immediately after the coup.[1]

Describing the immediate deterioration of the economic situation, and the difficulty of moving goods along the traditional communication routes or to traditional trading partners, the authors – one a journalist of *Le Monde*, the other a sociologist and author – write:

There is still some trading in agricultural products, but through a different channel. Chinese traders[2] buy them in Phnom Penh and send them to Saigon under the protection of the South Vietnamese army, which receives a commission. The Chinese agent in Saigon sells the rice, port, pepper, and fruit at profitable prices on the local market. Merchandise is bought in Vietnamese piastres, and the profits are exported to Hong Kong bank accounts in dollars. The Cambodian state gets nothing from these transactions, but its leaders are personally linked with the traffic. The Chinese henchman of Lon Nol is a certain Kuch Anh, a former supplier of rice to the NLF; that of Sirik Matak is named Nguy Canh, an importer and rice-mill owner, who formally ran a cinema specializing in films of People's China.

National trading, controlled by the state under the former régime, has completely disappeared. The new allies buy nothing in Cambodia. State trade has been replaced by a vast traffic in foodstuffs entirely controlled by people in Saigon. The role of the Cambodian elite, as always, is that of the parasites of the compradores, who have emerged again.

What a picture this gives of the two top personalities of the régime at that time, black-marketeering in foodstuffs of which there was a desperate shortage in Phnom Penh, in

1. *Des Courtisans aux Partisans*, Jean-Claude Pomonti and Serge Thion, Gallimard, Paris, 1971, pp. 264–5.
2. Usually resident for generations in Phnom Penh or Hong Kong.

order to swell their bank accounts abroad. A major pretext for my overthrow had been to 'end corruption'!

Lon Nol's compradore, Kuch Anh, was once caught in a flagrant act of corruption by Son Sann, when the latter was governor of the National Bank. I had Kuch Anh thrown out of the country, but Lon Nol brought him back from Hong Kong immediately after the coup. In his rice-buying operations to supply the NLF, he succeeded in fleecing Cambodian peasants, the government and the NLF!

In a speech given on 11 May 1970, while attempting to cast doubt on the genuineness of Peking's support for me, Lon Nol solemly 'disclosed' that, after my overthrow,

the Chinese secretly sent an emissary to me [Lon Nol] to ask whether we would give the same support to the North Vietnamese as in the past – intending by this to show that the question of Sihanouk and the Phnom Penh government was purely a Cambodian affair. Peking could be our friend . . . as long as we continued to supply the Vietnamese resistance forces as in the past. These secret contacts continued until 5 May 1970; that is, one month and twenty days after Sihanouk's deposition. Finally, as these démarches were fruitless, Peking decided to break diplomatic relations with Cambodia and to openly recognize Sihanouk.[1]

This was cabled abroad by the world press agencies and doubtless received some credence. It turned out that the 'emissary' was none other than Kuch Anh trying, perhaps, to persuade Lon Nol to play it both ways – continue the lucrative sales to the NLF and also open the black market route to Saigon. The date of 5 May 1970 was simply that of setting up the Royal Government of National Union recognized by China within hours of its formation. Probably, given Lon Nol's nature, he would not have turned a deaf ear to Kuch Anh's advice, had the profits been high enough, but the US–Saigon invasion of Cambodia (according to Lon Nol perpetrated without his permission or knowledge) on 30 April 1970, put an end to any such schemes, even in the most unlikely case that the NLF might entertain any further dealings with such swindlers.

1. Agence Khmère Press – Lon Nol's official news agency – 5 December 1970.

The evidence of the two French writers who, although they have never met me, showed a hostile attitude towards me in their book, regarding the sort of activities Lon Nol and Sirik Matak personally engaged in immediately after the 18 March coup, illustrated what I was up against in pushing through the 1965 commercial and financial reforms. To preserve our independence until the last possible moment, it was the only course to follow, as subsequent events were to prove. The natural alliance between corruption and treason reached its high point on 18 March 1970, but it was not long before those at the top were quarrelling with each other as to who was to get the lion's share of the booty, in power and dollars.

Chapter 11

Above All – Independence

From the first years of my reign as King of Cambodia, I had to grapple with the inescapable problem of independence. I was chosen monarch on 25 April 1941, the day following the death of King Sisowath Monivong. I was eighteen, a diligent student of rhetoric at the Chasseloup-Laubat Lycée in Saigon. I was home in Phnom Penh on school holidays when my grandfather died. I had never thought that I might be chosen to succeed him – nor had my mother. The choice seemed clearly to be between my father, Prince Norodom Suramarit, and my uncle, Prince Sisowath Monireth. Traditionally, the succession was decided by the Crown Council, consisting of the heads of the two Buddhist sects, the head of the Brahman sect, the President of the Council of the Royal Family, the Prime Minister, and other cabinet members. For the first time, the Crown Council was presided over by the French resident-supérieur, Monsieur Thibadeau. It was he who decided that I, and not Prince Monireth, who was in the direct line of succession as the eldest son of King Monivong, should succeed to the throne.

In acting thus, the French were correcting an irregularity committed by themselves nearly forty years earlier. Until they interfered, the line of succession of the monarchy was, as in most other countries, via the eldest son of the reigning monarch. King Ang Duong, the animator of a renaissance of patriotic upsurge in Cambodia in the mid-nineteenth century, had, as his first two sons, Norodom and Sisowath. When he died in 1860, he was succeeded by the eldest son, Norodom, in accordance with tradition. King Norodom's reign was during the period of resistance to, and annexation by, France. When he died in 1904, the throne should have gone to his eldest available son, Prince Sutharot.[1]

The French, however, gave the throne to Norodom's younger brother, Sisowath, who had collaborated with them in helping to put down a partisan resistance movement, which was clandestinely supported by Norodom. This was a clear break with tradition and was objected to by the people and, of course, by the Norodom clan. When Sisowath died in 1927, the French, under the pretext of reverting to the old ways, placed his eldest son, Sisowath Monivong, on the throne. This again caused resentment inside the country, because patriotic public opinion supported the Norodom branch. When King Monivong died, the French seized the chance of trying to placate both branches. They could have chosen Norodom's eldest son, Prince Sutharot, sixty-nine years old at the time, or the latter's son – my father, Suramarit.

They chose me. Why? Certainly because my father was a Norodom and my mother a Sisowath. The two branches of the royal family would be reunited, thus trouble would be reduced from that quarter. An additional reason was that I was young and had the reputation of being somewhat shy and scholarly. The French thought I would be more docile and malleable than my uncle Monireth, for instance, who, having served in the French Foreign Legion, had the reputation of being tough. According to the German writer, Klaus Mehnert, in one of his first books on Asia, the French chose me because they thought I was a 'little lamb' – later complaining that I had betrayed their faith by turning into a 'tiger'. In fact, on the question of Cambodian independence, I was always a 'tiger', but only a little one at the time they put me on the throne.

Those were the days of Vichy France, and the mentors who surrounded me from the moment I mounted the throne tried to instruct me in the moral and political precepts of Marshal Pétain, something I did not in the least appreciate. One of my first head-on collisions with the French was on a matter of personal independence. The Secretary General for

1. The eldest son, Yukanthor, as noted later, had been exiled.

Indo-China, Monsieur Georges Gautier, was obsessed with the notion of marrying me off to a wealthy mandarin's daughter of his choice. I vigorously opposed this and, after many long battles, I had my way. But a small coal of resentment glowed in my entrails at this early assault on my personal freedom.

The French Governor General for Indo-China at the time was Admiral Decoux, a fervent admirer of the authoritarian Pétain. I am grateful to the Admiral, however, for one thing. He strongly advised me to travel as much as possible inside the country, and learn to know it in depth. This I did, travelling to the remotest regions, often on elephant-back. In this way I had my first real contacts with our peasants and fishermen, and appreciated the varied beauties of my country. The results were probably the opposite to those intended by Decoux, because the more I got to know my country and the problems of my people, the more I began to detest the iniquities of colonial rule; the more determined I became that our country had to win complete independence. It was during those early years of my reign that I acquired the taste for conversing with peasants and even the tribespeople in the mountain areas and trying to understand their problems. My taste for intimate contact with the people has only grown stronger with the passage of time.

At that time Cambodia was a French Protectorate. The real meaning of that hardy colonialist term was revealed when Vichy France ceded Cambodia – and myself – to the Japanese in December 1941. If the French fired a few shots in their own defence, they certainly fired none in defence of the Royal Palace. During the first years of their occupation, the Japanese retained the French administration, ruling through it. I had little contact with the invaders. On 9 March 1945, however, the Japanese suddenly took over complete power. One of their first acts was to inform me that Cambodia, as from that date, was independent. This was another surprise, almost as great as the one four years previously, when I was informed that I had been chosen King. The price of this 'independence', I soon learned, was that I should place Cambodia at Japan's side in the war, and start mobilizing the country's human and material resources to this end.

I had no intention of doing this, but I was determined to squeeze every scrap of advantage I could out of our newly acquired status. Before I could do anything concrete, I explained to the Japanese High Command, I must have the documents establishing *de jure* independence. This produced an endless series of exchanges between Phnom Penh and Tokyo. I was thus able to keep Cambodia out of the war, and to later use the status of 'independence' as a bargaining counter with the French. During those five months of notes exchanged with the local Japanese commander and Tokyo – which went on until the Japanese surrender – I was under constant pressure from Son Ngoc Thanh, who had been brought in by the Japanese from Tokyo shortly after the 9 March coup and imposed on me as the Prime Minister, and whose bidding I was supposed to accept on all matters of state. I got the measure of this puppet's 'patriotism' at that time and never forgot it. He was after personal power then, and still is. It was because of his crimes at that time that, as soon as the French returned, they arrested Son Ngoc Thanh and sentenced him to death as a traitor.

When the French, with British help, returned to Indo-China in September 1945, they asked me to send a delegation to discuss 'questions of interest to my realm' with Admiral Thierry d'Argenlieu, the new French High Commissioner for Indo-China. Not much imagination was required to guess the main point at issue. My response, written on 28 September, read as follows:

We ask the Admiral to let us know if the delegates that we will eventually designate ... will be considered as delegates of an independent country.

Cambodia recovered its independence after the events of 9 March ... We are disposed to deal with France and to have friendly relations with her of a political, economic, and cultural nature; relations that, at the same time, must not be of a nature to endanger the independence of our country.

There was no reply to this letter, and the discussions with Admiral d'Argenlieu did not take place. Later the French made it clear that they wanted relations based as before on the 'protectorate' treaty of 1863, which had been imposed, after a four-hour ultimatum, on my great-grandfather, King Norodom – a treaty backed up by a French gunboat on the Mekong – and on the shameful Convention of 1884, extracted by even more brutal means. It seemed that I would have to go right back to the beginning to recover real independence if I accepted the French view.

Sceptics may think I exaggerate when I speak of the indignities and humiliations that colonialism imposed on successive Khmer sovereigns and, through them, on the Cambodian people. My adversaries like to refer to the 'folly' and 'hyper-sensitivity' of Sihanouk on matters of national and personal dignity. Let one example from the past suffice to answer them. In 1900, King Norodom sent his son and heir, Prince Yukanthor, to Paris to present a petition to the French government. He was showered with attention, and offered lavish gifts to make him forget his mission. But he persisted, and succeeded in making his speech. After expressing thanks for the manner in which he had been received, he pointed out that the generosity of his hosts in Paris was in great contrast to the policies from which his people were suffering in Cambodia 'In bringing the greetings of my father, I do not hesitate to open my heart and present his grievances,' which he then proceeded to do:

The French government doubtless cannot be aware of the means used to obtain the instruments which in 1897 marked the principal phases of the passing of royal powers into the hands of the Protectorate. In 1884, it was by a *coup de force*, by invading the palace and thrusting bayonets at the throat of the King, threatening to kidnap him, that treaties were obtained turning over political power in Cambodia.

In 1897, it was also by threats and by the use of force – less brutally perhaps, but just as mercilessly – that Monsieur Doumer got hold of what was left of administrative powers as well as economic rights, and the territorial possession of the Kingdom.

The Senior Resident at the time was Monsieur de Verneville. His excesses, together with those of his accomplices and mistress, Mi Moune, are notorious. This Senior Resident, enemy of the King because the latter protested against the abuses which brought such sufferings on the people, declared the King mad, locked him up, and after threatening to decapitate him, decided to dethrone him and deport him to the convict settlement of Poulo Condor.

Monsieur Doumer intervened to save the King, exacting as his price a revision of the 1884 Convention which placed the Sovereign and the Cambodian people in the hands of the Senior Resident, without redress of any sort, delivering them up to the arbitrary rule from which they suffer to this day.

In the long run it is the people who pay [continued Yukanthor, in presenting this remarkable petition which was to cost him the throne]. The people suffer also from the transfer of lands to the Senior Resident. Formerly all Cambodian soil belonged by law to the King. But in fact it belonged to those who occupied and cultivated it. This was in accordance with duties imposed on the throne by Buddhist laws. The soil belongs to God, committed to the protection of the King, and placed by him at the disposal of those who need it, without the slightest restriction. It is you who have established private property rights. It is you who have carved out big concessions. It is because of you that people have become impoverished: By force of arms you have made the Cambodian people pay dearly for the use of land which royal decree formerly granted them free of any payments.

Can anyone blame me for being furious on reading through such documents which I had found in the Royal Archives at the very moment I was under pressure from the French to turn the clock back to our days of colonial subservience. In presenting his petition, Prince Yukanthor detailed many cases of arbitrary arrest for the most trifling offences, especially any criticism of the French presence.

These arbitrary repressions, exile, convict prison, and sometimes decapitation are called political measures! The vengeance of the King's enemies, the madness of the Senior Residents – especially under the influence of alcohol, or opium, or the advice of their native mistresses and secretaries – have sown great terror among my people. If they complain, their liberty or their heads are at stake.

Prince Yukanthor informed the French government that, when the Senior Resident learned that King Norodom was sending his son to Paris, Yukanthor was threatened with arrest because the Resident was 'frightened that I would cry out the truth and perhaps be heard'. He spoke of the ageing King's suffering at the repression and indignities to which his people were subject and warned that if there were no redress, and if the King died of grief, as seemed probable, 'I will be justified in saying he was murdered.'

One would think that the government of what was considered the most civilized state in the Western world would have been moved by this dignified and courageous account of the situation in this faraway corner of the Empire. But what was the reaction? To issue a warrant for the prince's arrest soon after he had presented the petition. Yukanthor managed to escape to England, and eventually to Siam, where he died some thirty-four years later. Four years after he presented the petition, he should have acceded to the throne when his father, as Yukanthor had predicted, died of a broken heart.[1] A year before his death, King Norodom built what is known as the Silver Pagoda on the Royal Palace grounds, supervising the work himself. (From the time he was forced into signing the 1884 Convention, he never moved outside the palace precincts.) When the pagoda was dedicated, the King invoked Buddha as witness to his grief that he had to finish his reign in slavery and asked that the merits of building the pagoda should be 'transferred to descendants capable of restoring national independence and the former glories of Cambodia'. The French reply to that was to transfer the throne to his younger brother Sisowath, 'loyal' in all things to the French.

Is it surprising that I, the first of the Norodoms to ascend the throne after the death of my great-grandfather, should vow to acquire merit in the most sacred of all causes? It was to national independence that I applied myself with all my energy as soon as the French started their war for the reconquest of Indo-China. I was anxious, however, to avoid armed confrontation and bloodshed. That many of my compatriots disagreed with me on this was clear. Some chose to fight shoulder-to-shoulder with the Vietminh of Ho Chi Minh. In those days, due to the prejudices of background

1. Officially King Norodom died of cancer.

and education, I feared the Vietminh were fighting only to replace the French as masters in Cambodia. As things turned out, it was fortunate for Cambodia that a number of my countrymen acquired valuable experience in guerrilla warfare, serving with the Vietminh. After the war against France was over, unbeknown to me, they even maintained some of the resistance bases built up in those days in working order, just in case of renewed attempts at a colonialist takeover. The existence of these bases facilitated the amazingly swift appearance of our resistance movement in March 1970. Meanwhile, in that earlier struggle, I carried on as best I could by legal, constitutional means.

In 1946, and again in 1948, I studied military science in France at the Seaumur academy for cavalry and armoured units. Directing the academy, and in charge of the course that I took, was General de Langlade. Later, when I was showing excessive interest in our national independence, the French government sent de Langlade to head their High Command in Cambodia. They reasoned that, as I had been a very obedient pupil of de Langlade at Seaumur, I would continue to obey his orders in my own country. But just as de Langlade was 'king' at Seaumur, and acted as such, so I was King in Cambodia and also had every intention of playing this role. As we shall see, this led to a poignant incident. (The French, incidentally, had accepted me at their École Supérieure de Guerre but, as I was very fond of riding, I preferred to combine my military training with one of my favourite sports.)

In September 1949, I submitted a five-point demand to the French High Commissioner:
1. Genuine internal sovereignty for Cambodia.
2. Freedom to conduct foreign relations with the main world powers, and representation at the United Nations.
3. A progressive and rapid reduction of French military zones in Cambodia and the replacement of French presence there by a Cambodian presence.
4. Pardon for all resistance fighters.
5. A generous attitude towards freeing and according

complete amnesty to military and political prisoners and exiles – including Son Ngoc Thanh.

These demands were eventually met, and embodied in a new Convention. Cambodia was able to take part in the San Francisco Conference of September 1951. For the first time since the colonial occupation we acted as a separate entity, and signed, with forty-seven other states, the Japanese peace treaty.

Neither the people nor myself had been satisfied with the 1949 Convention, however. Although it was a big step in the right direction, it was still far from our aim of unconditional independence. In a message to the Cambodian people on 15 June 1952, I pledged to obtain complete independence within three years. That meant the transference to Cambodian competence of all those powers that France insisted on retaining, under the pretext that they were essential to waging war against the Vietminh.

I made my position clear to the French. Although I did not want the Vietminh on Cambodian soil, what they did in their own country was not Cambodia's business, and I did not want Cambodia to be used as a base of operations against them. I continued to push for complete independence.

My hopes were raised when I was invited to Paris to lunch with President Auriol on 25 March 1953. I had been assured that my communications to the French government had received the closest study. The luncheon discussion was sterile and President Auriol let it be known that the sooner I left French soil for Cambodia, the better pleased he would be. He went so far as to include in the official communiqué the offensive phrase that King Sihanouk 'should return to Phnom Penh within a few days'. A visit from the Minister for the Associated States, Monsieur Letourneau, made it clear that the steps I had taken in seeking independence were 'inopportune' to say the least.

I had fared better than my unfortunate great-uncle, half a century earlier, but I neverthless had no intention of being brushed off so easily. I decided to pursue my cause in the United States. Surely, in the citadel of freedom, untainted by colonialism in Indo-China, I would find the understanding and support I needed. Letourneau got wind of my plans and persuaded my francophile uncle, Prince Sisowath Monireth, to caution me that my 'crown' might be at stake if I engaged in 'anti-French adventures' abroad.

By this time, my main quarrel with the French had boiled down to their insistence, and my refusal, that Cambodia play a part in the war against the Vietminh, and remain within the French union. I had told President Auriol that it was

unnecessary for France to worry about myself or the throne, or the fate of the monarchy, or indeed that of Cambodia, but simply grant the total independence demanded by Cambodia – even if this means, as France had threatened, her total abandonment of our country. In this decisive turning point in the history of our country and our relations with France, I am forced to choose between France and my compatriots. Obviously I choose my compatriots.

Why a France that had so recently emerged from its own struggle against the Nazi occupiers could not understand the aspirations of the Cambodian people – indeed the peoples of Indo-China as a whole – was more than I could fathom. That a socialist president could take such an attitude was even more perplexing. Hints that I might 'lose my crown' if I pushed things too far also rankled. Was the crown really theirs to give and theirs to take away?

I took off for the United States via Canada on 13 April 1953, preparing en route a memorandum on the urgency of granting full independence to the three states of Indo-China, putting Cambodia's case in first place. I stressed that Cambodian participation in any activities in favour of the democracies could only be possible after real and total independence had been granted, and that was also true for the states of Indo-China as a whole.

That was the main theme of an hour-long discussion with John Foster Dulles. His reaction was sour, to say the least:

'Defeat communism in your area! Then we will put pressure on France to do what is necessary,' was the essence of his patronizing advice. His *idée fixe* was the urgency of destroying the Vietminh, and the importance of Cambodia's contribution to this.

As long as our common enemies, the Vietminh, are not crushed, and you know how capable they are of sweeping away your Khmer monarchy and your glorious traditions, your millennia-old civilization and your young democracy; as long as this great and possibly fatal danger is not repulsed – we must do nothing to discourage the French, who are making heavy sacrifices in Indo-China to defend our common liberties.

We are at the most crucial moment of the war. It has to be won. That is why more than ever we must unite our forces and our means and not quarrel and divide ourselves. Your dispute with France would only play into the hands of the common enemy . . . Without the help of the French Army, your country would quickly be conquered by the Reds and your independence would disappear.

I felt like telling him, as I had told President Auriol, not to worry so much about our affairs.

It is ironic to compare those words spoken in 1953 with the reality of 1970. Who has been trying to sweep away our traditions and civilization but the successors of John Foster Dulles, trying to implement his 'Asians fight Asians' doctrines? I refused to accept his arguments. I had nothing in common ideologically with the Vietminh, but I sympathized with their national liberation struggle. How could I do otherwise and remain a Cambodian patriot? We were after the same thing, but going about it in different ways. I hinted as much to Mr Dulles. His cold advice was an echo of President Auriol's: 'Go home and help General Navarre win the war against the communists!'

My next move was to set up an interview with the *New York Times*, front-paged on 19 April 1953. To a question about the 'communist menace', I replied.

'Among intellectual circles in Cambodia there has been the growing conviction during the past years that the Vietminh communists fight for the independence of their country.' I added that Cambodians who saw things that way did not see why they 'should die for France and help the French remain in Cambodia'. I pointed out the injustices flowing from French insistence on all sorts of extra-territorial rights and privileges, such as retaining command over Cambodian armed forces, controlling economic and financial affairs, and retaining other attributes of sovereignty. The reaction to the interview has impressed me ever since as to the power of the press, when it is disposed to act at the right time in the right way. Where I failed with Auriol and Dulles, I succeeded through the *New York Times*. Within four days, France invited a Cambodian delegation to come to Paris to negotiate the remaining issues.

I interrupted my return journey in Tokyo to await the results of the Paris negotiations. While there, I received a message from Dulles urging the necessity for Cambodia and France to work together in an atmosphere of complete harmony 'at a moment when the threat of a communist invasion from Laos is so apparent'. The United States, the message continued, 'is applying itself to intensifying and speeding up their aid to save the Khmer people from communist aggression'. Fine, I thought, what is clear is that Cambodia must rely on its own strength – and I was thinking in terms of military strength.

My detractors like to pretend that, somewhere in my development, I must have been brainwashed by Mao-Tse-tung and Chou En Lai. But it was men like Vincent Auriol and John Foster Dulles – and later, Richard Nixon – who were responsible for my political education. Independence, in the eyes of these leaders, was a bargaining counter to be offered or withdrawn according to how it suited their interests, not those of the little country concerned.

It was only after nearly half a million Cambodians had rallied to my appeal for armed struggle, if necessary, that the French started to show real interest in negotiations.

In September 1953, after the French had agreed to the transfer of military, police and judicial affairs, I had Premier Penn Nouth issue an appeal to the Khmer Issarak[1]-Vietminh and Vietminh forces in which the key phrases were: 'Although we are not communists, we do not oppose communism as long as it is not imposed from outside . . . What happens in Vietnam is none of our business.' I gave assurances that an independent Cambodia would not be used as a base for operations against the Vietminh. The proclamation

1. The Khmer Issarak was a loosely organized resistance group allied to the Vietminh.

brought down showers of invective about Cambodian 'neutralism' – the first time the term was used in relation to our country. It also brought a visit by the 'Senator for Taiwan', William F. Knowland of 'China Lobby' fame. He turned up with the US Ambassador to Saigon, Donald Heath, to insist that France must retain overall command in Cambodia in order to fulfil the main task of destroying communism. Sirik Matak at that time was Foreign Minister and Knowland had no difficulty in winning him over to his viewpoint, but I remained adamant.

Knowland's visit marked the beginning of the long process of US intervention in Cambodian affairs, culminating in the 1970 invasion. Both Knowland and Heath, supported by Sirik Matak, used every conceivable argument to force us to pledge Cambodia to aid in the 'common cause'. But we had set our course. They went away empty-handed and furious.

On 17 October 1953, the final questions regarding the transfer of military powers were negotiated and, on 9 November, all the attributes of independence were finally in Cambodian hands – but not before certain military show-downs with the French, and the actual disarming of some French units by our armed forces.

By exploiting the increasingly heavy pressures of the Vietminh in Vietnam and Laos, and the increasing resistance inside Cambodia, I was able to manoeuvre militarily and politically in such a way that the French either had to yield to my 'Royal Crusade for Independence' or strengthen their forces in Cambodia at the expense of other, more vital fronts.

When it came to the formal handing-over of powers, it was with my respected former cavalry instructor, General de Langlade, that I had to deal.

'Sire,' he said, 'You have "whipped" me.'[1]

'Mon général, it is not true,' I replied. 'But I had to show myself worthy of Général de Langlade's education. My success is yours, as it is you who taught me what I know of military science.'

'You are not very kind to your professor,' he continued.

1. Terms used in French cavalry circles.

'Mon général,' I said, 'I had to prove myself, as one of your pupils. I could not lose so vital a battle, with my country at stake.'

On the eve of the French departure, one of his staff officers whispered to de Langlade: 'The King is mad! Your former pupil is mad! He expels us from Cambodia, but without us he will be crushed by the Vietminh!'

De Langlade turned to him and other officers and replied: 'Gentlemen, the King may be mad but it is a brilliant sort of madness!'

Our independence received international recognition and guarantees at the 1954 Conference on Indo-China, but 9 November 1953 is celebrated as the day on which it was actually achieved. What seemed to me the end of a long and painful road turned out to be only the end of one phase of a struggle infinitely more complex than either myself or my ancestors could have imagined when the first colonial power offered its 'protection' over a century ago.

When I had the sad distinction of taking my place as an honour guard at the bier of the late President Ho Chi Minh, I thought how true is his phrase: 'Nothing is more precious than independence.' He was a life-long revolutionary of humble origins; I am an aristocrat from a long line of monarchs. He was of another generation, thirty years my senior. But we had one thing in common, unswerving devotion to our country's independence. He chose the stern revolutionary road, a course which appalled me when I was young and thought of the blood that would be shed.

Gazing for the first and last time at the serene, austere face of that incomparable patriot, I felt that, contained in his life and activities, was the history of generations of sacrifice by the peoples of Indo-China to be free of foreign domination. He was a thoroughly good and selfless man who had devoted his life to freeing his people.

In the end it was the Americans who drove home the bitter lesson that imperialists leave only one road to freedom, once they have marked a country down as their prey; that is the road of armed struggle as defined by Ho Chi Minh.

Chapter 12

Abdication to Deposition

On 2 March 1955, I sent an envelope to the Phnom Penh radio station together with instructions that it be opened at noon, and the recorded tape inside be played during the midday news. In this way the Cambodian people learned, to their great amazement, that I had renounced the throne. Members of the Royal family and the government were as astonished as everyone else. I had made the decision entirely on my own, and taken no one into my confidence. According to the 1947 constitution, in such a case the Crown Council must elect a successor from among the male descendants of King Ang Duong. That is, from the Sisowath or Norodom clans. They chose my father, Norodom Suramarit, then sixty years of age. I was thirty-two at the time, having been on the throne for fourteen years. In my broadcast statement, I made it absolutely clear that I would neither seek, nor accept, the throne again.

Why did I take such a step? And why at that time? There were many factors. Some related to internal, some to external, affairs. In 1952, I had pledged to win total independence for Cambodia within three years. I had achieved this with plenty of time to spare. Less than a month previous to my decision to abdicate, that is on 7 February 1955, 99.8 per cent of the population had replied 'Yes' to a referendum as to whether the royal mission to acquire independence had been accomplished to the satisfaction of our people. During that mission, I had accumulated experience in dealing with world statesmen, to a degree rare for someone of my years. I had lost any innocence *vis-à-vis* the 'disinterested' policies of major powers like France and the United States. Now that independence had been gained, the next problem was to see that it was maintained. The role of monarch, while suited for the royal crusade for independence, would not be suitable for the tasks ahead.

The International Control Commission was beginning to act as some sort of super-government. The Poles, considering me as an aristocrat, and therefore a sworn enemy of progress as well as the left-wing parties, were taking advantage of this. The Canadians, protecting US interests, from the beginning turned a blind eye to violations of our frontiers. The warring political factions within Cambodia wanted to make of me a mere figurehead who could be ignored in their wrangling. At least that is how I saw things at the time and this was the reason for my decision to renounce the symbolic role and step straight into the political arena.

On the external front, pressures were already building up for Cambodia to accept the SEATO 'umbrella'. Some of our rightists saw this 'umbrella' as convenient protection for their own political ambitions. Dulles had made it clear that he was prepared to send officers to help train the Cambodian Army 'provided they had full responsibility and would not be hampered by the French'. In that proviso was the clearly implied threat that US aims were to take advantage of the French departure to move in and replace them.

I also wanted to stand on my own feet politically and measure myself against my opponents in the political arena instead of basing my authority on my heredity. The Democratic Party, supported by the US, wanted to introduce Western, essentially French-style parliamentary democracy. The Poles in the ICC wanted to protect the interests of the pro-communist Pracheachon (People's) party. In 1947, I had transformed the absolute monarchy as it then existed, into a constitutional monarchy ruling through parliament. I considered later that the new system did not work well, mainly because our people had no experience of that formal type of democracy which consists of dropping ballots into boxes in favour of whomever had made the most attractive promises. When I dissolved the first elected parliament in

1952, in exchange for my promise to achieve independence within three years, I got a very critical letter from a fiery student, denouncing me for having destroyed our infant democracy. The student was Mou Youn, now one of the three key ministers leading the resistance struggle from inside the country. The truth is that we were all very inexperienced on how to create a viable democratic system in those days, one that really worked and could be maintained. We were not the only newly independent country to have such problems.

The example of the near-anarchy into which the French parliamentary system had degenerated in the postwar period, with governments falling every few months, was hardly an incentive to copy the same system in Cambodia. France had a well-established bureaucracy which functioned whether or not there was stability at the top. Cambodia, with its infant civil service, formerly staffed by French or Vietnamese, had no such institutional stability. I decided to halt what I considered a drift towards chaos by giving Cambodia an original system of a democracy, under which power could be exerted with a minimum premium on demagogy – the chief weapon of Son Ngoc Thanh, who by then was one of the leaders of the Democratic Party.

On 19 February, just three weeks before my abdication, I had proposed an amendment to the 1947 constitution providing for each commune[1] to elect deputies to a provincial assembly. The fifteen provincial assemblies would have wide powers in adminstering local affairs, and would elect deputies to the National Assembly. Candidates would stand as individuals, not as representatives of political parties, although the latter would continue to function. Cabinets, however, would be nominated by the King from among elected deputies. The National Assembly could revoke the mandates of individual ministers, but could not bring down the whole cabinet. The mandates of deputies could also be revoked if over half the electorate decided they were not doing the job for which they had been elected.

My idea in proposing this admittedly novel system was

1. An administrative unit grouping several villages.

or the people to elect candidates on the basis of their record in local activities and not on their skill as spell-binding orators. The opposition parties criticized the proposal, and even protested to the International Control Commission that it violated the spirit of the Geneva Agreements. The violence of their attacks, and the base motives imputed to me, were such that I felt it impossible to maintain my status as monarch. Either I had to maintain a politically aloof position as sovereign or step down and move straight into the political arena.

In the explanations I gave some two weeks after my abdication, I dealt with the difficulties of being a monarch and still having a real contact with the people, for which I had always yearned. I wanted to convince our youth, especially the students, that my efforts for the country had nothing in common with any desire to remain 'His Majesty the King' or to luxuriate in the pageantry and privileges of the Royal Palace. I explained that as long as I remained on the throne, I was not taken seriously by state officials when I exhorted them to abandon their pursuit of power and riches:

When I was confronted by the great powers in the struggle against foreign domination, my royal authority was essential . . . I needed my title as the legally qualified representative of my country . . . Had I not spoken as King, they could always have replied that I did not represent the whole of Cambodia . . . Today the situation is different. The main problem is internal.

If I remain on the throne, locked up in my palace . . . I will never really know the true situation or the abuses of which the people are the victim.

(I knew only too well that people with grievances were afraid to speak up openly in audience with me. There were too many officials around to reproach them afterwards, and even take reprisals if they spoke of things unpleasant for the officials concerned. How could I know what happened to them after they left the palace? My broadcast continued:

The palace is stuffed full of a hierarchy of court mandarins and intriguers. They are like the blood-sucking leeches that attach themselves to the feet of elephants.

Being a prisoner of protocol, fawned on by all sorts of time-servers awaiting my favours, was something I detested. And if I wanted to travel about and see things for myself, word was always sent in advance, so that anything disagreeable was hidden from sight. I saw only impeccably dressed citizens amidst banners and welcoming arches, and a wall of officialdom was raised as a barrier against social reality. I hated this but, as a God-King, I had to submit to it.

As more than forty states had recognized Cambodia after independence, most of my time was henceforth taken up by audiences with ambassadors and visiting dignatories, organizing receptions, banquets, Royal ballet performances, and so many official functions that I hardly had a moment free to visit the interior of the country. I remained the traditional 'God-King'. I summed all this up in my broadcast, adding:

This is why I took the definite decision to abandon the throne, its pomp and pageantry, in order to devote my whole time and energies to serve the people and their well-being.

To set at rest rumours that my abdication was a political manoeuvre, and that I would pick up the crown again when it suited me, I stated that: 'I categorically refuse to return to the throne no matter what the turn of events.' Many who should have known better did not believe this, although I stated it as clearly as possible as a 'promise made before the nation, before history, before our religion, and before the world'.

About a month after the abdication speech, I announced my intention of forming a new political grouping, the Sangkum Reaster Nivum (Popular Socialist Community), which would be the chief instrument in forging the national unity which I had set as my goal. I invited existing parties to bury their differences and put themselves inside the new organization, which I conceived as a front or movement, rather than a political party. The aim, I said, was 'to give birth to a truly democratic, equalitarian, and socialist Cambodia, to restore the past greatness of our motherland'. Many of my loyal supporters promptly forgot the words 'democratic, equalitarian, and socialist' and began to dream up ways to use the Sangkum to further their own private ambitions.

Within two months, the leadership of three right-wing political parties; the Khmer Restoration Party of Lon Nol, the Populist Party of Sam Sary, and the National Democratic Party of Oum Chheana Sun, dissolved their organizations and advised their members to join the Sangkum. The Democratic Party, the Pracheachon, the Liberal Party, and a few others announced they would contest the elections, scheduled for 11 September 1955, as autonomous entities.

The elections, supervised by the ICC and held in accordance with the terms of the 1954 Geneva Agreements, resulted in the Sangkum winning all ninety-one seats. I had never expected a victory of such embarrassing magnitude. The Sangkum received 83 per cent of the votes, the Democrats 13 per cent, and the Pracheachon only 3 per cent. The Liberals and four other small parties received a total of less than one per cent, and vanished from the political scene. Six months after I had abdicated, I found myself in the political forefront of the country as Prime Minister for a political grouping which held all the seats in the National Assembly!

Because the Sangkum, to all appearances, was comprised in its entirety of three right-wing parties, and because the Pracheachon had been so soundly defeated, Washington rejoiced in my victory – somewhat prematurely. Firstly, the Sangkum was by no means composed only of the three parties that had rallied to it; secondly, I had no intention of pursuing reactionary policies. I had been impressed by the popular support the left-wing groups had received in advocating neutrality, and opposition to American neo-colonialism. These were much closer to my ideas than the policies of the others. Dulles should have recalled – before the rejoicings in Washington – that I had visited Nehru just two weeks after my abdication. The Indian leader was enthusiastic that I had taken such a step, and strongly advised me to pursue a neutral course in foreign affairs, something which I had been turning over in my mind anyway.

Earlier, Son Ngoc Thanh had contacted Nehru seeking support for his policies, approaching him secretly during a visit by the Indian Prime Minister and his daughter, Indira, to the Angkor temples. Nehru apparently took the measure of this intriguer immediately. He advised Son Ngoc Thanh to forget his differences with me and cooperate in the interests of national unity. Thanh replied with a diatribe against me. Among the reproaches was that I was 'anti-American' which did not impress Nehru, who informed me of the whole affair.

The outcome of my eight-day visit to India had been an agreement to establish diplomatic relations between our two countries at legation level and, as set forth in a joint communiqué, to base our relations on the Five Principles of Peaceful Coexistence which had been formulated less than a year earlier during Chou En Lai's visit to New Delhi. Nehru and I got along well together, and he influenced me in opting for neutrality.

Two weeks after the elections, the first Sangkum National Congress was held. This was in line with my concept of giving the people a direct role in what the social scientists now like to call the 'decision-making processes'. Some historic measures were decided: the vote for women; the Khmer language as the only one to be used in public institutions. (This had long been a bone of contention between myself and the French. Gautier – the same Résident Supérieur who had tried to marry me off against my wishes – had gone as far as to suppress the Khmer script in favour of a Latinized version, solemnly assuring me that Cambodia would never become a modern state unless we did so.) Mandates of deputies, it was decided, could be withdrawn if a majority of voters in their electorate so desired. From that historic moment until December 1969, there were regular twice-yearly sessions of National Congress, with supplementary extraordinary sessions in case of a national crisis.

In the space of eight years, Cambodia had moved forward from an absolute monarchy to a constitutional monarchy with an elected parliament, and on to an original form of guided democracy via the National Congress of Sangkum. The role of the monarch had been reduced – at my initiative – to a symbolic one. Power of decision was in the hands of the

Prime Minister and his cabinet, reinforced by the direct participation of the people. The system worked smoothly for the next five years.

A crisis arose on 3 April 1960, when my father, King Norodom Suramarit, died at the age of sixty-five, six months after the lacquer-bomb attentat. Should the Crown Council choose from one of the 180-odd princes who were male decendants of King Ang Duong's two sons, and thus qualified as successors? (Although at the first National Congress we had taken the initial step towards equality of the sexes by giving the vote to women, there was no such equality in regard to the succession. Had there been, my mother would almost certainly have been chosen Queen.)

At the first meeting of the Crown Council, I pointed out that one of the great merits of the monarchy was that the throne was the highest symbol of national unity, but that there was now 'a group doing everything it can to weaken, and evidently destroy, the royal family and establish on the ruins a republic with Son Ngoc Thanh as president'. As a forecast of what was to happen almost exactly ten years later, I was not far off, except that in 1970–71, Son Ngoc Thanh was kept waiting in the presidential ante-chamber far longer than he had expected. There were strong pressures for me to take the crown again, but my decision was irrevocable. Many thought the choice should be from one of my sons, but I was against that, too. I told the Crown Council:

Nothing in the world will persuade me to permit one of my sons to ascend the throne. From my own experience I know only too well the terrible servitude and crushing responsibilities of a ruling monarch. On top of this, he has to endure intrigues, greed, and jealousies. I was spared none of this during my own reign, so I think you will appreciate why I want to save my children from the same fate.

The last thing I wanted was to see the country torn from top to bottom by a sordid scramble for power within the Royal family, with overtones of civil war. I knew in my own mind that in taking this stand I was, in effect, abolishing the monarchy in everything but the form. I had faced up to this with my own abdication. But the monarchy continued to be the greatest single unifying influence in the country, and a too sudden break would only benefit our enemies. I later said that the day the monarchy ceases to be 'a harmonious and effective framework' for national unity and progress I would not hesitate

to take the initiative myself in doing away with it, and guiding the nation along other roads, helping it to accomplish in peace, and without blood-letting, the revolution of its choice.[1]

The time had not yet come for this. For the people, the monarchy plus Buddhism equalled the nation. So while fighting to retain the monarchy, I opposed choosing a new monarch.

In the end it was decided, as a temporary solution, to set up a Regency Council presided over by my uncle, Prince Sisowath Monireth. He pledged his oath to the National Assembly on 4 April 1960. This did not end the crisis. There were floods of requests for me to propose some more permanent solution, and renewed demands for me to reclaim the throne. The solution was found in a proposal to amend the constitution so as to empower the Crown Council

in accordance with the expressed will of the people, to confide the powers and prerogatives of Head of State to an incontestable personality expressly designated by popular suffrage.

On 5 June 1960, there was a nation-wide plebiscite, and the proposal was approved by over two million votes against a few hundred. The amendment – Article 122, providing that once elected, the Head of State acquires 'the powers and prerogatives of a sovereign' – was approved without dissent by the National Assembly on 9 June and, five days later, on 14 June 1960, I was unanimously elected to the newly-created post. The Queen Mother remained as the symbol of the monarchy, while I exercised the 'powers and prerogatives' of a sovereign Head of State. The dynastic crisis was thus ended – as was the power of the monarchy.

In relation to what happened after March 1970, it is worth noting that Article 53 of the amended constitution states

1. *Réalités Cambodgiennes,* 3 August 1962.

that 'the person of the Supreme Head of State is sacred and inviolable', which means, among other things, that the National Assembly cannot depose him. The same article stipulates that all deputies must swear fidelity to the Head of State at the beginning of each legislature, and before assuming their functions. All those deputies who voted to depose me in March 1970 had sworn this oath. The provision that the Head of State was sacred and inviolable was transgressed not only by the act of my deposition in the coup of 18 March, but even more crudely in later condemning me to death for high treason.

Such flagrant illegalities did not prevent Washington from hastening to recognize the new régime and endorsing the 'legality' and 'constitutionality' of the methods by which it had seized power. Article 95 of the amended constitution provides for a referendum in case of important constitutional crises. It is difficult to imagine a more important one than that of deposing a Head of State, and switching from a monarchic to a republican régime. Obviously Lon Nol and his team never dared consult the people. Article 115 of the constitution specifies that 'dispositions relating to the monarchic form of state cannot be the object of any proposal for revision'. Article 92 provides for biannual sessions of the National Congress. As mentioned earlier, any question which the National Assembly and the National Congress could not solve between them should become the subject of a referendum. There have not even been any sessions of the National Congress since the coup.

All the democratic processes and safeguards that I so carefully built into our political institutions have been trampled underfoot to the accompaniment of approving cries from the 'free world' which applauded when I was overthrown in the name of 'democracy'. The voice of the people has been silenced. As another gesture of his devotion to 'democracy', Lon Nol, on 17 October 1971, dissolved the National Assembly: 'Let's stop playing this sterile game of liberal democracy if we want to win the war,' he explained.

Even Sirik Matak, who was forced for reasons of demagogic appeal to renounce his title of Prince, was led to admit that the Lon Nol state 'has no juridical, constitutional, or popular base, because a constitution has still to be drafted; a National Assembly has to be elected'. (This was before the electoral farce perpetrated on 6 June 1972, rigged by Lon Nol in the areas still under his control and by which he contrived to get himself 'elected' President.)

Whatever constitutional puppet-shows the Lon Nol–Sirik Matak–Son Ngoc Thanh putschists stage to try and give a legal veneer to their régime are of no importance for the future of Cambodia. The future is being created in the resistance areas, with elected bodies from the village upwards, something along the lines I had proposed before my abdication.

An ironic footnote is that, having plunged republicanism into discredit in record time, the plotters were advised by the Americans, in 1972, to restore the monarchy. The reasoning was that the 'republic' had become synonymous with corruption, an unprecedented assault on democratic rights, and above all for military and political catastrophes. So the new 'king-makers' of the world's strongest democracy started looking for a royal candidate for Cambodia. First choice was Prince Monireth, but it seemed my uncle had no stomach for the job. He was probably wise enough to know there was little future in it. The 'king-makers' then looked towards Monireth's eldest son, Prince Sisowath Retnara. The French had created the precedent, they argued, in choosing Sihanouk rather than his father Suramarit, so why not choose Retnara instead of his father Monireth?

As the disagreeable – for them – prospect hove in sight of having the Khmers Rouges in Phnom Penh, in the shape of Khieu Samphan, Hou Youn, Hu Nim and their comrades, the Americans frantically sought a nice, constitutional monarchy – without Sihanouk of course. But Lon Nol was not likely to give up easily, and waiting in the shadows for his turn was that inveterate would-be usurper of power, Son Ngoc Thanh. The scheme had to be put into cold storage for a time, but as the constitutional crisis of the Lon Nol régime is a permanent one, it would not be surprising if the Retnara-for-King advocates did not revive the idea at some point.

Retnara is a right-wing, anti-communist, pro-American functionary in Lon Nol's foreign ministry. In other words he has all the qualifications. Lon Nol likes him personally and, when he started to travel abroad immediately after the coup, he took Retnara with him. There is one flaw, however. Although Lon Nol likes Retnara, he does not like him – or anyone else – enough to cede his place as *de facto* King of the Khmer Republic. Lon Nol will never give up this post voluntarily. If Nixon decides to get rid of him the only way would be the method used by one of his predecessors, the late President Kennedy, in getting rid of the (also) late President Ngo Dinh Diem of South Vietnam. The Retnara 'solution' in any case, will fail – like all the others that the US has tried to impose on Cambodia.

The future lies in quite other directions, and I am happy to be associated with helping to lay the foundations.

Chapter 13

Cambodia's Fighting Role

Richard Nixon is Hanoi's most effective public relations officer. Thanks to him, future generations will say:

Those incredible North Vietnamese. They vanquished single-handed the mightiest of the imperialist powers. They took on the Americans in South Vietnam, in Laos and in Cambodia, with comparatively poorly armed ground troops, and fought off the US air armada and battle-fleet. What a people! Starting from Hanoi, they occupied and administered the whole of Indo-China. They were everywhere – even blowing up US planes in Thailand.

And there will be legends:

Once upon a time there was a race of God-Warriors that descended from Heaven. They were called North Vietnamese – the greatest warriors the world ever knew. They went everywhere and were invisible, appearing suddenly here and there in places thousands of kilometres apart, with weapons – even tanks – which were also invisible, until they suddenly appeared on battlefields to crush the greatest military power known till that time.

The North Vietnamese do their best to dispel this nonsense. When our Cambodian resistance forces win a battle, Hanoi sends them a congratulatory message, as they do for the Pathet Lao, when they overrun CIA bases in Laos or win battles against US mercenaries there, or for the NLF when there is a 'Tet' offensive or a victory in the Mekong Delta. 'But it's you . . . it's you, the North Vietnamese, that won those battles,' persists Nixon. 'It's you who are driving us out of Indo-China.' Reiterated denials from Hanoi have no effect.

To lend strength to the legend, if there is a victory by our forces in Cambodia, or the Pathet Lao in Laos, Nixon sends a few hundred planes to bomb North Vietnam, somewhat like the Nazis used to wipe out an Ouradour or a Lidice, if the patriots killed a *gauleiter* or some other Nazi big-wig. And they did this long before the 1972 'spring offensive' when, for the first time, the North Vietnamese really did come in large numbers and modern weapons to help their compatriots in the south.

It is true that the North Vietnamese, and the Vietnamese people in general, have performed miracles of courage and self-sacrifice and Vo Nguyen Giap is a military genius, undoubtedly the greatest strategist of our time and one of the greatest of all time. I was with him at the start of the invasion of south Laos by Saigon troops in February 1971. We spent an afternoon going over the situation in Cambodia, then had dinner together. To my surprise, there was a leisurely cup of coffee and some music after dinner, and Giap showed no sign of wanting to end the evening. In the end I said: 'I feel guilty, mon général. I have taken up so much of your time. I simply cannot understand you giving me so much time when such a tremendous battle is going on in south Laos.'

'Oh, that,' he said, with his calm, gently ironical smile, 'that's been prepared long ago. Our Pathet Lao comrades have everything necessary to deal on the spot with that. There's no need for me to bother. It has been expected for a long time. I listened to the radio today,' he added. 'Thieu says in Saigon that his troops will remain in Laos until May or June. In fact what's left of them will be out by the end of March, at the latest.' And they were. The last had left by 25 March.

I cannot say enough in praise of the Vietnamese, and how fortunate we are to have them as allies. I once said to my friend Pham Van Dong: 'Promise me one thing! When it is all over, tell me how you manage the miracle of getting supplies down the Ho Chi Minh trail despite hundreds of thousands of tons of bombs, and electronic detection gadgets and all the other American surveillance techniques. But don't tell me now,' I said, 'because I might reveal your secrets by accident.' He laughed, and promised that day we would drive down the Ho Chi Minh trail together, right into Saigon.

Why is it that in the West, any military action, anywhere in Indo-China, is officially presented as being between 'North Vietnamese' forces and those of the US and its allies? Is it perhaps too humiliating for a heavily armed super-power to admit military stalemate at the hands of South Vietnamese, Laotian and Cambodian peasant partisans? Must they elevate North Vietnam to their own level of armed might in order to be defeated by an equal? As for Cambodia, we have our own regular army and partisan detachments who together bear the main brunt of the fighting on Cam-bodian soil. And they have never been beaten in battle by Lon Nol's armies. But our victories are always credited to the 'North Vietnamese'.

In an earlier chapter, I mentioned that, at my request, General Giap sent military instructors to train military cadres for our own forces to reinforce a handful of veterans we already had. In quantity those that Giap sent were few – a couple of thousand – in quality they were superb. He had chosen magnificently, not only for their level of military skills, but for their human qualities. They came, did their job, and went home again. Long before the end of 1971, there was no more need for North Vietnamese instructors for, by that time, thanks to them, ninety per cent of operations were being waged by our own PNLAF, led by our own military cadres.

Only in the frontier areas did we sometimes combine operations with the NLF, and we always kept strictly to the letter and spirit of the decisions of the April 1970 Summit Conference of the Peoples of Indo-China, held at my initiative and which provided for the participants helping each other *when requested*. The North Vietnamese also had a small, virtually uninhabited area along part of the frontier to protect their communications with the south, and where they were responsible for any military operations. Apart from that our armed forces stayed within their respective national boundaries. Not that there is any reason why we should not cooperate militarily on a grand scale in certain situations.

172

Did not France, during the Second World War, join England and the U S A, and finally the Soviet Union, in order to beat the Nazis? Did national boundaries have to be respected then?

We will always be grateful for the help our Vietnamese comrades-in-arms gave us in the early days, for the arms supplied by the N L F and the instructors sent from the North. These men proved far more effective than the hundreds of millions of dollars the Americans sent to Lon Nol and Sirik Matak. As I explained to some French friends: 'In the old days I used to ask France for military instructors. But now – first of all you recognize Lon Nol and not me. Secondly, it's a different kind of war – the kind in which you were beaten by the Vietminh! So it is logical that I ask help from them – the best guerrilla-warfare experts in the world!'

We also have many local Vietnamese fighting with us, and Lon Nol served as our recruiting officer *par excellence*. In his barbarous massacre of ethnic Vietnamese in April 1970, he gave only three choices to the adults among the hundreds of thousands of Vietnamese residents in our country – most of whom had lived with us for generations. They could await the execution squads, accept deportation to South Vietnam and be press-ganged into the Saigon forces – or take to arms with the Cambodian resistance forces. Tens of thousands chose the last – women as well as men. In the long run most of them would probably have done so even had Lon Nol left them alone, for the overwhelming majority of our Vietnamese citizens sympathized with the Vietcong. From the start of the fighting in the south, there had been a steady trickle of young Vietnamese of both sexes across the frontier to join the N L F. We never interfered with this. With my declared policy of friendship with the N L F and the D R V, and the fact that the Americans used this friendship as the pretext to overthrow me, it was natural that the Vietnamese community became my staunchest supporters from the moment I launched the appeal to resist. But it was Lon Nol who left waverers no choice but to take to arms to survive. Thousands joined to take revenge for the murder of members of their families. They had 'blood debts to settle', as they expressed it.

The Saigon troops, with their savagery and rapacity, also helped forge our resistance movement from the start, by driving the people into our arms at a rate we could never have imagined. American reprisal bombings only accelerated the process. The dollar-grabbing mentality of the Saigon troops enabled us to arm our recruits almost as fast as Saigon's terror policies forced them into our camp. A Saigon officer once solemnly assured one of our procurement cadres: 'For dollars we can supply you with everything you want except helicopters – *for the moment.*' For helicopters we would have to be patient! In those turbulent early days, it was much easier and faster for our friends to make dollars available to us than have us depend on arms convoys coming down the Ho Chi Minh trail. I first told the press that our main source of arms would be the People's Republic of China, North Vietnam, North Korea, and Cuba – in that order. But I soon had to put South Vietnam in second place – an agreeable and unanticipated windfall. By 1972, our forces were capturing so many US arms, including tanks and artillery pieces, that I had to promote Nixon into first place as arms supplier!

I must say, though, that our resistance forces were from the beginning relatively well-armed. As mentioned earlier, in the period when the Khmers Rouges were in opposition to me, and even when Lon Nol was trying to wipe them out, the NLF, with whom they had contact, was reluctant to give them arms. They did not want a civil war which would endanger Cambodian neutrality and thus jeopardize the considerable material and political benefits from my support. The most they would do was to give temporary refuge to small groups of Khmers Rouges, if Lon Nol's troops were too hot on their heels in the frontier areas. But after I was overthrown, the situation was transformed: Khmers Rouges, 'Sihanoukists' and the NLF became allies overnight. From the moment of the coup the NLF knew it was only a matter of time before there would be a concerted drive against their bases and supply dumps in the frontier areas. So they started distributing arms, which would be lost anyway, in generous measure to our rapidly expanding resistance forces. Small wonder that the Americans were disappointed at the meagre stocks unearthed in the base areas. I always knew that recruits would be no problem. Arms and officers was another question. But the solution came far more quickly than I had thought possible.

There were large-scale desertions of Lon Nol units. In many cases units simply disbanded and handed over their arms to the partisans. A typical case occurred at the vital city of Kratié, capital of the province of the same name, and situated on the Mekong. Kratié and Mondulkiri, a neighbouring province, both have common frontiers with South Vietnam and constitute one of Cambodia's six military regions. On the eve of the coup, Lon Nol summoned the regional commander, Colonel Cheng Sayomboan, and the other five regional commanders to Phnom Penh. Although they were all his own appointees, Lon Nol immediately relieved two of them of their commands and placed them under arrest. He was not sure of their loyalty to treason. To the other four – including Cheng Sayomboan – and the two replacements for those arrested, Lon Nol revealed his plans for the coup, swearing them to absolute secrecy. Orders were to be given to their respective commands to maintain perfect order, but to deal harshly with any 'Vietcong disturbances'.

Back at Kratié, Cheng Sayomboan's deputy-commander, Major Tim Naing, a loyal officer from the days of the Royal Crusade for Independence, was temporarily in charge. He was puzzled when he heard of the coup. Next day there were, indeed, demonstrations, but he discovered immediately that the demonstrators were Cambodians supporting Sihanouk and not Vietcong, in spite of what the radio was saying. He ignored telephoned orders to suppress them. On 23 March, Tim Niang heard my Proclamation over Peking radio – and all became clear. Cheng Sayomboan had still not returned, but continued to give orders by telephone. Tim Niang then established contact with the resistance forces. He tried to persuade two battalions under him to do likewise, but opinions were divided, mainly because of family problems.

By the time Cheng Sayomboan returned to Kratié, Tim

Naing had disbanded the two battalions, given every soldier five hundred riels to go back to his village, and had handed over a stock of arms, including three mortars and twenty-three machine-guns to the partisans. He then took off, with the plans for the defence of Kratié in his pocket. The following day, the city was taken over without a shot, and the whole of the crucially important 6th Military Region was in our hands. Cheng Sayomboan was sent to set things in order, but it was too late. He was lucky to get out of Kratié alive, but he managed to make his way back to Phnom Penh, where Lon Nol promptly arrested him and sentenced him to death for having 'lost' Kratié. Eventually he managed to escape and make his way to Thailand. (He was more fortunate than Lieutenant-Colonel Tom Saravann of the Kep-Kompot military sub-division, who was executed for having 'lost' that region.) I know about the Kratié story in detail because Tim Naing, a first-class officer, after some extraordinary adventures, managed to get through to Laos and eventually to Paris and Peking, where he is now my aide-de-camp.

It was because of actions such as that at Kratié, that vast areas of the country were solidly in our hands within a few weeks of the coup. There was not a Vietnamese involved in the capture of the 6th Military Region, which Lon Nol and his Saigon allies have been unsuccessfully trying to take back ever since. What sort of supermen must the North Vietnamese be if, without any air transport and very few motor vehicles, they 'occupied' within weeks the major part of the country from the Gulf of Thailand in the south to the borders with Laos in the north; from South Vietnam in the east to Thailand in the west and north? As to how such myths are created and perpetuated, there was a revealing letter written by a Mr Jonathan Unger to the impeccably conservative *Far Eastern Economic Review* of Hong Kong and published in its issue of 10 April 1971. He writes:

Mr Ky Soth, Cambodia's Consul General in Hong Kong, in *Review* 13 (24 March 1971) disputes my contention that civil war is currently being waged in Cambodia.

Perhaps Mr Soth will explain why Phnom Penh – until at least late autumn 1970 – maintained an official policy of censoring the despatches of foreign correspondents which made mention of Khmers fighting for Sihanouk's government-in-exile. Perhaps the Cambodian government did not want foreign readers – and even Cambodian diplomats – to know that the Cambodian conflict is more than 'simply a national fight in legitimate self-defence'.

Gradually, the myth of the non-existence of Cambodian resistance forces was partly dissipated; first, by numerous journalists who had entered liberated territory uninvited, and very quickly found themselves prisoners – not of North Vietnamese or of the NLF – but of our partisans. (In most cases they had taken off for areas which Lon Nol's officers assured them were firmly under Phnom Penh's control.) Other journalists simply defied censorship. For instance, a UPA correspondent, Kate Webb, in a round-up for the first anniversary of the founding of the resistance government, wrote the following:

Intelligence sources say there are now hundreds of Cambodian communist training camps in central and western Cambodia. The presence of many Khmers Rouges on the battlefields of Cambodia in recent months show that training and propaganda have been very effective. Armed sabotage is carried out by Cambodians. The Cambodian communists and Sihanoukists are . . . mobile, moving, harassing, cutting roads, balking supply movements, almost at will.

(Incidentally, not long after she wrote that dispatch, Miss Webb was reported missing. There were reports that her body had been found. I gave instructions that at all costs we should find out what had happened and, if she were in our hands, standing instructions for good treatment and release as soon as possible should be implemented. Fortunately she had been captured alive and well and was soon afterwards released.)

Everyone, including our Vietnamese friends, were astonished at the speedy development of our resistance movement. But we had a big advantage. The NLF had had to get their arms slowly in hard, unequal battles with the enemy. Clubs and hoes at first, against pistols and rifles. Thanks largely to them, we had plenty of arms immediately. The Vietnamese were more politically and ideologically aware than the Cambodians, but President Nixon soon overcame this lag. With his bombs he performed the miracle of turning our people into revolutionaries within weeks. The hatred generated by the wholesale destruction of towns and villages was turned into anger and thirst for revenge. Our peasants make good raw material for guerrilla fighters, and once in the training camps described by Miss Webb, they learned tactics and how to handle modern weapons quickly.

Here it is necessary to digress for a moment to point out that resistance by guerrilla warfare is not by any means new to the Cambodian people. Most Western writers depict my people as passive, easy-going and rather indolent, and compare them to the more energetic, militant Vietnamese. They also sneer at the idea of a Prince heading armed struggle. Sometimes this has been done consciously to deride the idea of Cambodian armed resistance.

After the odious Convention was imposed on King Norodom in 1884, he started his own discreet revolt against the French by supporting, with arms and money, a revolt already started by his half-brother, Prince Sivotha, even before the Convention scandal. From research into official French documents of the period, it is clear that our Khmer guerrillas then were almost as effective against the French as have been the N L F guerrillas in South Vietnam against the Americans.

The new upsurge of revolt started in the first days of January 1885, in the region between Kompong Cham and Kratié – an area firmly held by our resistance forces today. By September of that year, the French 'Resident' in Kompong Cham, Monsieur de Lalande Calan, complained that all he held was a strip of territory about ten kilometres long on each side of the Mekong river. In a report to the French government, he wrote:

Outside these areas, the countryside is almost completely out of our control. None of the native officials [the Lon Nol puppets of those days, N.S.] dare to venture alone beyond the river banks or travel to the territories of which they are the chiefs; the non-occupied areas are administered by former rebel chiefs.[1]

1. 'Insurrection Nationale', Charles Meyer, *Études Cambodgiennes*, No. 11, July–September 1968.

The official French reports read just like the accounts of the first days of NLF activities in South Vietnam. The same sort of guerrilla tactics, ample use of traps and spikes; swift ambushes and fade-outs, the luring of French columns into exhausting expeditions then falling on them where and when the adversary least expected it. The people informed the guerrillas of every move made by the French while the latter were deprived of any valid information. Accounts written by French officers of their frustrating experiences are like copies of some of the diaries or letters home from American GIs in South Vietnam. The revolt was never crushed. It faded out only after the French restored many of the prerogatives – in 1886 – they had taken away from the King two years earlier. By the time the French backed down, the revolt had spread to many parts of the country. 'Pacification' operations inevitably ended with the guerrilla movement in the target areas stronger than ever.

Colonel Miramond, Commander-in-Chief of all French forces in Cambodia, who finally took over personal command of the operations, fared no better than Generals Harkins, Westmoreland and Abrams.

The traditions and natural aptitude for guerrilla tactics is in the blood of our peasants today. It is one of those factors which explain why, despite massive campaigns launched by Lon Nol and Saigon troops, seven tenths of the countryside and well over half the population were solidly in our hands before the end of the first year after the 18 March coup.

Five provinces, Ratanakiri, Stung Treng, Kratié, Mondulkiri and Preah-Vihear were ours. Unlike the liberated areas of South Vietnam, where provisional and district centres almost always remained under Saigon control, in that vast single block of territory mentioned, we controlled everything, including the towns. Not a vestige of Lon Nol administration was left. Most of the other provinces were from eighty to ninety per cent liberated, with Lon Nol troops clinging on to tightly encircled provincial capitals, isolated from each other and mainly supplied by air. In the four provinces of Kandal, Takéo, Pursat, and Battambang, where Lon Nol and his Saigon allies claimed 'maximum success', our control was between sixty and seventy-five per cent, even at the end of the first year and it steadily increased. Specifically, by March 1971, of the country's one hundred administrative districts, seventy had been liberated, and, of 1,129 villages, 751 were solidly in our hands. Six months later, our resistance administration was able to report that four fifths of the entire territory, populated by five million of the country's seven million population, were administered by the National United Front.

That this is neither exaggeration nor propaganda is shown by an Associated Press dispatch from Saigon on 10 December 1971, by correspondent, Richard Blystone: 'Highly placed official sources in Saigon estimated that enemy forces now control as much as eighty per cent of Cambodia.' It is worth noting that this dispatch was written several weeks after Saigon had sent another fifty thousand troops to invade us. By the end of 1971, our liberation armed forces controlled the villages and high ground surrounding Phnom Penh itself. How could anyone swallow the official fairy tale that the 'North Vietnamese' had accomplished all this, and had even set up some highly effective 'occupation administration' over almost all of Cambodia?

In those provinces where the resistance forces do not have complete control, the guerrillas are active day and night. All roads into Phnom Penh are either under our permanent control, or can be cut at will. We could easily strangle Phnom Penh. If we do not do it, this is because we do not want our compatriots to starve. American bombs and Saigon banditry have forced almost a million refugees into the city. The price of rice and fish soars every month. Our forces let enough food into the capital to keep people alive, but we must also maintain military pressure to keep our nation alive and win back our independence.

If we continue to hit Phnom Penh airport at Pochentong, it is because it is a military as well as civil airport. We also strike at military installations in the centre of Phnom Penh itself. Such attacks can only be carried out by our own people, helped by local residents – not by the Vietminh as Lon Nol claims.

An example was the first attack at Pochentong, which knocked out ninety-five per cent of Lon Nol's air force. The plans were prepared by an officer in the engineering corps of Lon Nol's army. They were relayed to Peking for approval, which was radioed back forty-eight hours before the attack. On the night of 21 January 1971, the officer and his family left for the Liberated Zone. They did not have to travel far, and he immediately sent me a message giving details of the attack. It was carried out by former Phnom Penh residents trained in commando techniques by our Vietnamese instructors. Inhabitants who could have been endangered by the attack were warned to quit the area beforehand, but to say nothing. Secrecy was maintained, which shows the mutual trust between our forces and the people. Lon Nol knew this was an 'inside job', and arrested a number of officers who had nothing to do with the affair. Tightened security after the first devastating attack did not prevent our commandos from hitting the airport again four days later, blowing up most of what had been left after the first attack. It was rumoured later that it was the destruction of his air force that brought about the stroke that left Lon Nol half paralysed for months.

Similarly, our guerrillas opened up with bazookas and mortars on oil depots in the outskirts of Phnom Penh at dawn on 20 September 1971, destroying them almost completely. Western news agencies reported that seventy-five per cent of Lon Nol's petrol reserves, including all his aviation fuel, were lost in that one attack. Security precautions were doubled and trebled around other oil depots but, in the week that followed, the remaining ones at Prek Thnot and Neak Luong were destroyed. The blowing-up of our only oil refinery at Sihanoukville was at my personal initiative, based on plans worked out at my Peking headquarters. It was a great success.

I have been asked if I do not suffer at the destruction of such installations, acquired at such great cost. Of course I do. We all do. But we do not hesitate. Petrol from those depots and the refinery went into the bellies of planes and tanks that massacred our compatriots. So we have no choice. But if it were North Vietnamese or any other foreigners who were blowing up our property our people would be very indignant, and there would be no cooperation.

Of course we cooperate with the resistance forces of Laos and South Vietnam in the border areas – we fight against a common enemy. But each is master in his own house, and if one or another of us wishes to cross a neighbour's threshold, we first ask for permission and then respect both house and master.

It is important for outsiders to understand that before the arrival of the French Indo-China did not exist as such. There were the separate entities of Annam (Vietnam), Laos and Cambodia. Tonking and Cochin China were created by the French. When the latter arrived on the scene, Cochin China was being fought over by the Annamites and the original Cambodian settlers in the Mekong Delta. Tonking, the northern part of Vietnam, was detached from the Annam Empire by the French and these components were lumped together with Cambodia and Laos to form what they called Indo-China. But the Vietnamese, Laotian, and Cambodian people wanted to get back their independence, and started to develop a sentiment of solidarity. When the Japanese occupied Indo-China, a further impetus was given to this. The French reoccupation and the United States invasion of Indo-China, starting with South Vietnam, drove the peoples of Indo-China even closer together.

Some 'experts' in the West like to write about the things which divide our three peoples, and dwell on 'traditional hostilities'. But we think more and more about the factors that unite us. Today, above all, it is the fact that we are victims of American aggression: aggression against South and North Vietnam, against Laos, against Cambodia. So we have to fight. We are three weak nations against a giant. Unless we stand together, we fall singly. It is 'unite and win' versus 'divide and rule'.

We rejoice in the fraternal aid we receive, thanks to our Vietnamese neighbours. But it is unfair to them, and to us, to attribute the victories of our liberation forces to the North Vietnamese. The Americans have learned to cry 'invaders' with every fabrication of a new 'North Vietnamese' victory.

Past sufferings at the hands of feudal Vietnamese and the succession of fascist régimes in Saigon, are used to invoke the theme of 'eternal hostility' between our two peoples. It is as though the French had cried 'invaders' when American and British forces entered their territory to deal with the Nazis; or political commentators had cited Anglo-French hostility during the Napoleonic wars as proof of General de Gaulle's treachery in collaborating with the British against the Nazis. Had anyone evoked 'traditional hostility' to oppose the Normandy landings, he would correctly have been branded a traitor.

On paper, the Lon Nol régime boasts an army of some 200,000 troops. The figure is inflated to justify the 501 million dollars Lon Nol received in the eighteen months between 18 March 1970 and September 1971. American journalists have revealed how boys from nine years upwards are registered as soldiers, and even their sisters' names are included on the lists, as are non-existent persons, or those killed in earlier battles, so that commanders can pocket their salaries. As those on the lists rarely get paid, they live on what they can loot from their compatriots. Lon Nol has an army of ghosts and gangsters. In fact, he has been able to mobilize about 100,000 men, of whom a maximum of 30,000 are genuine combat troops – or were before the defeats along Highway 6 in the last months of 1971. The rest are school-teachers, petty officials, students, and children, rounded up by Lon Nol's press gangs. Our forces have orders not to shoot at such youngsters and, when possible, to warn them of impending attacks so they can get out of the way. A steady flow of conscript deserters come over to our side. We put the youngsters into our schools, older ones who want to fight are welcomed in our ranks. Others can return to their villages.

In connection with the phantom warriors on the Lon Nol payroll, a cable from United Press International, datelined Phnom Penh, 13 December 1971, is eloquent:

One of the most common forms of corruption in the fledgling Cambodian army is listing on paper more men in a battalion than there really are, and at times non-existent battalions have been listed. The officers responsible then collect the pay . . . Sources say one of the High Command's major difficulties was that when battalions were called up from the provinces to help out on Highway 6 and around the city of Phnom Penh 'they were found to exist only on paper'.

Just a week later, UPI correspondent Kim Willenson, writing from Phnom Penh on the same theme, was even more explicit in commenting on the 'Chenla 2' defeat on Highway 6:

Perhaps worst of all, the army is riddled with corruption and its units are under strength. Battalion commanders assigned to recruit and pay their own troops have found it possible to reap vast profits by maintaining paper soldiers on their payrolls . . . On 13 December, he (Lon Nol) took a snap survey of the army to eliminate the payroll ghosts and get a true picture of military strength. Already more than thirty battalions, totalling over 15,000 men, have been disbanded because they were seriously under strength.

My Chinese friends have told me that collecting pay for non-existent troops was an old trick of the Kuomintang army in China: one that Lon Nol's officers have picked up with as great a rapidity as Lon Nol and Sirik Matak acquired the trick of pocketing a goodly share of the Pentagon millions. Those officers who come over to our forces, on the other hand, quickly develop into politically conscious patriots who share and share alike with the troops on an equal basis.

Our armed forces are an integral part of the resistance forces of Indo-China as a whole. The Americans have long used Indo-China as a single battlefield. They use Saigon troops in Laos and Cambodia; Thai troops in South Vietnam, Laos and Cambodia. They use sanctuaries in Thailand from which to bomb the four components of Indo-China. Lon Nol commandos are trained at US bases in Thailand, Laos and South Vietnam. There is military coordination on various fronts. When the operation into south Laos was launched in February 1971, a parallel and coordinated thrust was also made into Cambodia to try to reoccupy the Kratié area. (The Saigon troops involved, despite US air support, suffered a crushing defeat and never got within sight of their objective.)

We, the peoples of Indo-China, must also consider the whole area a single battlefield and coordinate our activities. This was the central idea of the Summit Conference of the Peoples of Indo-China on 24–25 April 1970, just five weeks after I was deposed. We agreed that while each component would retain its separate entity, we would combine our efforts until final victory. For the first time, the Indo-China put together by the French would become a living reality. For that, at least, we owe our thanks to Richard Nixon. The invasion of Cambodia in April and May 1970, and of south Laos in February and March 1971, cemented this solidarity still further, and paved the way for still greater victories by our forces along Highway 6, in August to December 1971, and those of the Pathet Lao forces in the Plain of Jars and Bolovens Plateau in December 1971 and January 1972.

Cambodia has made a far greater contribution to the joint struggle than I imagined possible when I launched my call to arms on 23 March 1970.

Chapter 14

New Life

Those of us at the rear base await with impatience, even with anguish, news from home. Not just that contained in the military communiqués, but information from the grassroots level. How are our people living, how are they adjusting to wartime life and the merciless air bombings and incursions into their villages by marauding Saigon and Lon Nol soldiery? It was with considerable emotion that, in the first days of January 1972, I opened two reports straight from the forward base. The first was from Vice-Premier and Defence Minister Khieu Samphan, the second was from Hou Youn, our Minister of the Interior, and for Cooperatives and Communal Reforms. He had just completed a visit made from 13 October to 3 December 1971 to the liberated provinces of Kratié, Stung Treng, Preah Vihear, Kompong Thom and Siem Reap. His was the first comprehensive report I had had from a large cross-section of the countryside. He wrote:

Elderly people, especially the grandmothers, cannot say enough in praise of the good conduct and exemplary moral behaviour of our troops. They insist with great emotion on speaking of the radical transformation of rural life. Villages and hamlets have started to take on an orderly, even radiant aspect. Household quarrels, exchanges of insults, all sorts of wrong-doing including drunkenness and debauchery, are things of the past. The peasants are loud in praise of the fact that acts of brigandage and theft of cattle have ended in the Liberated Zones. These days, if someone forgets an axe or hoe in the field, he is sure to find it where he left it.

Clearly a new life had already sunk its roots deep into our national soil, I think never to be effaced. Burgeoning there in our villages, the backbone of the nation, despite the bombs and napalm, is the kind of society I had dreamed of on a national scale, and which I had wanted to bring about – a democratic, creative organism whose members would live together as one family in social and racial harmony, in accordance with what is best and most progressive in our Buddhist precepts and our ancient Angkorian heritage.

In my second message to the nation, on 4 April 1970, I had said that the aim of the resistance struggle would be

to ensure to our nation for the first time in history, a new life based on complete social justice; a really popular democratic system under which all powers will be exercised directly by the people, or by the intermediary of its progressive youth and working people, within the framework of national independence and territorial integrity, and under the protection of Buddhism, our national religion.

These ideas were later embodied in the Political Programme of the Cambodian National United Front. Now according to these official and detailed reports, these ideas were becoming living reality.

Some may protest that Khieu Samphan and Hou Youn are well-known Khmers Rouges and have a vested interest in telling Sihanouk such agreeable things. How can he really know what is going on, sitting thousands of kilometres away in Peking? In fact, these reports are but a synthesis, or confirmation, of others I have received from dozens of different sources. And I can find no other explanation for the enthusiasm with which the peasantry has hurled itself into the struggle. It is another of the keys to the swift advance of our resistance forces.

'To get the active cooperation of the people and to act with rapidity – these are the two keys to the situation,' reports Khieu Samphan, in explaining the enemy's defeat in their ill-fated 'Chenla 2' campaign.[1]

The people are with us and fight against the enemy. Along Highway 6, from the first days of the enemy attack, following our appeal, and with the help of our people's organizations, the overwhelming majority of the population evacuated the villages. The

[1]. Of 20,000 troops committed to the 'Chenla 2' operation, seventy per cent were killed or wounded, thousands more captured in an operation from 20 August to 3 December 1971.

enemy, deprived of human and material resources to replace the
losses we inflicted, was soon demoralized under our repeated blows.
... It was not only the cadres and combatants of our PNLAFC
who took part, but the whole of the people, including Buddhist
monks living along Highway 6.

The total support of the people explains why our num-
erically inferior forces, with no heavy equipment to oppose
the enemy's tanks, artillery, and planes, could bring off the
victory. The 'Chenla 2' battle was not an isolated one, but
was coordinated with our military initiatives on all fronts.
Such popular support presupposes that the people had, and
have today, more than an ordinary stake in victory: the
'new life' in the villages announced in the NUFC programme.
Thus Richard Dudman of the *St Louis Post Dispatch*, captured
a few days after the NUFC was formed and its programme
broadcast, wrote after his release:

I saw the early development of what appears to be a Cambodian
people's movement ... The Cambodian countryside, where most
of the population lives, is being radicalized and quickly turned into
a massive, dedicated revolutionary base ... At each plantation or
farmer's hut ... we have seen evidence of allegiance to Sihanouk
and of its counterpoint – extreme hatred of the United States and
President Nixon ...[1]

About a year after the March coup, I began to receive
messages from old acquaintances – people far removed
ideologically from the Khmers Rouges – but who could no
longer stand the rottenness of Phnom Penh, and had found
their way to the Liberated Zone. One thing common to all
these messages was insistence on the free and democratic life
they had found. Typical was one from Ros Chet Thor, former
director of *Neat Cheat Niyum* (the *Nationalist*) weekly. After
describing the degradation of life in Phnom Penh and the
reasons that prompted him to flee with his family, he wrote:

The Liberated Zone is the authentic new Cambodia – independent, democratic – really marvellous. People live here in honour
and dignity. They are really masters of their villages. The joy and
enthusiasm on people's faces – from the old to children and young

1. The *International Herald Tribune*, Paris, 29 June 1970.

people – is clear evidence of their faith in final victory and a radiant future . . . All that we have seen with our own eyes in the Liberated Zone has filled us with faith and pride in our people and the NUFC.

There was a regular exodus of professional people and intellectuals from Phnom Penh about the time Ros Chet Thor fled. In early March 1971, I received a joint message from one such group, which included Phnom Penh's most famous surgeon, a dentist, several engineers, and civil servants. They wrote:

The Liberated Zone starts not very far from the capital, but we had an impression of entering an entirely different world. No barbed wire around administrative buildings! No puppet troops with bayonets on their rifles and hatred on their faces searching passersby from head to toe! No bribes, police raids, curfews, humiliation of young women. Knowledge is respected; talent appreciated and encouraged. Intellectuals, all patriotic and progressive individuals can put their ideas of democracy, patriotism, and feeling for the people into practice. Everyone's dignity is respected.

Why were they so impressed? The comparison with the fascist prison and paradise for criminals that Phnom Penh has become is only part of the answer, I believe. The other part is because justice and human worth, the qualities that most Cambodians place far above material belongings, are respected in the Liberated Zone, according to every account I have received.

A radio-electrical engineer, Chhon Hay, who fled a few months after the aforementioned group, wrote:

I find here an atmosphere of friendship, solidarity, democracy. No more secret agents, police, and puppet troops swarming around! We live like brothers and sisters, people at one with us and with our combatants, who are sons and daughters of the Cambodian people, in mutual respect, mutual aid and moral purity. No gangsterism, no gambling, no corruption . . . This is the source of our enthusiasm and confidence.

When I studied in Paris, I often dreamed of such a society. Now I have found it. Under the leadership of the NUFC, headed by Prince Sihanouk, a really democratic régime has been set up. Every sector of society – workers, peasants, Buddhist monks, intellectuals, business people, small manufacturers – all are accorded consideration, support, and personal freedom.

The majority of those who sent such messages are not, or were not, politically orientated, but Lon Nol and Nixon have changed them. They are middle-class professional people, civil servants, and intellectuals, who went about their daily tasks, and were probably not much concerned over the 18 March coup. Many of them were led astray by demagogic assurances of the bright future which the setting up of a 'republic' would usher in. Among them, for instance, was a young woman, Madame Khau Vanny, a French-trained pharmacist. She came from a wealthy bourgeois family, and had opened one of the most flourishing pharmacies in Phnom Penh. But a few months of Phnom Penh life under Lon Nol was enough. She risked her life and abandoned her wealth to come to the Liberated Zone. If one had to pin a political label on such people, it would probably be that of 'liberal centrists'. Had they been 'progressives', they would have left a year earlier. I say this not in reproach, for many honest and patriotic people were taken in by the Lon Nol–Sirik Matak régime. I say it to underline that they cannot remotely be accused of being Khmers Rouges propagandists.

The most surprising message, in the form of a long letter, came from my own son-in-law, Prince Sisowath Doussady, a conservative young man who had never knowingly met a Khmers Rouge in his life until he arrived in the Liberated Zone at the end of August 1971.[1] I esteemed him as an upright, responsible person, and when he asked for the hand of my youngest daughter, Princess Botum Bopha, I gave my consent. He had been educated for the civil service, and at the time of the 18 March coup (he was then twenty-nine years old) was on the managerial staff of the Phnom Penh State Department Store. Because of his family connection with me, he was immediately dismissed. After eighteen

1. Prince Doussady was the son of Prince Sisowath Entaravong, elder brother of Prince Yutevong, first President of the Democratic Party when it was founded in 1946.

months under the Lon Nol régime, during which his wife was arrested and charged with high treason, Doussady managed to escape to the Liberated Zone, from where he sent me a letter dated 1 October 1971. If his language sounds somewhat vehement for a man of his background, it is probably due to the contrast of his life in the liberated countryside with his traumatic experience in what he referred to as 'that fascist concentration camp which Phnom Penh has become'.

Patriots in Phnom Penh all speak the same language today. 'If we don't strike the traitors, they will strike us down. If we want to live in honour and dignity; if we want to remain free men in an independent and sovereign country, we must dare to stand up and fight for the noble ideals set forth in the political programme of the NUFC. Dare to fight now means to dare everything! It means to take up arms and overthrow the Lon Nol–Sirik Matak–Son Ngoc Thanh clique. There is no other road to national liberation and independence.'

In joining the Liberated Zone, I have chosen the path of dignity and honour . . . I have been considerably moved here to rediscover the true face of our motherland . . . a smiling affectionate face; that of a fond mother finding her children after a long separation . . . Here in the Liberated Zone everyone really lives in an atmosphere of solidarity and harmony. I can testify by my own eyes that 'liberty, equality and fraternity' are words without meaning in the pseudo-republic of Lon Nol . . . Here, liberty of thought, expression and belief, are guaranteed and scrupulously respected. There is no discrimination because of class or sex. Private property is respected.

Despite enemy air attacks, our compatriots are valiantly struggling to build up the economy, mobilizing all resources for the national liberation struggle, and improving living conditions at the same time. Famine, poverty, unemployment are non-existent. Knowing they are masters of their fate and the country, our compatriots work with an enthusiasm that has to be seen to be believed. One detail I found especially moving: people help each other in all their activities: mutual aid in combat with the enemy, mutual aid in working the fields, mutual aid in the cultural and social fields, with the setting up of schools for children and adults of all ages, and of training centres for nurses and public health workers . . . Life here is really dynamic!

None of this would have been possible without a political line which corresponded to the real aspirations of the people . . . Passing from the hell of Phnom Penh . . . it was impossible not to be overcome with amazement . . . Personally I feel as if I have been born again – started a new, clean life – one full of purpose and value.

Prince Doussady has now become a NUFC cadre, together with my son, Prince Racvivongs who, despite a weak heart and lungs, and a frail constitution, also found the strength to gain the Liberated Zone. Young Doussady has turned out to be a fine person, and fully deserved the confidence I had in him when I agreed to his marrying my daughter. Needless to say, to receive such a letter from a close member of my family made a deep impression. Every word gave me more confidence than ever in the reports from our resistance headquarters.

Doussady said he had been born again. In reading through his and so many other accounts, I felt this to be true of the Cambodian nation. The Political Programme was not just so many empty phrases, but a guide to day-to-day action that was being implemented in the spirit and the letter – for instance:

> Guarantee to all Cambodians, except known traitors, freedom to vote; freedom to stand for election; freedom of speech, opinion, association, demonstration, residence, to travel at home and abroad . . . Safeguard the inviolability of the person, property, wealth, and privacy of correspondence.

(Freedom to travel at home and abroad might sound academic at present, but it was expressly included to stress the difference in ideology between our government and the Lon Nol régime where that particular 'freedom' could only be enjoyed at the cost of very heavy bribes, or for some exceptional services to the ruling clique. Furthermore, those who did get permission to go to France and elsewhere could only do so by leaving their wives and children as hostages in case of their non-return.)

Most Cambodians, irrespective of rank, background, or political colouring, are patriots who admire patriotism in others. They are also devoted to democracy. Even Lon Nol and Sirik Matak grasped that, and that is why they like the word 'republic' with its overtones of being more democratic than a monarchic system. But true democracy exists only in the liberated areas. It was spelt out in our Political Programme that the 'democratization of Cambodian society is being carried out in the Liberated Zone at present and will be carried out on the whole country later'. From the hamlets and villages upwards, this has been done. Committees of from three to seven persons, according to the size of the community, are elected. Members of these committees in turn elect a district committee, and members of the district committees elect a provincial committee. Such committees, in the name of the National United Front, exercise administrative power. It is not as in the old days when those seeking office were after personal advantages – the job of collecting taxes for instance – and the posts were paid. Today, it is those who are prepared to sacrifice their unpaid time and take on irksome, at times dangerous, duties who volunteer for election. There is no campaigning, but frank discussions between villagers and candidates as to who is most suitable for the three primary tasks of the village committee: military and security affairs; economic production; and general political affairs, which include education and public health. The whole village takes an active part in electing the committee. At the beginning it was often those who could talk best who were elected; later it was those who had proved themselves in work and combat. But in any case it is always the people who survive.

The criterion for candidates is that they be devoted to the anti-imperialist struggle, lead an exemplary life, and be totally devoted to the people and their interests. NUFC cadres live with the people and take part in production. Through various social organizations of youth, women, Buddhist monks, peasants, and others, the elected committees maintain close and permanent contact with the people. On the military side, there is a National Military Committee presided over by Khieu Samphan, with a general staff headquarters and local military committees and headquarters for the different military regions.

Khieu Samphan mentioned in his report that when the enemy attacks the villagers, helped by the local organizations, make an orderly withdrawal to the rear areas, 'taking with them all their belongings and foodstuffs, rice, poultry, pigs, etc. leaving a vacuum for the advancing enemy'. Such evacuations are organized by the NUFC committees. There is rarely any panic, I am assured. The enemy has to make noisy, large-scale preparations, with the troops and tank concentrations, so there is always plenty of advance warning from this alone – not to mention tip-offs from patriots on Lon Nol's staff. The villagers are helped to move to a safe area where other NUFC committees will organize their housing. All this is done in a spirit of solidarity and, as Doussady said, 'of mutual aid' that accords with the best traditions of Cambodian hospitality. Usually such evacuations are temporary. But if the occupation of an area is prolonged, then labour-power is pooled to build another village. Our forests abound in raw material for the simple structures to which our peasants are accustomed. If some houses in one village are destroyed by air attacks, the inhabitants of that village cooperate to replace them. If an entire village is levelled, it is rebuilt with help from neighbouring villages.

Another of Hou Youn's impressions after his long tour was that:

The warmth of the atmosphere and popular enthusiasm wherever I went proves the importance, the depth and breadth of our national liberation movement, which has the total support of the people. An example among many:

In one place where I stayed overnight with a NUFC cadre, there was a moving scene. Three girls came to his house to ask to be admitted to the NUFC and be sent straight to the battlefront . . . When our cadre advised them to stay in their village to help with production and thus contribute to the struggle, they burst into tears. I might add that they had no idea that I was there.

This one example among thousands illustrates the extent to which patriotism and revolutionary enthusiasm are fairly bubbling over in the hearts of our young people . . . In every village hardly a day passes without young people coming to enlist in the PNLAFC, the girls offering to work in hospital and other NUFC organs . . . We can have as many recruits as we want, and that is why effectively we are on the constant increase . . . In remote places where arms are in short supply, the young people are active in making traditional arms, crossbows, local firearms and grenades. All the young people serve in the village militia.

It is difficult for outsiders to understand the depth of Cambodian patriotism. It is a matter of survival, imposed upon us by our fate of being squeezed in between stronger, hostile neighbours. In the past we invariably had to fight or disappear as a nation. Today it is the same. The Americans pretend we are fighting for some ideology. This is not true. We fight to survive. The young girls in remote villages instinctively know this. The Buddhist monks know it, for throughout our history they have played a patriotic role because of their close links with the people. It was no surprise for me to learn that monks are important in encouraging the people to take to arms. Death in the villages often comes from afar – from B 52s, which are neither seen nor heard. But the girls continue to make crossbows even when the B 52s are overhead. They cannot shoot at planes but, if an American or a soldier in American pay appears, they will shoot at him with their crossbows. The patriotism and heroism of our people were always there, like mushroom spore lying dormant under the earth's lid. Treachery at home and aggression from abroad provided the right conditions, and guerrilla units, like mushrooms, started popping up everywhere.

Equality of the sexes is part of the new life. At the First National Congress of the Sangkum, in 1955, women had been given the vote, but today complete equality is being put into effect in the villages. Hou Youn relates:

Making my way from one district to another one day, I saw some militia women pounding rice. As soon as they saw our little group, they presented themselves with grace and courtesy – but also with their rifles – asking to verify my travel papers.

Armed women, questioning men in such a way! It showed not only how vigilant the peasants have become, but also how quickly the women have accepted promotion in their responsibilities.

Khieu Samphan explained in his report how important is the 'battle for the population'. The enemy needs people in its hands for cannon fodder. The fact that, within months of the March 1970 coup, Lon Nol decreed general mobilization of persons of both sexes between the ages of eighteen and sixty-four shows how desperate he was from the beginning. Boys from nine years upwards were snatched from their families or school desks during 1971 and pressed into service. At first the Lon Nol–Sirik Matak régime had within their grasp recruits drawn from the hundreds of thousands who had fled to Phnom Penh and other 'safe' areas to escape American bombs. In Phnom Penh, this created more problems than it solved. The population almost trebled in the first year of the war. Three times as many mouths to be fed and few of them productive. Food prices doubled, trebled, quadrupled while, in the Liberated Zone, even the Phnom Penh press had to admit that prices remained stable. Next came 'pacification' on the South Vietnam pattern, with 'strategic hamlets' and 'self-defence militia' to enable Lon Nol to control the peasants, and force them to grow their rice in the perimeter areas just outside the barbed wire. But for Cambodian peasants freedom is as essential as air. If professional people and intellectuals living in comfortable circumstances found the primitive conditions of villages in the Liberated Zone a paradise compared to Phnom Penh, it is easy to imagine how peasants compared the new life conditions with the 'strategic hamlets'. Most of them already knew the difference, for those herded into the 'strategic hamlets' were mainly from former liberated areas reoccupied by Lon Nol with the help of Saigon troops.

Khieu Samphan relates what occurred in three districts about ten kilometres south of the provincial capital of Kompong Cham, the isle of Koh Sotin in the Mekong river, and Rokar Koy and Krakor on the opposite right bank. This area had been liberated shortly after the coup, but recaptured by Saigon troops early in 1971, and handed back to Lon Nol. The local inhabitants were concentrated in groups of ten, fifty, and a hundred houses, each group surrounded by barbed wire and watched over by four military posts garrisoned by about eight hundred regular troops supplemented by a thousand 'self-defence militia', scattered among the villages. This was a considerable military force for such a small area. Khieu Samphan reported that:

Despite this, by patient clandestine work, we managed to control all the villages politically. We were thus able to bring about sixty per cent of the self-defence militia under our control, and elements of the PNLAFC, in close cooperation with the local population, managed to re-liberate Koh Sotin on 18 November 1971, and Rokar Koy and Krokar the following day . . . Over 20,000 inhabitants were freed, some 400 rifles as well as ammunition and other military supplies were seized.

Three of the four military posts were wiped out in the operation. There were simultaneous actions to the north of Kompong Cham, and the Lon Nol troops were too scared to move out of the city to the rescue. The essential factor, Khieu Samphan stressed, was the yearning of the peasants to lead an unfettered life.

In general, the Liberated Zone acts as an irresistible magnet to attract the peasants away from areas still controlled by Phnom Penh. Fortunately we have a vast hinterland to accommodate them. At the end of 1971 Khieu Samphan reported:

At the present moment, in the area west of Phnom Penh, the main part of the population, who have long placed their hopes in our victory, follow us. In tens of thousands, they have evacuated the combat zones for safer rear areas. They refused to side with the traitors. It had become impossible for them to support the sufferings under the Phnom Penh régime.

Thus, the unpopular régime not only became increasingly isolated politically, but has already become physically detached from the rural masses. More and more, the only Cambodians seen by the Lon Nol–Sirik Matak apparatus are those with weapons in their hands – and these are usually seen too late!

The NUFC programme stipulates that peasants have the right to the land they cultivate. This had been the rule up to the time of the reign of my great-grandfather, King Norodom. As Prince Yuhanthor pointed out (see Chapter 11), the French tried to put an end to this – they wanted to carve out

197

huge plantations for themselves. Under the NUFC programme the ancient custom has become law in the Liberated Zone. It also provides for a fair system of land rent and low interest on loans. The latter are vital. Rural moneylenders have been the scourge of the Cambodian countryside ever since money was introduced into our country. No way was ever devised to limit their extortions. Rates were set in private bargaining between moneylender and peasant, the latter having no real bargaining power. Compound interest was set on a monthly basis, and at the end of a year could run up to 200 per cent of the original sum borrowed. I had tried to counter this by setting up rural credit cooperatives. But the moneylenders, by the political influence their wealth gave them, found means of sabotaging these measures. Moneylenders still exist, but rates in the Liberated Zone are now in the region of five to ten per cent annually.

Because of the elections at the base and all the way up the pyramid of power to the provincial level, it is in effect the poorer peasants who are in charge of implementing NUFC policies. One can be certain that they will be diligent about this, for tremendous burdens are removed from their shoulders the moment their villages are liberated and they will be vigilant in ensuring they are never reimposed.

Provision is made for the confiscation of the

land and property of traitors who are active accomplices in the pay of American imperialists and who have committed crimes against the people. The land and property seized will be distributed among the needy peasants.

Large tracts of land belonging to Sirik Matak, Cheng Heng, Lay In and other feudal-type landowners have been seized and distributed, though not yet definitely confiscated. Final expropriation will be carried out by legal process. Much of this land has been turned over to evacuees from other areas who may wish to return to their original villages after the war, so it is better not to make a final distribution at this time. Traitors, however, have no prospects of ever getting their hands on their properties again.

The Political Programme also provides for developing the

'good traditions of our Angkorian civilization . . . building up a national culture on the basis of patriotism, love for work well done and love for art, and protecting historical relics and monuments'. All reports show that this aspect of the programme is also being faithfully applied. As mentioned elsewhere, the vicinity of the Angkor temples is solidly under the control of the resistance forces. The only danger to them is from the Lon Nol vandals, the air power they command, and their long-range artillery, which has already caused serious danger to Angkor Wat, the main temple. Elsewhere, culture and revolutionary art, based on our excellent artistic traditions, are flourishing at village and district level.

An extra fillip is given by the influx of intellectuals, including specialists in the fine arts, into the Liberated Zone. It is noteworthy that virtually all intellectuals of any reputation were already with the resistance forces by early 1972. This includes the overwhelming majority of doctors. Lon Nol has been forced to try to replace them by doctors from France, who were soon complaining of fatigue brought on by impossibly long working hours.

A medical faculty has been set up in the Liberated Zone under one of Cambodia's outstanding surgeons, Dr Thiounn Thioeunn, formerly head doctor at the Cambodian-Soviet Friendship Hospital. In addition to the training of qualified doctors and surgeons, we have also started a system comparable to that of China's 'barefoot doctors'. Trainees, sometimes illiterate, are taken in and given three months' rudimentary medical training combined with a course in reading and writing. They are then sent out to practise for nine months, returning for another three months' training, then nine more months of practice and so on. It is above all an excellent method of bringing notions of public health to the frontier regions. Among the mountain tribes, for instance, it was customary for a woman to go off into the jungle alone to have her baby. Now she has them at home, or in the village clinic under hygienic conditions introduced by our 'barefoot doctors'. The result has been a dramatic drop in the rate of infant mortality – very important for the tribespeople, whose population growth has been stagnant or decreasing for decades. Thanks to people like Madame Khau Vanny, we have been able to establish a modest pharmaceutical industry, turning out over thirty types of medicines. Many other small industries have been started with the know-how of persons like her. They keep coming from the towns to contribute their technical skills to the struggle.

War was the last thing we wanted, and we made every effort to avoid it. Nevertheless it has come, and I must say that, in addition to the devastation wrought by Nixon's bombers, it has stimulated our people to superhuman efforts in all fields of activity. Problems which would have taken years to solve in our peacetime rhythm are now solved in weeks and months. Nixon unwittingly forged a high level of national solidarity among our citizens within a matter of weeks, and made us revolutionaries without having to read Karl Marx. It is this new-born revolutionary spirit that has transformed the countryside and introduced a new life from which the people will never turn back.

Chapter 15

Peking – Rear Base

When I stepped out of the plane at Peking airport on 19 March 1970, I started my seventh and longest visit to the People's Republic of China. The number 'seven' turned out to be just as lucky as the number 'thirteen' – the date of my arrival in Moscow – turned out to be unlucky. It was the difference between recognition and non-recognition, one of those fateful accidents of history. Many journalists still ask – but why did you go to Peking immediately after the coup? The answer is that Lon Nol and Sirik Matak decided it that way. It was these plotters who drew up the timetable for the coup. My itinerary had been decided long before. They struck at a point in time and place that left me no choice. Next stop after Moscow was Peking and in view of my immediate resolve to fight back, the fact that Peking was next on my travel schedule could not have been more opportune. What could I have done, in any case, in view of the fact that I learned of my deposition a few minutes before stepping into the plane? Had I stayed on in Moscow my critics would have been just as severe. Was I expected to try and hijack the plane of the President of the Soviet Union and force the crew to fly to Sweden or some such neutral haven?

I could have been *en route* to any one of half a dozen capitals. But fate, activated by the Phnom Penh plotters, pointed its finger in one direction. I knew I would find immediate support in Peking. My friendship with Chou En Lai, and the affection that Chairman Mao had manifested convinced me of this. As I saw from the plane window the crowd of welcomers, then the diplomats and, as the plane taxied to a stop, Chou En Lai walking towards it with a group of official dignatories, I knew things were as I thought. When Premier Chou embraced me and said: 'You remain the Head of State. We will never recognize another;' this was but confirmation of what I had felt in my bones.

I had met Chou En Lai first at the Bandung Conference in April 1955. It was a case of 'love at first sight'. It had been the same with General de Gaulle, and was to be the same later with Mao Tse-tung. Just those three giants! What did they have in common that attracted me? The simplicity of the great, and their respect for the small. Respect for a small country and for the leader of that small country. All three set high value on national and personal dignity, and were patriots who esteemed patriotism in others. Despite the different background and ideology of the Chinese leaders and de Gaulle, I found these common traits. It did not surprise me to learn later that the Chinese leaders also held de Gaulle in high esteem.

Before meeting Premier Chou in Bandung, I had asked about him from our delegation to the 1954 Geneva Conference. 'A very seductive personality,' I was told. 'He knows how to explain things, how to put across his line. He says he only wants friendship with Cambodia and that, if we remain independent, that's enough as far as China is concerned. "But don't fall into the hands of the imperialists again," he said. "If you remain independent, we'll support you and we can be friends."' It was a very right-wing delegation including Sam Sary, Tep Phân[1] and others like them, so they added: 'Of course, he's a communist, so be careful. He's all the more dangerous because of his allure.'

At our first meeting, I found him open, friendly and very straightforward. There was a complete absence of superior airs, but I felt in the presence of a 'big man'. His simple, modest bearing was in contrast to some little men strutting around in the big boots of US imperialism. He immediately congratulated me for my stand on neutrality, and said that China would always support our independence and neutral-

---

1. Tep Phân was then Foreign Minister and later governor of Phnom Penh.

ity. We hit it off straightaway, and a friendship born at Bandung has only developed and strengthened since. Chou En Lai invited me to visit Peking, which I did the following year to the great consternation of the free world, especially the United States and my immediate neighbours. (Even the British Chargé d'Affaires from Peking, whose country had long since established diplomatic relations with China, thought it necessary, at a dinner offered me by the British Governor in Hong Kong in 1955, to give me an avuncular warning that 'frankly he would not wish me to visit Peking'.)

During my first visit in 1956, I met Chairman Mao several times, as I have during every visit since. He has always found time to see me, and never have our discussions lasted less than an hour. The first impression was that of being in the presence of a giant among men. His gentle, reflective face radiates wisdom, calm and strength. The fact that he received me so often, and for so long, I took as a symbol of China's interest in, and respect for, small nations. I was made to feel that patriotism and courage in standing up to imperialism was more important than social background and formal ideological labels. It was clear that my immediate liking for Chairman Mao was reciprocal and, as time went on, I felt that he had developed an affection for me as I had for him.

At our first meeting, Chairman Mao set forth the broad lines of China's policy, the importance attached to countries being really independent and not falling under the domination of others. China, he explained, believed in the principle of equality among nations, big, medium and small. There was no reason why small Cambodia and big China should not be friends on an equal basis, and develop relations on the basis of mutual benefit. Mao agreed that neutrality was the best course for Cambodia to steer. China would always support this. From that time until now China has kept her word.

In August 1958, Mao Tse-tung received me at his presidential palace soon after my arrival. It was very hot in Peking, and we continued our talks the following day under a tent set up in a garden on the edge of a swimming pool. Our conversations continued at a seaside resort. Premier Krushchev had visited Peking some weeks earlier, and one of

Chairman Mao's aides told me that I was the only statesman who had so many meetings with Chairman Mao in a single visit apart from Khruschev. Premier Chou En Lai had personally escorted me to the seaside resort.

Was all this done just to impress me? To brainwash me? I can understand such suspicions. In fact, Chairman Mao was really interested in our problems, our relations with our neighbours, my estimation of American intentions in the area, and many other problems of mutual interest. Perhaps he was seeking also to understand my personality and motives. It is possible that the image of a prince-patriot intrigued him. But, from the beginning of our relationship he took me seriously; he treated me as an equal which is more than I can say of some Western leaders, with the notable exception of General de Gaulle.

Great Britain, for instance, several times proposed that I should pay an official visit to that fellow kingdom, but the proposals were so vague, wrapped up with such ambiguities and restrictions of dates and reminders of the many obligations of Her Majesty the Queen and her ministers, that I preferred the more straightforward invitations from the socialist world, especially those from China. At the 1960 session of the United Nations, for instance, British Prime Minister Macmillan invited me to visit England, assuring me that the Queen 'will be delighted to receive you'. The following day he confirmed the invitation in writing, adding the proviso that the visit would 'not be official'. But I am not a tourist, wasting the time and money of my country in attending Royal garden parties. As I also had many other official duties and invitations, I promptly declined, which brought the British Foreign Minister, Sir Alec Douglas-Home, knocking at my door to try to rectify the gaffe. I never did make either official or unofficial visits to England.

I hasten to add that it was not only capitalist powers that made such gaffes. In 1965, I was on my way for official visits to a number of socialist states, including the People's Republic of China and North Korea in Asia, followed by the Soviet Union, Poland, Czechoslovakia and Bulgaria, at the invitation, and according to dates and itineraries proposed by these governments. But in the North Korean capital, Pyongyang, I received a visit from a diplomat of the Soviet Embassy. He held up a piece of paper which was a telegram from Moscow abruptly 'postponing' my visit, without proposing a new date, because the Soviet leadership was suddenly 'very busy' at the time proposed. I racked my brains to recall whether I had said something in Peking or Pyongyang to offend them. I could think of nothing, and no explanation was ever offered. I cancelled the rest of my trip and returned to Phnom Penh.

For Chinese leaders, such behaviour cuts across their concepts of equality among states regardless of size. This was a point I made quite early in my relations with China in an article I published in the 22–29 March 1958 issue of *Réalités Cambodgiennes* – partly under the influence of the real respect for national and personal dignity and equality that I found during my first visit to Peking. I wrote:

Premier Chou En Lai has spoken of great power chauvinism. The communist governments know that Asians, and small nations, are particularly sensitive about the respect due to them, and the application of the UN principles of the equality of great and small powers. The inequality and discrimination in the protocol arrangements for the treatment of guests, is the basis for much of the disillusionment that no one can deny exists among Asian nations in respect to Western governments.

Questions of honour for Asians of standing are much more important than those of money. The materialistic Westerner, if he ever becomes aware of this, is astounded.

I pointed out that China gave material aid 'without any unpleasant remarks, without conditions. The utilization of Chinese aid is completely free and practically without any limitation of time.' I compared this with constant US complaints about our neutrality, and that they constantly make us feel, 'that they have had, they continue to have, and they will have in the future, enormous problems in getting Congress to continue aiding a neutral Cambodia'. This is pushed to such a point, I wrote, that we felt they had no interest at all, 'to help under-developed peoples raise their standard of living and defend their freedom, but rather they want to buy up their consciences and, as the communists say – to use them as cannon fodder ... But what is the worth of an army of mercenaries? If it agrees to fight for he who pays for it, it will be quite capable of betraying him to rally around a master who pays a higher price.' I do not have to revise this because it remains more than ever true today with the Nixon Doctrine and the attempted Vietnamization of Indo-China which has ended in a humiliating defeat for Nixon, precisely because of the worthlessness of mercenary armies when the real moment of truth arrives.

The Chinese leaders never tried to push us around. They never said – independence yes, but it must be 'red' independence. Neutrality yes but it must be a 'leftist' neutrality. Independence and neutrality were good enough without any qualifications, good for Cambodia and South-East Asia as a whole. Chairman Mao or Premier Chou never subjected me to the homilies, the admonitions, warnings, 'friendly advice' and so forth that I had to endure from Western leaders and their Asian satellites. And what the Chinese gave in the way of economic aid, they gave modestly, usually with the preface: 'We wish it were of better quality – but we are still a developing country. We wish it were more – but our own production is limited. We hope that as we build up our industry we will be able to give our friends more effective help.'

Never were we subject to the continual type of pressures that we had from the Americans: 'We have no idea whether we will be able to continue this next year,' with the implicit warning: 'Unless you change your policy of neutrality.' From the West we were constantly subject to unsolicited advice. The Chinese leaders never undertook such initiatives. If I asked their opinion on a specific subject, they gave it with the reservation: 'When we were faced with a similar problem, we solved it in this way ... But China is China and Cambodia is Cambodia, so we cannot say that this way of doing things is good in your case.'

In the Moscow-Peking plane, with Premier Kosygin's warm offers of support ringing in my ears, I toyed with the idea of having two centres abroad for the resistance government. One in Peking, if the Chinese agreed, to handle military affairs, technical, supply and communications problems, because Peking was closer to the scene and neighboured on North Vietnam with whom we were bound to depend for transiting supplies. Another in Moscow, to handle foreign affairs, diplomacy and propaganda. Due to its contacts with the European socialist states and the Western world, Moscow was ideally placed for this. I would divide my time between these two capitals. But Moscow did not want to see me again. The Soviet government preferred to retain its ties with Lon Nol. (We kept to this concept of separation of spheres of duties, however, by stationing Foreign Minister Sarin Chhak in Cairo, and our minister for special missions, Chau Seng, for the greater part of his time in France. Thus we maintain flexibility of movement and contacts with the outside world on as broad a front as possible.)

Where in the wide world could I have found a more ideal capital for that half of the government which has to remain abroad? Material support, including weapons and the means of getting them into the hands of our fighters, has been generous beyond measure. As was previously the case with economic aid, it is given with such modesty and tact that I am made to feel that we are doing a favour in accepting it.

'We're not arms merchants,' replied Chairman Mao when I once raised the question of repayment. 'For some services you can call it a loan and there can be some book-keeping – but not for arms.' Political and diplomatic aid is just as total and unconditional as is material aid.

The Chinese government evacuated its entire foreign ministry – housed in the beautiful and spacious former French Embassy – and turned it over as a residence for a 'deposed' Head of State and his suite with the remark that this was the inviolable territory of the Kingdom of Cambodia for as long as I wanted. A wing of another important, newly-built block of buildings was placed at the disposition of our resistance government – even before we had our armed forces organized to resist! All facilities from a temporary secretarial staff – until we were able to staff our own from patriots abroad who rallied to our cause – to a fleet of cars and day-to-day necessities, were provided, and we were always made to feel that we were doing a favour by accepting.

At my meeting with Chairman Mao on 1 May 1970, I said: 'Monsieur le President! China has heavy burdens. She gives much help to third world countries and now I am an additional burden with my suite, my companions and my staff.' He replied:

'I ask you to burden us still more. The more adherents you have the happier I shall be. The more there are around you the better I'll be pleased. Think nothing of it. Bring as many as possible to support you. If they can't go to fight on the battlefield, let them come here. Six hundred, a thousand, two thousand or more! China will always be ready to support them and to provide all facilities.'

That has been the attitude from the start. Ask us for more. Order us around. Tell us what you need. They have been open-hearted and open-handed from the beginning and are constantly inventing new ways to help us.

Chairman Mao is indefatigable in our conversations about Cambodia. Once he said: 'Prince Sihanouk – I like to talk with you. You speak out frankly and express your ideas courageously. You're not afraid to say what you think.' It became clear to me at an early stage in our friendship that he likes to speak with someone who opposes certain of his ideas. 'You deserve to be a communist,' he observed after one of our chats.

'Monsieur le President,' I replied. 'Really, I can't.'

He laughed: 'You're intelligent,' he said, 'you're hard-working. You could start studying.'

'I'm too lazy to plough through the works of Marx, Lenin and the others,' I said.

'We have condensed versions of these texts now,' he continued. 'Extracts. There's no need for you to read the entire works of Marx and Lenin to grasp the essence of their ideas.'

'Monsieur le President,' I replied. 'I prefer to read the works of Mao Tse-tung.' It is true that these works are easier for me to understand than those of Marx or Lenin. Perhaps because I am not an economist. I have read some extracts from Marx. They are interesting but I consider that he wrote in a determined context and that things have evolved since. Perhaps because I am an Asian, I find that what Mao has written will always remain valid. He has found a link between that which is most logical in Marxist concepts and that which is best in Asian civilization and traditions. His ideas about humanity are more philosophical than political and are not in contradiction with the best in Buddhist humanist concepts. I feel that his ideas will hold good for generations to come.

Mao's ideas on military affairs I also find of passionate interest. Just as Xenophon and other classical Greek strategists wrote passages that remain valid today, I am sure this will be true of Mao because what he writes rings of classical universal truths. He manages to combine clarity and logic with common sense.

Like de Gaulle, Mao has a prodigious memory. At our 1 May 1970 meeting, he reminded me of things I had said in 1956, in 1958 and during other visits. He quoted exact phrases to ask how I saw things at the moment. Conversations were recorded in his mind to be evoked at will. He had followed events in Cambodia from the time of our first meeting in such detail as to amaze me.

'You were reproached for having opened a state casino in Phnom Penh,'[1] he said to my great surprise. 'As I see it,' he continued, 'it was better to open a casino than to accept US aid. I know that it was not for your personal gain. You had budgetary difficulties and so you opened a state casino to nourish state revenue with the profits. Your people gamble a lot anyway. Why should the state not get the profits instead of letting them swell the private pockets of the gambling-den owners? From the time you had those temporary financial difficulties, I can see that the choice had to be between US aid and an alternative source of finance.' This is what we talked about on the evening of 1 May, as everyone waited for

1. The state casino was opened in 1969 as a means of swelling state revenues, just as many countries run state lotteries for the same purpose. It was seized on by my enemies, those who were most expert in corruption for their own ends, as a great 'scandal', and was advanced as one of the reasons for my deposition.

Chairman Mao to appear on the tribune at Tien An Mien Square as the signal to start the fireworks display. Later I learned that diplomats and the press were speculating on the state of Chairman Mao's health as a possible reason for the delay.

'They reproached you for opening the casino,' he repeated, 'in order to raise some funds for the state. Look at what Lon Nol is doing with the hundreds of millions of dollars he gets from Nixon! Now that he has unlimited dollars your people really suffer. Opening a state casino was infinitely better than accepting US aid.' I was amazed how well-informed he was about this. It had been a highly controversial question. Those who were up to their necks in corruption were those who cried loudest about the 'immorality' of state-sponsored gambling. But Chairman Mao had put his finger on the crux of the question, which was to divert some of the ill-gotten proceeds of gambling and corruption into the state coffers.

An aide came and made a sign that it was time to go on to the tribune. 'Wait, wait,' said Mao. 'I am having a most interesting conversation with Prince Sihanouk.' He continued to question me about Cambodia, about the personalities of Lon Nol and Sirik Matak. Sirik Matak had been in Peking as ambassador, Chairman Mao had seen Lon Nol some seven months earlier but had no clear impression of either of the two chief architects of the 18 March coup. For two hours he questioned me in great detail about the situation. Just twenty-four hours before, US–Saigon troops in great strength had invaded Cambodia. Less than three weeks later – on 20 May 1970 – Chairman Mao made one of his rare and historic public declarations in which he said, among other things that:

I warmly support the fighting spirit of Samdech Norodom Sihanouk, Head of State of Cambodia, against US imperialism and its lackeys; I warmly support the Joint Declaration of the Summit Conference of the Peoples of Indo-China; I warmly support the setting up of the Royal Government of National Union under the aegis of the National United Front of Cambodia.

It was then that I understood the reason for his long questioning.

If the assembled diplomats and public had, unprecedentedly, to await a full hour beyond the scheduled time for Chairman Mao to appear on the Tien An Men tribune as a signal to start the 1 May fireworks display, it was because Mao wanted to have the most complete information possible from the Head of State of a small country that had just become a victim – hours previously – of a most brutal act of aggression!

What better illustration of the difference between two worlds than the manner of this invasion and that of my treatment in Peking? Lon Nol feebly protested that neither had his permission been asked nor had he been warned in advance. This could be true seeing that the Americans had invaded South Vietnam five years earlier without bothering to secure a formal invitation from the Saigon régime! It would have been forthcoming from Lon Nol, as from the Saigon régime at the time. But puppet-masters are not used to seeking permission from their creatures. Top US and Saigon generals came and went into Cambodia as they pleased. If President Thieu wanted to fly into Cambodia, they never dreamed of asking Lon Nol's permission. Thieu even summoned his sub-puppet, Lon Nol, to give him instructions – on Cambodian soil! In Peking, no Chinese official – or anyone else – would dream of trying to enter the compound of my resistance without going through the protocol procedures which govern the relations between sovereign states. Cambodian sovereignty in Peking is most rigidly respected in the spirit as in the letter, *de jure* and *de facto*. My residence is scrupulously respected as Cambodian territory.

Although I am obviously in Peking for a long stay, there is not a hairsbreadth deviation in the treatment, including respect for protocol, which I have always been accorded during visits as Head of State, or – during the 1956 and 1958 visits – as Prime Minister. Regarding my long stay, I am plagued with almost wearisomely standard questions as to why I do not quit Peking, and return to Cambodia to lead the resistance forces in the field. Some of my more suspicious ministers, studying the standard form of such questions submitted by journalists of marginal reputations, believe they represent a new variant of the continuing CIA plot to take me out of circulation. Because of my impulsive nature, it is perhaps hoped that I will be goaded into heading south for the Liberated Zone just to prove my courage! When such questions come from French journalists, I sometimes feel like replying:

When the Nazis invaded France, General de Gaulle did not lead the resistance from inside his own country. He directed it from London, because England was an ally and offered a secure rear base. De Gaulle did not, in fact, return to France until his country was liberated. Does anyone question, however, de Gaulle's courage or patriotism?

Because of improvements in communications technique, we in Peking probably have more rapid and constant contacts with our resistance headquarters inside Cambodia than had de Gaulle from his London headquarters with the resistance bases inside France. The Chinese have put an excellent tele-communications system at our disposition.

To state things more exactly. There is a division of roles between that part of the Royal Government of National Union based inside the country and that based abroad. The two parts are perfectly integrated. For every minister in Peking, there is a vice-minister in the Liberated Zone. For the three key ministers in the Liberated Zone, there are vice-ministers in Peking, or attached to the Peking headquarters. In the exchange of views before setting up the resistance government, it was agreed that only the half to be based in the Liberated Zone would have the necessary knowledge to decide which ministers, including the Head of State, should take up their posts inside the country – and when. There are obvious difficulties in travelling back and forth. I have been assigned tasks in the diplomatic and information fields which can best be accomplished from my present base – which Lon Nol and his CIA backers would dearly love to see closed down.

From the start I had asked to set up my own base inside Cambodia, but I am bound by the same discipline as other NUFC leaders. The definitive reply came in a message from

Vice-Premier and Defence Minister, Khieu Samphan, dated 30 April 1971, which reads in part:

Our important victories are the result of the struggle, and the perfect unity between that part of the NUFC which is abroad, and the part which is inside the country. It is this unity that the enemy is trying to shatter and to attain this end it would like to disperse Samdech, Head of State, and the other NUFC leaders somewhere away from Peking. In Peking, in fact, the possibilities of assuring close and direct liaison between us are very favourable . . . Apart from that, the material and moral conditions for the fight for that section of the NUFC which is outside the country are better than is possible anywhere else, such as the possiblity of taking part in the fight inside the country through the intermediary of Radio Peking; the facilities for contact with the press and progressive political circles, etc.

The presence of Samdech, Head of State, and the other leading members of the NUFC in the Liberated Zone would undoubtedly strengthen our struggle. We would sincerely like this if the problem of your security was not a cause for concern. Obviously Samdech and other leading members of the NUFC are not primarily concerned about their personal security. But in the interest of our national struggle, all our compatriots are concerned about preserving all our leading organs. At the present time our Liberated Zone is vast, and our armed forces are sufficiently strong to effectively prevent any enemy incursions. However, the US Air Force tries its best to wipe us out. Its particular target is our leading organs.

Taking into account the present conditions of our struggle, and in the interests of our people, it is therefore indispensable that Samdech, Head of State, and other leading members of the NUFC, remain in Peking.

That is the definitive instruction on this subject until some new qualitative change occurs in the situation. For those in the outside world who are so impatient to see me back inside Cambodia leading in person the resistance struggle (or is it to see me abandon the Peking rear base), I can only comment that they are in no way as impatient as I, myself, to be back on the soil of my beloved Cambodia. As a footnote to that, I must add that it is a source of infinite encouragement to my people, above all to our resistance fighters, to know that we have built up a solid rear base in such a country as China. It is, in part at least, the guarantee of our victory on the battlefield and, in the future, on the field of reconstruction. No resistance movement could ever dream of having such conditions as have been placed unconditionally at our disposal by the Chinese leadership to live, to work and to fight. Had Lon Nol, Sirik Matak and the other plotters foreseen this, they might have changed the timetable of their coup!

Chapter 16

I Accuse

If I write with bitterness about some personal and family matters, this is not to complain about my own sufferings in exile. Nor is it to compare the fate of my family with that of tens of thousands of compatriots who have suffered atrociously for resisting the Lon Nol dictatorship. If I write of the fate of my family it is to expose the true face of the Phnom Penh plotters, the moral concepts of these self-appointed defenders of the Buddhist faith, and champions of a holy war.

At the time of the coup, the ringleaders had no thought of setting up a republic. It was the last thing that Sirik Matak, for instance, wanted. He had illusions of filling the vacant throne himself. After all, he is a Sisowath, of the same branch of the royal family as my mother, Queen Sisowath Kossomak. At first they tried to expoloit the name of my mother to legitimize their régime by sending cables to the outside world that the Queen Mother had approved the coup – had approved my deposition.

In fact, my mother behaved with courage and dignity. When Lon Nol and Sirik Matak tried to her to get her to endorse the coup, she said: 'No! My son is my son. You have deposed him. You have slanderered him. You have dragged his name in the mud. He has done nothing to deserve this after thirty years of service exclusively for the good of the country, for the good of the people. I'll have nothing to do with you.' She was adamant and they were furious. It frustrated their scheme to exploit the continuity of the monarchy as a constitutional cover for their régime. It was only after my mother's refusal to lend her name to their treachery, that they decided to play the card of the republic.

With the help of psychological warfare specialists from Indonesia who had engineered the slander campaign against the late President Soekarno, Lon Nol and Sirik Matak whipped up a campaign against the monarchy. To 'act in the name of the people' they had young rightist intellectuals and army officers present petitions demanding its abolition. The Queen's portraits, and my own, were removed from all public buildings. Slogans such as: 'The Monarchs Were Always Traitors' were hung up. For two thousand years, shouted these pseudo-republicans, the monarchy has always betrayed the people. Even King Jayavarman VII, the builder of Angkor Thom and Bayon,[1] was a 'traitor', according to them. He had ill-treated the people by forcing them to build temples and palaces and had bled the nation white, so it could not resist the Siamese and Annam invaders! And, they proclaimed, it was my great-grandfather Norodom, who had 'sold' the country to the French in 1863. As I was not in their hands, it was my mother who must pay for all these crimes! Had she lent her name to cover their treachery, the monarchy would have obviously continued to be a most noble institution!

My mother had her home apart, in a building inside the Royal Palace. Soon after the coup, as the anti-monarchy hysteria was whipped up by Lon Nol's toughs, the new rulers demanded that she quit the Royal Palace. At first she refused.

Apart from the fact that Lon Nol and Sirik Matak detested my mother because she had refused to back the coup, they also hated her for having insisted that they apologize to the Vietnamese for the sacking of the embassies and pay compensation. (Of course, the compensation was never paid, but an apology of sorts was made.) Because of her firm stand on this, they now called her 'traitor'. She had sided with the Vietminh and Vietcong 'against her own people'! The Khmer Krom hirelings of the CIA, who had carried out the sackings, and wreaked terrible vengeance on Vietnamese residents in Phnom Penh, had now become her 'own people'.

1. Two of the masterpieces of Angkorian civilization among the Angkor complex of temples and other buildings.

Lon Nol, Sirik Matak and In Tam – chairman of the National Assembly at the time – sent a delegation to the Queen Mother. 'If you don't leave the Royal Palace we will throw you out,' they said. 'You and your son side with the Vietnamese against your own people. Good! If you don't leave, we are going to pile up the corpses of the Vietnamese dealt with by the people, outside your villa. You can watch the vultures pick the flesh off their bones. You sold the country to the Vietnamese so we'll bring their corpses and stack them up under your windows. There they'll rot and stink you out.' That was the way Lon Nol, Sirik Matak and In Tam – the latter an arch-monarchist turned arch-republican – treated my mother, an ailing, ageing woman, over seventy years of age, who had done nothing but good in her life. She had shown nothing but kindness to those who now vilified her.

The Queen Mother had always exerted her influence to avoid disunity at the top. She had not wanted to play politics, but she did try to avoid dissensions between the various political tendencies. Many of these political mandarins abused her good nature by trying to gain political favours, sometimes even at my expense. Sim Var[1] was a typical case. He would hang around the Royal Palace, morning, noon, and night. I had open quarrels with people like Sim Var and his entourage. They wanted to change my policy of neutrality and turn Cambodia to the right. Such people fawned on my mother to try to persuade her that they were the staunchest pillars of the throne. My mother would send me notes: 'Try to compose your differences with Sim Var and the others. They are not ill-intentioned people, and are completely loyal to the monarchy.' Even though she was in poor health, she would find the time and strength to listen to these people and write me letters: 'Do not be too harsh with them. Be kind to them.' In Tam, for his part, would follow up with a speech: 'Peace – this means the throne. Independence – this means the throne. Tranquillity – synonymous with the monarchy.

1. One of Lon Nol's righthand men immediately after the coup; he had served with Son Ngoc Thanh under the Japanese. Lon Nol later appointed him ambassador to Japan.

One country and one leader – Prince Norodom Sihanouk.'
My mother would beam and say: 'You see, it is as I say, In
Tam is a real pillar of the throne.' Sim Var worked on my
mother, trying to separate her from me, but did not succeed.
For the Queen Mother, I was her son, and neither Sim Var
nor anyone else succeeded in turning her against me. But it
was not for want of trying. My mother, however, always
considered Sim Var, In Tam and other such sycophants
among the most stalwart supporters of the throne and she had
a good deal of maternal affection for these worthless cour-
tesans.

It was a heavy blow for her when they bared the fangs of
ingratitude. Those who had been most abject in their fawn-
ing attentions were those who could not do or say enough to
dishonour her in the most ignoble terms.

For many years prior to the coup, the Queen Mother's
main activities had been developing our classical ballet. She
had personally trained most of the ballerinas and supervised
the productions that were so much admired by foreign
visitors. She is a kindly and sensitive person, loved and
respected by all who knew her. Her good works were repaid
by driving her out of her home with the stench of rotting
corpses of those martyred because of their race. My mother,
like other members of the royal family, was proud of our
multi-national society and felt that our racial harmony was a
good example of Buddhist tolerance that could well be
copied by other countries. She had been deeply grieved when
news of the massacre of the Vietnamese reached her.

To the threats of the Lon Nol delegates, my mother
replied: 'No need to bring the corpses – evidence of your
crimes. I shall leave the Royal Palace. Give me the house
where my son was born and let me live there.' It was the villa
where she had lived with my father before I was chosen as
King. I had later given it to the nation as a national museum.
(Some Western journalists wrote that I created it for my own
glory. It was not so. I placed in the museum the various
documents relating to our independence struggle and the
gifts I had received as King, later as Head of State, from
foreign governments. I regarded these as having been given

to me for the nation, which is why I displayed them for all to see.) The museum, in any case, had been dismantled as soon as I was overthrown, so it was agreed that my mother could have her old home back. What Lon Nol and Sirik Matak did with the documents and valuable gifts, I do not know. Perhaps like other precious relics looted after the coup, they can now be bought in antique shops in Hong Kong and Singapore!

My mother's new residence was surrounded by Lon Nol's military police and anyone entering or leaving was most rigourously searched – in the most humiliating way for women visitors. During the first months after the coup hardly anyone dared approach her. As the fortunes of war went badly for the régime, people plucked up courage to pay her a visit. Some later came to France and relayed messages to me: 'Don't be too sad about me,' was the first message I received. 'I fight back and will do so to the end. I am proud of you. My only fear is that I might die without seeing you again. Apart from that I regret nothing.'

Old and sick as she is, alone and deserted, forced to listen to the most degrading insults almost daily, my mother retained her courage and dignity. Everything is done to discourage and humiliate her, to break her spirit. On 9 October 1970, for instance, the day the 'Republic' was proclaimed, a gang of Lon Nol storm-troopers carried my effigy to burn at the Phnom – the temple-crowned hill from which the capital takes its name. But before the burning ceremony, they paraded the effigy before my mother's villa, insulting me – and thus her – in the crudest, most revolting terms. They insulted not only us, but all our forbears and two thousand years of Cambodian history – right in front of my mother's windows. Among the paraders were many students, competing with each other in inventing the most vulgar and offensive epithets.

There was an ironical sequel to this particular incident, which my mother appears to have endured with her usual fortitude. The French government continues to give scholarships to enable the Lon Nol régime to send students to Paris – also for young officers to pursue technical courses in military affairs. On one occasion, a member of our representation in Paris, who had managed to flee Phnom Penh some months earlier, was at Orly airport when a group of students arrived. No sooner had they passed through the controls, than most of them started shouting: 'Down with Lon Nol and Sirik Matak! Long Live Samdech Euv!' He was even more astonished to recognize among them some who had shouted loudest in front of my mother's villa during the Republic Day celebration. He accosted one whom he knew, heatedly recalling the incident. 'But that's the only way to get out of the country,' the student replied. 'You have to shout insults or do something similar to please the régime to get a scholarship, an exit visa and air fare.' Other students crowded around and confirmed that it was only those who proved their ardour for the régime who had any chance of getting scholarships and thus fleeing the country, avoiding, among other things, military service which they equated with certain death. They explained that this was true for anyone, including the military trainees competing for the chance to be sent to France. In any case, for the students, it has remained true that at least seventy per cent of those that came to France declared themselves for the NUFC on arrival at Paris airport.

It has always been the dream of Cambodian males to go to France. The best reward you could offer anyone in the past – and more than ever after the 18 March coup – was the chance to complete their training in France. Before, it was the attraction of France itself – even the girls, lovely, friendly, no racial prejudices. Cambodians like the French way of life; they have a sufficient taste of it in Phnom Penh and other cities to whet their appetites for more. Students are fairly well steeped in French history and culture. Added to all this today is the extra bonus of escaping Lon Nol's press gangs, and gaining the chance to strike a blow for patriotism. My mother was thus unwittingly the target of thousands of rivals, each inventing new ways of demonstrating he was the worst enemy of Sihanouk in order to prove later that he was the best friend of Sihanouk! When the bourses are handed out the French have no idea what they are getting. Their motive, unfortunately, is to turn out good cadres for the Lon Nol régime, including the army. For this I sometimes attack France, despite my admiration for so many of its qualities. But then these students, including officers and technical cadres, come to our mission in Paris and say: 'Please accept and excuse us. The only way we could come was to insult Sihanouk. In reality we are for the N U F C. Please tell us what to do.' The French government knows this – but what can it do?

If my mother survives, she will laugh when we explain that she was an involuntary recruiting agent for the resistance forces. She has a strong sense of humour – but at the time the insults must have been hard to endure. She was left quite alone, no one to serve her, no one to comfort her. Later when people saw the wind was blowing from another direction and started to visit her their names were noted and their families often had police visits. But many risked police reprisals in order to take out an 'insurance' policy on the future. Through such people I have received many messages from my mother.

The scandalous treatment she has received is typical of the régime. It is normal if there is a change from a monarchy to a republic to permit the reigning family to go into exile. My mother demanded permission to leave after the coup. It was refused. Later, a former friendly country, perhaps because of conscience pangs for its attitude during and after the coup, offered to help my mother to leave the country. The proposal was that she should retire to Luang Prabang, the royal capital of Laos (as distinct from Vientiane, the administrative capital). The Laotian royal family offered hospitality, my mother accepted. It was a quiet, out-of-the-way place and there was no risk that my mother would use Luang Prabang as a centre of political activity. But Lon Nol and Sirik Matak demanded as the price for an exit visa, that I cease all political activities and resign all my functions. My mother would be held hostage until I paid their political ransom. As an example of the morality of these usurpers, it is supreme!

Dearly as I love my mother I had no choice but to refuse. Apart from anything else, I represent, by my person, the legitimacy of the resistance struggle. Even if they threaten the life of my mother, or of those of my children still in Phnom Penh, I have no choice. It was heartening to receive a message from the Queen Mother, urging me to stick to my position and that she would disapprove if I acted otherwise.

Lon Nol's military tribunal sentenced me to death for high treason, but even this in civilized societies is not considered grounds for persecuting a mother and children. Part of the moral code is not 'to visit the sins of the father' on his sons, and even less on an ageing mother. What is depressing is that Western monarchies with which my Cambodia had such good relations in the past, have not lifted a finger to intercede for the Queen Mother. Is it a question of the colour of the skin? That because we are 'only' an Asian monarchy the customary norms of chivalry are scrapped? On two occasions since the 18 March coup I have had the humiliation of having had communications addressed to European monarchies sent back marked: 'returned to sender'.

There were some Americans who wrote to the State Department, some Australians and others who wrote to US Embassies and asked why the US government did not use its influence to stop the Lon Nol government from behaving in such a barbarous way. Why not let members of the royal family go into exile? The Nixon administration invariably replied:

The Lon Nol government is a sovereign government. Cambodia is an independent state. We cannot do anything. It would be regarded as intolerable interference in the internal affairs of a sovereign state.

Greater hypocrisy is difficult to imagine. The American press itself writes that Lon Nol lives entirely from Nixon's dollar handouts. The CIA can intervene to overthrow a legal government? The US army can invade – according to Lon Nol without even asking *his* permission. The B 52s and helicopter gunships can come and massacre our peasants by the thousands, but when it comes to permitting an aged, ailing woman to go away quietly to die in peace, Nixon throws up his hands in pious horror at the thought of violating Lon Nol's sovereignty!

A sovereign state! A cable from UPI correspondent Ken Willenson from Phnom Penh on 20 December 1971 is eloquent in this respect. Commenting on the threat of a coup following the disastrous defeats of Lon Nol's troops in the 'Chenla 2' operation, Willenson comments:

However the United States is not going to countenance a coup by just anybody . . . Any forceful change of government . . . would require at least the tacit consent of the United States which is providing 341 million dollars in aid to Cambodia for the current fiscal year.

As to why a US-controlled change at the top was necessary, Willenson could not be more explicit:

The hard fact remains that *the Cambodian army has not fulfilled the role the United States assigned to it*. (My italics.)

US News And World Report of 29 November 1971 sums up the farce of the 'sovereign state' even more pointedly:

Cambodia, teetering from one crisis to another, cannot stand by itself. It is completely dependent on hundreds of millions of dollars' aid from the US, on military guidance from Americans, and a helping hand from South Vietnamese troops . . . If it were not for US air power and South Vietnamese soldiers now in Cambodia, Phnom Penh would be no match for . . . Red Forces that already control huge sections of the country.

When it comes to slaughtering our people, Cambodia's sovereignty is non-existent; when it comes to helping an aged, innocent woman to retire into exile, sovereignty is invoked as a reason to refuse. How ignoble can President Nixon become? America's allies act similarly. On 11 May 1972, the leader of the Labour Party opposition in the Australian parliament, Mr E. Gough Whitlam, was man enough to ask the Minister for Foreign Affairs: 'What has the government done to secure the release of Prince Sihanouk's mother?', a subject which Mr Whitlam to his great credit, has assiduously pursued. Foreign Minister Bowen, after noting previous queries as to the 'situation of Queen Kossomak, Prince Sihanouk's mother', replied that it 'was decided that it would not be proper for the Australian government to interfere in the domestic affairs of another state.' Australia, which set up for

Son Ngoc Thanh a radio station in Thailand from which he broadcast daily exhortations for my overthrow; which today provides instructors and transport planes for the Lon Nol army, to be so delicate about interfering in 'domestic affairs'!!!

It is not only my mother who has suffered. My daughter Botum Bopha and my sons Naradipo and Ranaridh[1] also had to suffer for my 'sins'. At first my two sons were placed under house arrest, then all three children were arrested on charges of 'high treason'. While under house arrest my sons were subject to the same treatment of organized insults as my mother, with the added threats that they were to be taken out and lynched to expunge their father's crimes. My daughter had never taken any part in politics. Only nineteen years at the time of her arrest, she had always been rather sickly, but was already the mother of three children, it being the custom for girls to marry early in my country. Together with her two brothers, she was accused of 'political homicides', of heading a terrorist movement accused of carrying out bomb and grenade attacks – including one against the US Embassy – during the last months of 1970.

Her real offence was to have given way to her emotions at the funeral of one of her favourite uncles, shot down in the street a week earlier by a captain in Lon Nol's army who had pledged 'to wipe all blood-sucking princes from the face of the earth – in the name of the republic'.

'What sort of a republic is it?' cried Botum Bopha at the funeral ceremonies. 'It's a republic of gangsters when officers can commit such murders! Where are the laws? Where is there any justice in this republic?'

Sirik Matak, cousin of the murdered prince – a major in the army – had her arrested. 'You're my niece,' he said, 'a distant niece, but still a relative, so I shall try to save you. You have insulted our republic. You must apologize. Take back your words.'

'I will not take back a single word,' my daughter replied. So her uncle sent her to the military tribunal which could impose the death sentence. But the Americans apparently realized that to sentence such a frail princess, mother of three,

1. Born respectively in 1951, 1946 and 1944.

would be bad publicity. They advised that she be acquitted and this was done. It was a few months after this that her husband, Prince Sisowath Doussady, escaped, with his wife's encouragement, to the Liberated Zone.

My two sons were accused of having spent many thousands of French francs to publish leaflets, manufacture grenades and to 'hire brigands' to distribute the leaflets and hurl the grenades! Where my two sons would have found 'thousands of French francs', I have no idea. On the day following the coup, precisely on 19 March 1970, they had both asked permission to go into exile. The response was for both of them to be placed under house arrest with the strictest surveillance. Not to mention the constant parades of insult-hurling mobs outside their home. How they could have organized plots or attentats is difficult to imagine.

The complete lack of evidence of any sort did not prevent Naradipo from being sentenced to five years' imprisonment for 'passing intelligence to the enemy'. In fact he was sentenced for political motives. He is the most political-minded of my children – or was then – and I had sent him to study in Peking. Chou En Lai had been generous enough to take him under his personal supervision and had taught him – not how to become a good communist, but how to become a good Cambodian; how best to be useful to our country after completing his studies. Naradipo had assiduously studied agronomy and Chinese language and literature. He acquitted himself well enough to serve later as an interpreter in my secretariat. He went off on labour projects with other students in China and integrated himself thoroughly with the activities of Chinese students. When his studies were interrupted by the Cultural Revolution, he returned to Phnom Penh where he became editor of the state-published newspaper in Chinese. I had publicly expressed the hope that if anything happened to me, he would become my 'political successor' because I was impressed by his patriotism, his concepts of service to the people and by his political maturity.

In the context intended by Lon Nol, millions of Cambodians could be charged with 'passing intelligence to the enemy' as the enemy for him is the people and their resistance forces.

Naradipo was sentenced for having been named my 'political successor'.

Among the charges against Ranaridh was 'irrefutable proof' of his possession of subversive literature. This turned out to be clippings from the respected French evening paper, *Le Monde*! Ranaridh was acquitted, not because of the absurdity of the charges and the 'proof' presented in court, but because my mother spent a large part of her fortune in buying an acquittal. Ranaridh is her favourite grandson. Many people are arrested under the Lon Nol régime as people are kidnapped in the West – to raise huge sums of ransom for their release. As the police can arrest anybody without the formality of a warrant, members of the military tribunal and other legal extortioners have an inexhaustible source of revenue.

Later, two more of my sons, Racvivongs and Khemanurak[1] managed to flee Phnom Penh. Racvivongs succeeded in reaching the Liberated Zone. News agencies announced the disappearance of Khemanurak from his Phnom Penh home on 17 September 1971, stating it was believed that he had fled to Paris via Thailand. He has not been heard of since.

At the trial of my three children, two of the accused who were supposed to testify against them charged they had been tortured to produce false evidence. One of them, Huoch Smoeurn, started to undress in court to show scars of burns from electric torture. He maintained in court that he alone had been responsible for preparing and distributing leaflets. He repudiated all testimony involving my children. He was sentenced to life imprisonment. A former servant of Botum Bopha, according to press reports of the trial, explained in court how the police had tortured her into testifying that she had acted as an intermediary between Botum Bopha and the heroic Huoch Smoeurn. She withdrew her testimony in court, and was sentenced to ten years hard labour. By such infamous means Lon Nol and Sirik Matak tried to do away with my children, and savagely punished those who refused to cooperate.

My own trial *in absentia* at the beginning of July 1970

1. Born respectively in 1944 and 1949.

took place in circumstances which made a mockery of all normal legal practices, starting with the fact that I was forbidden under pain of death to face my accusers. A typical press account of this farce was that of *Le Monde* of 7 July 1970.

Staged over three days, the proceedings against Prince Sihanouk turned out to be the usual type of scenario written in advance; the whole farce proceeding to a logically predictable ending. The lawyers appointed by the authorities made the court laugh at the expense of the accused. A procession of prosecution witnesses was paraded before about a hundred and fifty people, the régime being unable to muster any popular audience which might have given the trial some real weight. Incidentally, since 18 March, the date of the coup, there have been no spontaneous mass demonstrations in favour of Lon Nol.

If the charges reflected anything real at all, they were, in fact, an indictment of the present régime, the direct successor of the preceding one . . . They accuse Sihanouk of 'not keeping the peace in Cambodia', never mentioning that from 1953 to 1970, no one made greater efforts than he to keep the Kingdom out of the Indo-China conflict. The rural inhabitants, ravaged by B 52s, by toxic gases, by operations launched by American, South Vietnamese, and now Thai, troops, could not be represented at the proceedings. They know that peace came to an end on 18 March, with the removal of Sihanouk.

When one looks in retrospect at the 'crimes' for which I was condemned to death, then one sees how correct was the comment of *Le Monde*'s correspondent that the charge represented, in fact, 'an indictment of the present régime', not for what happened in the past but for what happened after the coup. I was accused, among other things, of being despotic. But if we examine this aspect of the Lon Nol–Sirik Matak régime, one sees against whom the indictment should really have been levelled:

18 March 1970: Even before the final act of my deposition was completed, the constitution was suspended for six months under an emergency law.

28 March 1970: Clarifications of the 18 March decisions were given. Firstly the 'emergency law' is renewable; secondly, during the period of its operation the government is empowered 'to take appropriate measures concerning the police and justice, press and public opinion, assembly and private corresponence' (the suppression of the democratic rights exercised under Sihanouk's despotism).

30 May 1970: Without waiting for the six months period to expire, the Lon Nol–Sirik Matak régime prolonged the 'emergency law' indefinitely and also imposed 'martial law'. It provided that:

Those who participate in, or openly incite, revolt or insurrect against the government, who knowingly conduct subversive propaganda by word of mouth or in writing or by any visual or oral means, or who spread panic in the army or defence forces, are to be punished by execution by shooting.

Those who listen to radio broadcasts from Peking, Hanoi, the Vietcong or other enemy broadcasts are to be sentenced to from five to twenty years' hard labour.

18 October 1971: Dissolution of the National Assembly and the institution of government by decree: 'We have had enough of sterile liberal democracy,' explained Lon Nol.

17 December 1971: Decrees were issued banning all political meetings, anti-government demonstrations, and giving the police

unlimited powers to investigate and detain suspected subversives . . . to search and arrest suspects at all hours . . . to search private homes, day and night, without warrant . . . The emergency laws do not permit general rights granted under the pre-war constitution including freedom of speech and association and secrecy of correspondence.[1]

On the question of despotism, the record is clear. I was also charged with having 'sabotaged the national economy'. As shown in a previous chapter, Lon Nol and Sirik Matak, as individuals acting through their compradore agents, had siphoned off proceeds from sectors of the national economy; the dollar profits dropped into their own pockets, more specifically into their bank accounts abroad. (I have never

1. Quotations from Reuter and UPI dispatches from Phnom Penh, 1 December 1971.

owned a bank account in a foreign bank.) Still more serious, due to the consequences of Lon Nol and Sirik Matak having called in the US–Saigon invaders to save their régime from collapse, rice production had dropped by 60 per cent in the first months of their rule; rubber production was nil; exports were non-existent; food prices in the enclaves controlled by their régime had risen by three or four times; the official value of the riel had fallen to about one fifth of what it was before the coup. B 52s, napalm, toxic chemicals – employed to keep the Phnom Penh usurpers in power – have utterly ruined the national economy.

A further charge was that I had helped 'Vietnamese communists' to occupy portions of Cambodian territory. The total of territory ever held by the resistance forces never exceeded a few square kilometres, a few strips of territory never more than five hundred metres in depth. The resistance forces never harmed our people or affected our economy except to stimulate trade in the frontier areas. Their temporary presence never infringed upon our *de jure* territorial integrity, our sovereignty or our neutrality.

What is the position today? The Saigon régime has annexed areas of Svay Rieng, Prey Veng, Kompong Cham Kampot and Takeo provinces – certain parts of which are now included in the Saigon postal maps as constituting South Vietnamese territory. The ferry town of Neak Luong, forty miles from Phnom Penh, has been baptized 'Little Saigon'. Our coastal islands have been annexed by Saigon troops. Our air space is almost permanently occupied by US, South Vietnamese and Thai planes. Who is guilty of losing territory to foreign occupiers?

I was charged with rebelling against the 'legitimate' régime of Lon Nol and Sirik Matak. That I direct an armed struggle against that régime, I admit. I also contest that the régime – despite the presidential electoral farce of June 1972 – has the slightest shred of legitimacy. And I have the weight of international constitutional law on my side.

In condemning me to death on such trumped-up charges, Lon Nol and Sirik Matak and the other conspirators have woven a rope which in due time will be dropped around their own necks. Even within the terms of the indictment drawn up to convict me – it is they who are many times guilty on all charges. But much graver accusations will be added to the list when the time comes. The sentence pronounced against myself will be executed against those that framed the indictment. The crimes committed against my person and my family are insignificant in comparison with those committed against the nation as a whole. For these, our people will demand retribution. I am not a hypocrite so I declare clearly that the ringleaders of the 18 March coup, who have wrought such incalculable damage to the nation and brought such atrocious sufferings to our people, will suffer the same fate as the Quislings and Lavals of the Second World War.

Chapter 17

The Spring Offensive

If the Saigon forces suffered shattering blows on all fronts in the spring of 1972, this was because of superb coordination between the armed forces and peoples of all Indo-China. It was by coordinated and joint efforts of Giap's troops from North Vietnam with their tanks and heavy weapons; of Pathet Lao forces in Laos protecting north-south supply lines in depth, combined with diversionary attacks in the western regions of Laos; of NLF regular and guerrilla forces launching attacks and uprisings in every province of South Vietnam; of our own PNLAF in attacking the enemy in our eastern and south-eastern provinces. The latter were especially effective in the Parrot's Beak area, along Highway I, linking Phnom Penh with Saigon, and at key points along the Cambodian-South Vietnamese frontier. The peoples of Laos, South Vietnam and Cambodia exerted heroic efforts for a year or more before the spring offensive, by helping to transport and hide enormous quantities of supplies, despite ferocious enemy air assaults.

The shortest road – militarily speaking – to Saigon lies through the Parrot's Beak in Cambodia. Large areas of the strategic Central Highlands of South Vietnam are adjacent to our completely liberated north-eastern provinces. The easiest way to infiltrate troops with heavy weapons is to join up with the guerrillas in the Mekong Delta, the latter including veterans from the several hundred thousand strong Cambodian minority there, in through our south-eastern provinces. Thus, in the final stages of the liberation of South Vietnam, Cambodia plays a key role. We have always felt that the liberation of South Vietnam is inextricably linked with our own final victory. While defending our own liberated areas and continuing heavy attacks on enemy installations in Phnom Penh itself, our forces launched their main attacks in the frontier areas to open up infiltration routes for our allies into South Vietnam.

Such coordination of efforts was foreseen at the Indo-China People's Summit Conference in April 1970, at which the final communiqué states that:

proceeding from the principle that the liberation of each country is the affair of its people, the various parties pledge to do all they can to give one another reciprocal support according to the desire of the party concerned, and on the basis of mutual respect.

It was further stated that:

the three Indo-Chinese peoples, by the impetus of their victories, will make the fullest use of their positions of initiative and offensive to push ahead and step up the fight without respite on all fronts.

Each of us has loyally carried out this concept. Throughout 1971 and the first months of 1972, when the main scene of action seemed to have shifted to Laos and Cambodia, it was the coordinated activities on all fronts that pave the way for the spring offensive in South Vietnam.

On the very eve of the offensive, our armed forces carried out heavy attacks in the Phnom Penh area. On 16 March a big munitions depot at Phnom Penh's Pochentong airport was blown up; on 21 March there was another heavy attack against the airport's military installations and against the capital's main radio station. The central section of the vital Chruoy Changwar bridge over the Tonle Sap river, in the heart of Phnom Penh was destroyed on 24 March. These attacks inside Phnon Penh, forced the enemy to withdraw troops from other areas to defend the capital. Our forces were not inactive on other fronts. On 20 March, our commandos destroyed an important munitions depot of the Saigon troops, twenty-five miles south-east of Phnom Penh, and partially destroyed another five miles further east. These were just a few highlights of actions aimed at effecting the maximum dispersal of enemy forces before the main blow was struck.

232

Overall strategy was discussed when I went to Hanoi in February – on the eve of President Nixon's arrival in Peking. My North Vietnamese friends, also those of the NLF and Pathet Lao in Hanoi while I was there, were in total agreement that we were not going to be cheated of victory by some new variant of a Geneva Conference. We felt we had been tricked too often by the West and that this time it was necessary to smash the US puppet régimes.

Having studied all aspects of the situation in Indo-China, we agreed that we were now sailing downstream with a spanking wind behind us. Giap was convinced that the Saigon puppets could no longer undertake operations such as that into south Laos and Cambodia in March 1971, nor could the Lon Nol army support another 'Chenla 2' operation along Highway 6 in Cambodia during August-December of the same year. Attacks on such a scale were henceforth impossible because of the heavy losses inflicted on the best-trained, best-equipped units of the puppet armies. Our forces, however, as Giap asserted, were capable of going over to large-scale offensives this year because they had grown continuously in both total and relative terms. The Americans could react by stepping up their air raids, extending their so-called electronic battlefield of detection gadgets, but supplies would get through and the Americans would be powerless to stop this without physically occupying the terrain. They had tried this in the south Laos and Kratié operations into Cambodia in March 1971, and they had ended in disaster. Without the physical presence of US forces, the combat capacity of the puppet troops rapidly declined.

The latter are divided among themselves. South Korean mercenaries despise the Saigon troops. Elite units of the latter despise the regular army. The Saigon army despises that of Lon Nol. Thai troops and Meo mercenaries despise the Vientiane troops in Laos. All these feelings are mutual and sharply detract from overall morale. In our camp we are more united than ever. At the same time as our armed forces were developed, we reinforced our capacity for coordinated efforts and the spirit of solidarity which springs from identity of aims. The high ideological motivation of the armed forces of our three peoples precluded any trace of racism.

By his folly in wasting the strategic reserves of the Saigon army in adventures into Cambodia and Laos in the spring of 1971, Nixon created excellent conditions for our forces to take the offensive in 1972. The spring tide for the revolutionary forces in Indo-China was approaching its high point as the time of my visit to Hanoi. Giap was in a most optimistic mood as we went over the situation on the military maps.

Our Cambodian forces are the youngest of the Indo-China family. If I use their development as a yardstick, I have some idea of the quality of their veteran elder brothers. In an incredibly short time our forces have become battle-hardened, audacious, and expert in handling all sorts of weapons which did not exist in our armed forces before. Just as the enemy had reached a low point of demoralization on the eve of the spring offensive, so the morale of ours had never been so high. All reports from the resistance bases confirmed this. The combination of a just cause, battlefield victories and close support from the people, is unbeatable in promoting a high *éspirit de combat*. Of crucial importance was our assessment, at the Hanoi meeting, that no matter how savage Nixon's reactions to battlefield defeats – and none of us underestimated his capacity for beastliness – these would only heighten the morale and determination of our forces.

It was Nixon who had thrown down the challenge to each of our three peoples in turn. It was he who decided on a trial of strength and left us with no choice but to pick up the challenge. We decided to use our combined forces against him, or whoever succeeds him as President of the United States if he pursues the same policy, until total victory. We have suffered too much; we have been humiliated too long. Our aims are modest – leave us alone to settle our own affairs. We agreed in Hanoi that we had to go all out, united as one people, for complete victory. This is the essence of the conclusions arrived at in my talks with the leaders of the Democratic Republic of Vietnam, including President Ton Duc Thang, Premier Pham Van Dong, Defence Minister Vo Nguyen Giap, the Lao Dong Party Secretary, Le Duan, and others.

Our identity of views and aims is expressed in the communiqué I signed with President Ton on 5 March 1972, which includes such passages as:

As long as the Nixon administration pursues its neo-colonialist aims against the countries of Indo-China and continues to apply the 'Nixon Doctrine' to Indo-China, the Cambodian and Vietnamese peoples are determined to fight shoulder-to-shoulder with all our strength until total victory ... The Cambodian people, for their part, are determined to fight on without any compromises or waverings in order to kick the American aggressors and their Saigon and Bangkok valets out of our country, together with all their armed forces and personnel; to overthrow and wipe out the fascist, anti-popular, anti-national, anti-constitutional régime of Lon Nol, Sirik Matak and Son Ngoc Thanh, puppets of US imperialism, and to build up Cambodia as an independent, sovereign, neutral, pacific, democratic and prosperous state, enjoying complete territorial integrity.

Neither brute force nor insolent threats, nor perfidious intrigues of the US imperialists, can make the three peoples of Indo-China deviate from their noble aim of liberating the whole of Indo-China and turning it into a peninsula of peace comprising independent and sovereign states, thus ensuring for South Vietnam, Cambodia, and Laos, the right to follow the path of independence, peace, and true neutrality.

Perhaps little notice was taken of this historic document at the time, world attention still having been focused on the aftermath of Nixon's visit to the People's Republic of China, but it was under this banner that the spring offensive was launched; it was in this spirit that our three peoples cooperated before and during the offensive, to achieve victories on a scale unprecedented in the history of the peoples of Indo-China.

Regarding the Nixon visit to Peking, neither our Chinese friends, nor my Vietnamese and Laotian friends, nor myself had any illusions but that one of Nixon's aims was to try to drive a wedge between the Chinese and our national liberation movements. Premier Chou En Lai gave me a frank evaluation of the situation in the small hours of 12 July 1971, shortly after Kissinger left Peking for Washington after his first visit. And a few days after Nixon left Changhai, at the end of his tour of China, Premier Chou came to see me while

I was still on my visit to North Vietnam. In a three-hour meeting, he told me of his discussion with Nixon. As far as Indo-China was concerned, they went as follows:

Chou En Lai made it clear to Nixon that if he wanted to settle the Cambodian problem, or that of Vietnam or Laos, he should address himself to the leaders of the Cambodian, Vietnamese and Laotian resistance movements and handle the questions directly with them. Nixon showed no enthusiasm for seeing me, Premier Chou explained, because to have done so would have meant the immediate collapse of the Lon Nol régime and Nixon was not prepared to envisage that! The leaders of the resistance movements of Indo-China will not give up their sovereignty in such matters and the Chinese viewpoint is the following: the United States should recognize that it is the resistance fighters who are the true representatives of their respective peoples because they fight for their country's freedom and independence, whereas the US puppets do not represent any national aspirations. President Nixon should firstly decide to negotiate with the resistance leaders. Secondly, he should pay serious attention to their demands which are legitimate ones. Thirdly, China advises the United States to leave the Indo-Chinese people alone.

Go away! That is what you ought to do. If you do not, we Chinese, faithful to our conceptions of justice and of solidarity with all oppressed peoples, will give the Indo-Chinese peoples all necessary aid – everything they may need to liberate themselves. We will support them to the end. We will never retreat from this position, and it is better that you should know this. Our conversations should deal with matters of bilateral interest between China and the United States. The question of Indo-China is one between you and the Indo-Chinese. It is not one that you can settle with us. We only tell you what we think you ought to do and, as far as we are concerned, we inform you that we will never halt our total support and aid to the resistance movements.

Nixon's reactions at this point, Premier Chou said, was simply to note that this was the Chinese position, but the question came up again in discussions on Taiwan with Nixon's assertion that US troops would remain there 'until tension in the areas was lessened'. Chou En Lai insisted that tension exists in the area above all because of the war in Indo-China. 'But you are not yet ready to quit Indo-China,' he told Nixon:

You continue your policy of Vietnamization of the war, of Khmerization and of Laosization – policies not acceptable to the peoples of Indo-China and their real leaders. You continue with troop withdrawals but you also continue to bomb the peoples of Indo-China. You try to maintain your position there through mercenaries – people in your pay. As long as the Indo-China war continues there can be no easing of tension so you will stay in Taiwan until the end of your lives. We say – if you are sincere in wanting to improve relations with us – then stop interfering in Indo-China. Then there will be no more tension. We will never attack the United States, and you have no right to remain indefinitely on Taiwan. In order that there should be no more tension in the area so that you can leave Taiwan, you have to end the war in Indo-China. This is impeccable, irrefutable logic.

At the beginning of our conversation and again at the end Premier Chou expressed himself as follows: 'We Chinese are in complete solidarity with you, the peoples of Indo-China. The big question between the United States and us is that of Taiwan. But in Taiwan there is no war whereas in Indo-China war is still raging. Your peoples are suffering. If we can do something to end those sufferings, we will do our best to do it. That is why we tell the Americans that "as far as Taiwan is concerned we can be patient. But as far as Indo-China is concerned we want you to end this war. This you must do if you want to normalize relations with us."'

As for a new Geneva-type conference – a question raised by Nixon – Chou En Lai told him that China could not accept such a conference because the principal parties concerned in Indo-China did not want this and China would act in accordance with their desires. Premier Chou knew quite well that neither the Vietnamese, nor the Pathet Lao, or myself, want anything to do with such a conference.

Concrete proof that China's support would not waver as a result of the Nixon visit was that stepped-up aid for our resistance forces – already considerable – was offered soon after Nixon's departure in just those materials we most needed – plus the means of transporting them.

Probably one of the reasons behind Nixon's visit to Peking and later to Moscow was that Nixon had hoped by this means to ward off an offensive during the last operational season before the presidential elections. He had failed in his two 'war-winning' offensives against Cambodia and Laos, in 1970 and 1971 respectively, and he must have feared what was coming in 1972. If he expected the Chinese to exert any pressures aimed at warding off an offensive, he was badly informed. Chinese aid to ourselves and our Vietnamese comrades-in-arms was steadily increased throughout 1971 and the first months of 1972 and Chinese encouragement to push on with plans for the spring offensive never faltered.

The situation in Cambodia on the eve of the spring offensive was summed up in the end-of-the-year report of Defence Minister and Vice-Premier Khieu Samphan, mentioned earlier. It is a document of fundamental importance:

All enemy plans aimed at encroaching into our liberated areas, at pillaging the people's economy, at conscripting manpower into the Lon Nol army and thus changing the balance of forces in their favour, have been successfully repulsed. The enemy cannot get fresh recruits because of his failure to seize and 'pacify' liberated territory. His existing forces have been severely weakened, the morale of the remainder drastically lowered by a long series of defeats unrelieved by a single victory. Thus the Nixon Doctrine has not found a favourable terrain in Cambodia.

Khieu Samphan went on to summarize four characteristics of the situation which help explain the contribution our forces were able to make to the spring offensive.

1. Consolidation of Our Armed Forces

This was reflected in 'more generalized, more intensive, systematic and continuous offensive activities' resulting in the failure of the Lon Nol troops to loosen our grip of Highway 6 – which leads north from Phnom Penh to Kompong Thom via Skoun, Baray, and Taing Krasaing, and then west from Kompong Thom to Siem Reap and Angkor. Also the failure of the Saigon–Lon Nol troops to dislodge our forces even from the immediate vicinity of Phnom Penh. Khieu Samphan assessed this as proof of 'a fundamental change in the general balance of military, political and social forces' as between ourselves and the enemy. He pointed out that in the first months of armed struggle, our forces had to withstand strong attacks aimed at smothering them at birth. They had to take the initiative themselves to liberate large areas and, at the same time, build up the armed forces and an administrative infrastructure. His report read:

> But at the present time our regular, regional and guerrilla units have, between them, established a fine-meshed network over the whole country so that even if the enemy shows the tip of his nose he feels the iron fist of our PNLAF.

Defence Minister Khieu also stressed the continuous improvement in combat efficiency and morale, shown by the ability

to combine guerrilla warfare with regular warfare; to effect excellent coordination between regular forces, regional units and village militia, and between the three branches of the armed forces and the people's political organizations.

As a result of the changed balance of forces, the enemy could no longer switch units from one area to rescue those under attack elsewhere – as they had been able to do up to mid-1971. 'We can now immobilize enemy forces, denying them the possibility of going to each other's rescue.'

2. Disintegration of Enemy Forces

The battle of 'Chenla 2', later analysed in detail by Khieu Samphan, had shown that, even with massive air and naval support, the enemy was unable to crush our resistance forces and completely went to pieces when under counter-attack. The report continued:

> At present, the traitor army is literally paralysed by the psychosis of defeat. As distinct from the situation in our armed forces, there is a complete lack of solidarity. No unit even thinks of coming to the help of another even when they are engaged in the same operation. The Phnom Penh leadership is only concerned with the fate of the capital – of defending their last hide-out.

Khieu Samphan remarks that the Saigon puppets, by late 1971, 'had lost much of their arrogance of a year previously'. He considered that if the enemy mobilized sufficient numbers of men and weight of equipment he could 'push in here or there', but that whatever force was employed 'the enemy can in no way improve the disastrous situation of the Lon Nol army. The further enemy troops advance into our areas, the more vulnerable they become.' Khieu Samphan predicted correctly that, in 1972, 'the enemy can certainly not do more than in 1971. In such conditions it is quite certain that we will inflict on him still greater defeats.'

3. Improved Coordination of Military and Political Struggle

Our Defence Minister here stresses the vital importance of the 'active cooperation between armed forces and people', especially in view of American attempts, first to 'Vietnamize' the war in Cambodia and, when that failed, to Cambodianize it. We consider, incidentally, that the death blow dealt to Nixon's attempt to 'Vietnamize' our war was dealt during operation 'Total Victory' – the ill-fated attempt by Saigon troops to capture Kratié on the Mekong, during which most of the attacking force's armour and artillery was destroyed or captured by our forces. The Saigon officer commanding the operation, General Do Cao Tri, was killed when his helicopter was shot down, and the attacking forces retreated in disorder, never having got within sight of Kratié. This coincided with the death blow dealt to Nixon's attempt to 'Vietnamize' the war in Laos, crowned by the crushing defeat of the invasion of south Laos. Khieu Samphan considers that the 'Cambodianization' of the war was essentially defeated in December 1971, with the débâcle of Lon Nol's much-vaunted 'Chenla 2' operation.

It is because of the support of the local people that our elite units have been able to carry out such feats as that in October 1971, when they infiltrated the most intricate defence installations to destroy the main military post at the district centre of Kompong Trabêk, on Highway 1, wiping out a complex of support posts, and liberating tens of thousands of peasants rounded up during an operation by Saigon troops two months earlier.[1]

As explained elsewhere, an essential element of 'Cambodianization' of the war was the herding of the peasantry into barbed-wire-surrounded 'strategic hamlets', as in South Vietnam, guarded by 'self-defence' units to ensure they had no contact with the world outside. A major task of our armed forces was to help the peasantry escape from such concentration camps, and from enemy control in general. This meant also helping them to withdraw in time from the path of enemy offensives. As a typical result of this, Khieu Samphan reported that, when Lon Nol's forces lost 12,000 men in the battles along Highway 6, they were unable to scrape together more than 1,000 replacements in the area. As one of the main aims of such enemy operations was the rounding up of cannon fodder, Khieu was correct in describing such examples as crushing defeats for 'Cambodianization' of the war, and thus for Nixon's overall strategy in Indo-China.

4. Reinforced Unity at Home and Abroad

In this section, the report stressed the high degree of combat solidarity forged with the fraternal peoples of Vietnam and Laos, and the vital support from the peoples of China, Korea and other friendly countries. As a general conclusion, Khieu Samphan observed that

while the enemy is retreating on all fronts . . . we are advancing in closely united ranks at home and with the fraternal countries. We are on the crest of a revolutionary wave.

Khieu Samphan predicted that, by continuing to combine the offensive in the months ahead,

in the military, political, economic, diplomatic and psychological fields, inside the country and abroad, we are sure that during 1972 we will be able to change the general balance of forces still more

1. Kompong Trabêk, a key town on the main Phnom Penh–Saigon highway, was captured by the PNLAF in April 1972, paving the way for clearing Saigon troops out of the whole Parrot's Beak area, and leading to the liberation of the strategically important town of Bavet, on the frontier with South Vietnam, little more than forty miles from Saigon.

decisively in our favour and accelerate the death throes of the Lon Nol, Sirik Matak, and Son Ngoc Thanh régime.

When I first studied this report, I felt that, with understandable optimism, Khieu Samphan was painting too bright a picture, but events have confirmed that this was a sober, realistic evaluation.

As future historians will probably assess the 'Chenla 2' battle as a decisive turning point in the fighting in Cambodia, Khieu Samphan's analysis of what happened is important. He stresses that this was but the most ambitious of a series of operations launched simultaneously by Lon Nol in the second half of 1971, in a major attempt to crush the resistance forces. 'Chenla 2' had two main aims: (a) to regain control of a vital, fifty-mile stretch of Highway 6, between Skoun and Kompong Thom: (b) to win back a rich and densely-populated triangular area bordered by Highways 6 and 7, and Road 21. Within this triangle lay the districts of Baray, Chamlar Loeu and Stung Trâng, either athwart Highway 6 or to the east of it.

Khieu Samphan continued:

If this region fell into Lon Nol's hands, his forces would have plundered all local resources; forced the peasantry into 'strategic hamlets'; rounded up all of military age for the army, and built up the area as a base for attacks into other liberated areas in the provinces of Kompong Cham, Kompong Thom, Preah Vihear and Siem Reap. Over fourteen infantry brigades and other units, totalling more than seventy battalions, were committed, supported by the US air force, the Lon Nol navy, tanks and heavy artillery.

We fought this battle in three phases. From 20 August to 25 October, we used mainly guerrilla tactics – ambushes and swift hit-and-run attacks. We put over five thousand Lon Nol troops out of action in this phase. A major task was also to help the local people escape from enemy control and thus thwart 'pacification'. On the success of this depended that of the next two phases.

The second phase started on 26 October with the blowing-up of the key Prek Trâs bridge at Batheay, about halfway between Skoun and Kompong Thom, and violent attacks against enemy posts along Highway 6, from Prek Trâs–Batheay to Santouk, isolating enemy units from each other and cutting their supply line to the rear. One after another, posts along Highway 6 fell into our hands while we started to tighten pincer movements around the enemy's main command posts. This phase ended on 13 November when we attacked, after a siege of nineteen days, the headquarters post of the 46th Infantry Brigade at Rumlorng. We wiped out the post and its garrison. Four thousand more Lon Nol troops were put out of action during that second phase. This was a fatal blow, preparing the way for the third and final act.

From 14 November to 3 December, we launched all-out attacks at the main command posts of 'Chenla 2', starting with heavily fortified posts at Baray and Kompong Thmâr and all other key posts – ten in all. After the first two were wiped out, the rout started. Cut off from each other, the command posts destroyed and the whole command system disrupted, the rest of the forces started a headlong retreat. Of about 20,000 Lon Nol troops thrown into this operation, we killed, wounded or captured over 12,000. Not a single battalion escaped without severe losses.

During the 'Chenla 2' adventure, Lon Nol lost over half of what were considered the best of his troops. Still more serious for him was the fact that, apart from the seventy battalions decimated in that operation, the rest of the army – beaten on all fronts – can no longer be considered frontline combat troops for use in the defence of Phnom Penh or anywhere else. Their morale is at zero level. They were defeated at every point where battle was engaged. This marks the first strategic turning-point towards total defeat of the 'Cambodianization' of the war; a defeat for 'pacification'; for the setting up of 'strategic hamlets' and 'self-defence' forces . . . the collapse of the spinal column of the Nixon Doctrine for Cambodia.

A victory of such dimensions is a measure of the great progress achieved by the PNLAF during 1971. It must be stressed that it was the simultaneous military actions carried out by the whole of our forces on all fronts that enabled us to bring off such a victory. In 1971, the enemy was able to limit his defeats along Highway 4 – linking Phnom Penh with our only seaport at Sihanoukville – by reinforcing the troops there with those withdrawn from other regions. But this time Lon Nol's troops were pinned down on all fronts. None could be withdrawn. Appeals by 'Chenla 2' commanders for help fell on deaf ears. There were no reinforcements available. Even the Saigon interventionists had no troops to spare. Our forces had pinned them down east of the capital.

A key ingredient in this victory, Khieu Samphan concluded, was the fact that 'the armed forces had the support of a solid military political and social base'. His assessment was strikingly confirmed by a spate of Western news agency dispatches from Phnom Penh, about the same time that I received the Khieu Samphan report. Robin Mannock of Associated Press, reported on 4 January 1972, that:

> Government troops, their morale sapped by a string of recent defeats, are weaker than they have been in many months in the opinion of long-term residents here. Even the increasing flow of American-made weapons cannot change that ... Morale hit a new low and stayed there after the costly collapse a month ago of operation 'Chenla 2', a campaign personally devised by Premier Lon Nol to regain control of the north-east part of Cambodia.
>
> The communist command let 20,000 Cambodian regulars advance up Highway 6 without opposition, then chopped them up when their supply lines were stretched thin. The Cambodians were then forced into enclaves that shrank and fell, despite heavy US and South Vietnam air support.

(Note that, for Robin Mannock, as for most Western reporters, the patriotic force are 'communists', presumably stateless – when they are not North Vietnamese – whereas the Lon Nol traitor troops, puppets of the USA and Saigon are 'the Cambodians'. As for the myth that the campaign was 'personally devised by Lon Nol', it is unthinkable that such an operation could have been launched unless it had been approved – if not totally conceived – by Lon Nol's US military advisers. After all, they are there to see that efficient use is made of US-supplied weapons!)

In any case the 'Chenla 2' debacle provoked the gravest, till that time, of the endless series of political crises that are a permanent feature of the Lon Nol régime. As to who dictates the solutions to such crises, there was the fascinating 'special report' – presumably for editors' eyes only – from Kim Willenson of United Press International, of 20 December 1971, to which I have briefly referred in a previous chapter. Because of the 'Chenla 2' disaster, Willenson spoke of rumours of a 'government reshuffle that would kick Lon Nol upstairs to a position so high, "to the planets or even the stars", as one source puts it – that he would be little more than a figurehead'. The UPI reporter continues with the passage quoted in an earlier chapter, to the effect that the United

States was 'not going to countenance a coup by just anybody', however.

Information reaching my Peking headquarters at that time was that the US Embassy in Phnom Penh had prepared the list of a new cabinet to be installed after a palace coup had eliminated Lon Nol. But, it seems, there were CIA-State Department divergencies, also troubles with the French. The French Ambassador in Phnom Penh was reported as having said that if the new 'strong man' was to be the Son Ngoc Thanh that France had condemned to death as a traitor (and who had been saved from execution by my intervention), France 'would no longer collaborate', implying that, at some level, France had 'collaborated' with the Lon Nol coup against Sihanouk! Another cause of dissension was that the CIA wanted to replace Lon Nol by his younger brother, Lon Non, but, as the latter had become involved in supplying drugs to the GIs in Vietnam from Laos, through the medium of a training centre set up in South Laos to train Lon Nol commandos – soon transformed into a relay post for opium traffic – the State Department objected. Lon Non's involvement had been inadvertently discovered when a US Congressional investigation team, sent to discover the source of 'pot' for the GIs, put its finger on the CIA-run training camp for Lon Nol commandos as a key link in the chain of distribution of everything from hashish to heroin![1]

Son Ngoc Thanh applied blackmail by threatening to withdraw his ten thousand CIA-trained Khmer Krom commando battalions – on which Lon Nol mainly relied for the defence of Phnom Penh – unless he got a top post. By this time a large part of the forces nominally at Lon Nol's disposal were lined up protecting the various factions from being devoured by their rivals! Eventually the crisis was temporarily solved by Lon Nol dumping 'President' Cheng Heng and 'Prime Minister' Sirik Matak, inaugurating himself as President – in a ceremony which virtually all diplomats in Phnom Penh boycotted. He later gave Son Ngoc Thanh a consolation prize as 'Prime Minister'. The wheel of treachery

1. Running the camp – which was closed down – was a protégé of Lon Non.

in the latter's case, had now made a full turn. First time Prime Minister as a puppet of the Japanese. Second time Prime Minister as a puppet of the United States. In neither case did he hold any real power. But in both cases it was a symbolic reward for 'services rendered'.

Lon Nol by this time was completely isolated, deserted even by those who had been closest to him during the 18 March coup. In Tam had turned against him after the dissolution of the National Assembly. Sirik Matak had been politically decapitated, Cheng Heng was flung aside with little ceremony. Even Sim Var, brought back from Japan as a possible candidate of the premiership, took a brief look at the situation in Phnom Penh and refused the job. (He founded a newspaper in which he editorialized among other things that corruption under Lon Nol was 'a hundred times what it had been under Sihanouk'! This was doubtless because he discovered that Lon Nol and Sirik Matak and a few others had already monopolized the main channels for siphoning off the Pentagon millions into their foreign bank accounts.) Lon Nol had mobilized the students in demonstrations to support his drive to eliminate Sirik Matak. The students cooperated with enthusiasm, but once Sirik Matak was downed, they turned their wrath against Lon Nol and Son Ngoc Thanh. The result was that on 27 April 1972, military police, on the direct orders of Lon Nol and Son Ngoc Thanh, opened fire on student demonstrators from the Law Faculty of Phnom Penh University, killing and wounding at least thirty students. The dead were taken off and secretly buried by the Lon Nol police. This provoked still more violent demonstrations, in the heart of Phnom Penh, with parents and relatives demanding at least the bodies of the victims. Students and parents chained themselves to the Independence Monument in the centre of Phnom Penh, and with Buddhist monks in the vanguard there were mass demonstrations of sympathy for the victims and their relatives until Lon Nol mined the gardens surrounding the monument, causing further deaths and mutilations.

By the time the spring offensive was launched, the Lon Nol régime was literally falling apart. When our commandos penetrated the city outskirts on the night of 6 May 1972, blowing up an oil depot, attacking Pochentong airport and engaging the Lon Nol troops in hand-to-hand combat in several sectors of the city, there were no Saigon troops to come to the rescue. 'Are you crazy?' is said to have been the response of Nguyen Van Thieu – having just lost Quang Tri province and with Hué seriously threatened – when Lon Nol used the 'hot line' between Phnom Penh and Saigon to ask for help.

One would have thought that the clear demonstrations of the isolation of usurpers like Lon Nol and Son Ngoc Thanh would have caused Nixon to reconsider his attitude towards Cambodia. Apparently, to expect that, is to overestimate his intelligence and realism. Anything less than a complete US puppet at the helm in Phnom Penh – or Saigon – is equated with the 'humiliation' of President Nixon, and prejudicial to the 'respect of the office of the President of the United States'. Thus we learned, on 24 April 1972 – from the *Washington Post* – that the United States 'will have a defence commitment to Cambodia even after all US troops are withdrawn from South Vietnam'. This revelation was based on a Pentagon demand for the United States 'to build a Cambodian force level of 220,000 in fiscal 1973'. As there are approximately two million Cambodians in that part of the country controlled by Lon Nol and the number is shrinking every day, the figure is 'optimistic' to say the least, especially as a high proportion of the two million are women, children and the aged who have fled from US bombing of the rural areas. That Lon Nol is capable of producing on paper an army of 220,000 – and salting away the payroll of the non-existent effectives in a Swiss bank account – is very possible. In the Willenson report quoted above, it is noted that 'battalion commanders assigned to recruit and pay their own troops have found it possible to reap vast profits by maintaining paper soldiers on their payrolls'.

That which the battalion commanders can pocket is petty stuff compared to the tens of millions of dollars siphoned off by Lon Nol and the handful of political tricksters with whom he shares power and profits at the top. The corruption itself is a minor point compared to the implications of the new commitments.

The Nixon administration is serving notice that Cambodia is to remain indefinitely an American fief. In justifying this, the US Under-Secretary of State for Asian Affairs, Marshall Green, outdid himself in hypocrisy by telling the US Congressional Foreign Affairs Committee that the United States 'had an interest in the Cambodians being able to form a government of their own choosing'. Throughout almost seventeen years of peace after Cambodia won her independence from France, the top level of our armed forces was around 35,000 men! The director of the US Security Assistance Program, Lt. General George M. Seignious, was less hypocritical, but more cynical, in backing up Green when he stated: 'I think we may have a United States interest, and policy reasons, that would indicate that it was prudent and *in our interest*, to continue some form of support to Cambodia after the US forces have withdrawn from South Vietnam.' (My italics.)

This is a naked declaration of intention of a permanent puppet role for Cambodia, in keeping with Willenson's report that 'the Cambodian army has not fulfilled the role the United States assigned to it: harassing communist rear positions so the United States can more easily pull out of the neighbouring South Vietnam'. At first there must be a Cambodian puppet army so that the United States may safely withdraw its troops from the more dangerous South Vietnam, then there must be a puppet army to protect United States interests in the area!

As was made clear during the 'spring offensive', the Cambodian people and their armed forces see their role quite differently – that of 'harassing the rear positions' of the Saigon and Phnom Penh puppets so the 'spring offensive' could sweep on from victory to victory to ensure that the peoples of Indo-China could really win the right to decide their own fate, and to form 'governments of their own choosing', without American guns in their backs or American puppets in control at the top.

Chapter 18

The Future

Will we win the battle for national survival? If so what comes after? Many of my correspondents in the West seem interested only in the second question! The answer to the first is directly linked to the outcome of the struggle between the NUFC and the present régime in Phnom Penh or whatever the United States imposes in its place. Such régimes can only be maintained by the physical presence of foreign powers. So in the long run the perpetuation of such régimes would spell the end of our national survival. In precise terms, it would mean dividing up Cambodia between our traditional enemies, represented today by the inheritors and continuators of the worst features of Vietnamese and Thai expansionism – the military dictatorships in Saigon and Bangkok.

It is the Cambodian resistance forces that will win, however, just as the resistance forces in South Vietnam will eventually sweep the Saigon dictatorship into the sea. Sooner or later, depending on how far and how fast the Bangkok régime permits itself to be pushed by the United States into adventures against Laos and Cambodia, the people of Thailand will also deal with their dictatorship. (If the USA does succeed in unleashing Thai aggression against Cambodia, the present resistance front between the three peoples of Indo-China will expand into a militant front between our three peoples and those of Thailand. Our ranks will be reinforced by the inclusion of the Thai Patriotic Front, and we will coordinate our activities in the west, as in the north and east.)

The future of Cambodia is the NUFC. In this respect there is an important difference between our position and that of the NLF of South Vietnam. There, the Thieu régime – or whatever succeeds it in Saigon – is some sort of successor to the Bao Dai régime set up by the French. The latter was succeeded by a whole series of dictatorships of dubious legal status, from that of Ngo Dinh Diem to that of Nguyen Van Thieu. What they all had in common was that they existed solely by force of US dollars and arms and, finally, by the physical presence of US military power. There is also the Provisional Revolutionary Government which represents the national liberation forces. By their heroic and victorious struggle, the leaders of the PRG have won on the battle-field the right to claim state power. In fact, they have never claimed to represent the whole of South Vietnam just as the NLF has rejected any monopoly position in deciding the country's future. The NLF has asserted from the beginning that it fights to create the conditions for the people of South Vietnam to decide their future, free of foreign domination and foreign puppets. The PRG-NLF demand that the Saigon régime be changed from one bent on waging war against its own people on behalf of the USA, to one seeking peace and independence. With such a régime, the PRG is prepared to negotiate a peaceful settlement, and also to par-ticipate with elements of that régime in a provisional coalition government.

In Cambodia the situation is quite different. The Phnom Penh putchists have violated the constitution to illegally, and temporarily, seize power in Phnom Penh. They are main-tained in power by the armed forces of foreign states. They are traitors and outlaws in the juridical sense of the term, guilty of unspeakable crimes against my people. We will never negotiate with them; we will never enter into any coalition or other compromise with them. They will be wiped out and, if any of the ringleaders fall into our hands, they will inevitably be executed. They are conspirators and quislings who took part in an international plot to destroy our independence. No matter what sort of *post facto* legalistic trappings they, and their patrons, give their régime, the NUFC will maintain only one policy towards it – wipe it out or accept its surrender.

The Royal Government of National Union is the sole constitutional government of Cambodia. It has adopted the Political Programme of the NUFC, and it is on the basis of this programme that the struggle will be waged until victory. The key to understand 'what comes after' is therefore found in this Political Programme in which is set forth, for instance, that: 'The foreign policy of the NUFC is one of national independence, peace, neutrality, non-alignment, solidarity and friendship with all peace-loving peoples and governments.' Neutrality is spelt out in precise terms – no participation in military alliances, nor the protection of any country, nor foreign military bases or foreign troops on Cambodian soil. During the common struggle, Cambodia cooperates with Laos and Vietnam:

according to the principle that the liberation and defence of each country are the affair of her own people . . . In addition, Cambodia is ready to make concerted efforts with Laos and Vietnam to make Indo-China genuinely a zone of independence, peace and progress wherein each nation preserves its integral sovereignty.

In its relations with the outside world, Cambodia will thus remain much as it was before; friendly with all countries that respect our independence and sovereignty. We will have especially close and friendly relations with the only type of South Vietnam and Laos that we can envisage emerging from the victories of their respective resistance struggles. We will have friendlier relations than ever with North Vietnam and China, born from the comradeship-in-arms with the one and the generous support from the other. Such relationships should ensure an era of peace and stability in our corner of the globe as has not been known for centuries. We will all need this, apart from any other reason, because of the terrible problems of reconstruction that lie ahead. US air power adds to these problems every day that the war continues, with its policy of destroying that which the US puppets cannot control.

What our future relations with Thailand will be depends on how things evolve. If Thailand takes the fatal step of attacking us, with the help of the Thai people and our

Vietnamese and Laotian comrades-in-arms, we will strike back. We will win. The Thai military dictatorships – no matter who is in power at the time – will be overthrown and a new era of friendship between our two countries will be inaugurated. Bangkok may well hesitate about making such a move, especially after the catastrophic defeats inflicted on Thai troops during the battle for the Plain of Jars and Long Cheng in Laos at the end of 1971 and the beginning of 1972. It is possible that Thailand may not want to be the last bastion of US imperialism on the South-East Asian mainland – or the last country in the area to mend its fences with the People's Republic of China.

In my view, the future for South-East Asia is that of neutrality. It can have different nuances according to the various countries' individual preferences. It is a solution supported by Hanoi and Peking as the best guarantee of keeping the area really independent and thus locking the doors to further imperialist incursions. Whatever the nuances, this has to be an anti-imperialist neutrality. A pro-imperialist neutrality is a contradiction in terms, imperialism being synonymous with intervention. Behind-the-scenes schemes by Western powers and others at the end of 1971, to capitalize on the trend towards neutralism by sponsoring their own version in South-East Asia can come to nothing. South Vietnam, Laos and Cambodia, have already opted for a progressive type of neutrality – as expressed in the final documents of the Summit Conference of the People's of Indo-China, in April 1970. There are strong tendencies in Thailand and Malaysia towards a neutralism which will permit a more effective type of independence. This represents the best guarantee for keeping the small and medium countries of the area out of the grasp of the super-powers while maintaining their own political and social systems. Dulles used to say that neutralism was 'dangerous and immoral'. Since then the countries of the area have seen what the contrary to neutrality means in terms of national disaster. Neutrality is something that China can accept for South-East Asia because it represents no danger to her interests. To have China's support and friendship is of crucial importance and will become more so as years go by. Because of the clearer ideas I and my companions now have of Peking and Hanoi policies – our exile has inevitably brought about more intimate contacts with the leaders of China and North Vietnam and their thinking on matters of common concern – I am more than ever convinced that neutrality for South-East Asia affords the optimum conditions for peace and mutually friendly relations between all countries of the area. It is imperialism that has whipped up ancient hostilities and set us at each other's throats over the past century. Neutrality is the best umbrella under which a new era of peace and stability in the area can be developed, and outsiders with hostile intent kept at a distance.

Our internal policy will be socialist and progressive, but not communist. State, state-private, and private enterprise will coexist. 'Social justice, equality and fraternity' are the aims as set forth in the Political Programme. There are Marxists and non-Marxists in the NUFC leadership and, as they cooperated in drawing up the Programme, there is no reason to doubt similar cooperation in applying it. This has been proven by developments in the Liberated Zone. The Programme itself is a good compromise between differing ideologies. The spirit of fraternity and solidarity forged during the resistance struggle is the best basis for cooperation later. Our socialism will be to the left of the Buddhist socialism we tried in the pre-coup years. Above all, the rightists, the corrupt, the black-marketeers and other swindlers – all those willing to sell out the country for dollars – will be excluded from public life for a time. They have taught us a good lesson and will need to prove their repentance by their behaviour.

Although the writing is on the wall for US imperialism in our area, we have to keep our eyes on future dangers – the rising role of Japan for instance. Her agents are already solidly implanted in Cambodia – as well as elsewhere in South-East Asia, including South Vietnam and Thailand. The only real guarantee for maintaining non-alignment is to neutralize the forces of internal reaction, and this we are determined to do.

Non-alignment, it is now clear, can only survive if we

have national unity without the inclusion of reactionary groups and individuals, insignificant in numbers, but powerful because of their wealth. In internal affairs, in other words, we will be to the left of any of our pre-coup Sangkum Governments, or at least more energetic in ensuring the strictest application of the most progressive measures envisaged at that time. Buddhism remains our state religion, but the Programme 'recognizes and guarantees freedom for all other religions and beliefs'.

That part of the government which is based in Peking carefully studies the experiences of the People's Republic of China, North Korea and North Vietnam, in tackling their problems of postwar reconstruction. North Korea, for instance, had been totally devastated by 'United Nations' air power in the 1950–53 war. The manner in which the country has been developed since is an object lesson for us. We study China's way of doing things and, when I make state visits to Pyongyang and Hanoi, ministers responsible for postwar planning accompany me. They are given every facility to study aspects that interest them. This does not mean that we will blindly copy things done elsewhere. Cambodia will retain its own personality, but we find much in the experiences of our Asian neighbours that can be adapted to our needs.

We are already drafting postwar reconstruction plans, and being based in Peking is propitious for this. We watch everything going on around us. Our ministers were impressed, for instance, by an institute for training civil servants in North Korea. Most of such cadres in Cambodia had some training in France, but this was for a sclerotic-type administration that had little in common with Cambodian realities. It was divorced from the people and their needs. In Korea we found that the accent was not only on serving the people but that cadres were trained to be practical and efficient, and to deal with very down-to-earth matters. We need something like that – not for a paper administration.

I am personally interested in the people's communes, of which I have visited many of varying size in China. They have many obvious advantages, but one above all others appeals to me. Even small communes cover several square kilometres, englobing big communities of several thousand families. Young people go to school in the communes, including secondary and technical schools. When they complete their education, they are not uprooted from their localities as was the case in my country. We invested a lot of money in education and were proud of our network of secondary and technical schools – 279 of them with an enrolment of 124,000 students by 1968, compared with seventeen and 5,600 students at the time we regained our independence. But they were almost all in the provincial capitals. By the time students had finished their studies they no longer wanted to go back to the villages. The kind of jobs for which they were educated were often not available in their home villages. The fact that the secondary school is on the spot – right where the students live and their parents work – is of capital importance.

While studying they take part in the life of the commune. Teachers are usually also from the commune, especially in the practical and technical subjects which are taught in all commune schools. As the communes run small industries in addition to agriculture, there is no problem in finding jobs on the spot for those who prefer technical work. The fact that young people remain rooted in their native soil is of great importance. The uprooting of our young people was one of the biggest problems we had to face and this is true for many other developing countries. The knowledge they acquire in the town schools does not come back to the village and students often turn into hoodlums and petty criminals in the cities rather than go back 'to vegetate' in their home villages. In the communes there is a bit of everything, agriculture, small industry, handicrafts, repair works, teaching jobs, public health – a great variety of outlets for all of which training facilities are available on the spot.

The young people know from the beginning what real life is about. They visit their friends in other parts of the commune – if they are children of workers, they find out about agriculture and vice-versa. I have seen factories for all sorts of consumer goods on the communes – turning out goods of exportable quality; handicraft products also – of very high quality. Everyone in the area is included in the commune, so they often have handicraftsmen with a highly developed sense of art, plus an art school to develop it still further. Those who are outstanding artisans become whole or part-time teachers of their craft. There are special schools for truck and tractor-drivers; for lathe workers and technicians for machine maintenance, running small electric plants – jobs to which technically-minded youngsters turn naturally.

Before I made my first visit to a commune, I had read that they were something like prisons – husbands and wives living in segregated barracks, both separated from their children. Of course this is nonsense. Families live together as always. There are nurseries for the babies and toddlers. This is practical. Perhaps the husband works in an agricultural team, his wife at a noodle factory. Whoever goes to work last in the morning leaves the baby at the nursery, whoever finishes work first in the evening collects it. I saw for myself that the nurseries are very well run, with specially trained women in charge. In the evening and on rest days there is normal family life. I visited homes wherever I went. If it were the evening, there were always children. Babies at the mother's breast, a child on his father's knee – these were typical sights in the evening when one visited commune members' homes.

Far from separating families, the commune preserves the family concept. Under our system with the secondary school in the provincial capital, families broke up because children did not want to go back to village life. Their interests and way of life had changed: the commune holds the family together. It has become a vital element of cohesion in the new Chinese society. I do not know about Europe, with its own traditions and concepts, but I feel that, for Asia, the commune is a real discovery. It is the way to fix the young people and to make rational use of their labour power and to develop their talents. It stops the drift to the towns where, in many cases in Cambodia in the past, youths with secondary education only wanted to get lucrative jobs in the administration – preferably in the police and customs service where they could grab other people's money. The 'help-thy-neighbour' spirit in the communes promotes the opposite sort of mentality.

The communes have their own shops, clinics, cinemas, theatres and sports fields. They have their own cultural and artistic groups and represent almost autonomous, integrated communities. The commune is the state in miniature. Because they are politically self-administering, the development of the communes had led to a great dismantling of central government departments. In any case, the problems that plague young people in many parts of the world today, including the gap between education and the realities of the life for which they are supposed to have been prepared in school, do not exist in the communes where the overwhelming majority of Chinese young people live, study and work today. They are morally, mentally, and physically better off than young people in any other country I have visited.

On the economic side, there are certainly great advantages also – the communes represent a great decentralization of economic and administrative power – but the aspect of human relations is that which impressed me most. Inside the commune one has the feeling that members belong to one big family, the components living in harmony with each other. If China has had an unbroken run of ten good harvests and grain reserves have reached record heights, I believe this is not so much due to the absence of floods and droughts but to the built-in strength to absorb natural disasters that the commune system provides. The scope of irrigation and flood-control works which a single commune undertakes is something that could only be tackled by the state or huge capitalist agricultural enterprises in other countries. The basis of the abundance of consumer goods which one sees wherever one travels in China today – and I have travelled very widely since March 1970 – is, in my opinion, the commune. I believe this new way of organizing the countryside is something from which Cambodia can benefit. To a certain extent, working the land and harvesting in common, has always been a fine tradition of the Cambodian peasants.

We are going to need to do a lot of new thinking and new organizing to cope with the terrible problems created by America's air aggression and the depredations of the Saigon troops. Tens of thousands of head of oxen and water buffalo, our main draught animals, have been slaughtered, thousands of others driven off as loot to South Vietnam. Mutual aid and cooperative effort is going to be a 'must' to overcome shortage of farm animals and implements.

One of the most alarming things, however, is the deliberate war against nature. This is, in effect, war waged against the future. Cambodia is normally considered an extremely fertile country. This is a relative truth. We have three categories of soil and they are by no means inexhaustible: alluvial soil along the Mekong and its main branches; red earth mainly towards the border areas with South Vietnam, and the fertile black soil of the Battambang plains. Together they cover only a small part of our territory and are restricted to certain determined areas. There are continuous assaults by B52s – each wave of three planes dropping almost a hundred tons of bombs in a tightly concentrated area. Other planes are using bombs of all calibres, as well as napalm and a wide variety of vegetation-destroying chemicals. This combined assault against nature is having a disastrous effect on the soil itself.

A special target, even before the 18 March coup, has been the rubber plantations in the red earth areas. Repeated bombings, and chemical warfare, have destroyed large areas and also vast tracts of forest in adjacent red soil regions. As the trees and undergrowth are destroyed, their roots also die and can no longer hold the topsoil together. When the heavy tropical rains come, the topsoil is washed away by the thousands of tons, leaving only sterile laterite. The soil can never be replaced; the affected area becomes as dead and barren as the Sahara desert. Such vast tracts of dead land are expanded every day and, even if the bombing and chemical warfare were halted immediately, and irreversible process has started – the sterile areas will continue to expand as forest tracts already doomed gradually die out.

When napalm is used against certain types of alluvial soil,

the top layer cakes as hard as stone. Nothing can grow there. The earth itself is burned with such heat that the micro-organisms, on which soil fertility depends, are killed. The chemical composition is changed and the earth becomes sterile. This is especially true where the fertile soil exists in depth. There are also hundreds of thousands of overlapping craters where fertile and infertile soil have become so inextricably mixed that it will take decades for the land to regain its original fertility – if it ever does. This war against nature gives us one of our greatest headaches for the future. It represents an aspect of long-range genocide. There are, alas, far too many of our people with arms or legs blown off, who will no longer be able to contribute to reconstruction. But at least they can reproduce children who will replace them. Soil is more vulnerable than man. It dies more easily – and leaves no successor.

There were those of us who thought – once the war is over we will replant the heveas trees and in five years or so we will have rubber again. It is not true. Once the top soil disappears – as is already the case in very large areas – nothing will grow. The Americans and their puppets want to prevent the revolutionary peoples of Indo-China from surviving. They say in effect: 'If you do win and we have to go away – there will be nothing left for you. You will be destitute for ever. Not because you lack courage or vigour but because we will have killed even your soil.' This is an extraordinary criminal aspect of American use of air power. It is worse than what Hitler did. Many of my American friends will be horrified at such an observation. But what is the difference between burning and gassing people in ovens and doing it to a whole nation out in the open? That is just what the United States of President Nixon is doing today. Everyone knows of the horrors of Auschwitz and other extermination camps. But Nixon is waging a war of extermination against the entire people of Indo-China. And if one can bandage up the wounds of the survivors, many of the wounds of nature can never be healed. How will our forests, among the richest in the world, which have taken generations to grow, ever be replaced? The whole life cycle has been destroyed and over vast areas they will never grow again. According to ancient records, certain regions of what is now desert in Africa were once flourishing rain forests, as we had in Cambodia. It was the fault of man that they were transformed into desert. In Cambodia, it is happening before our eyes as part of deliberate US policy, specifically that of the Nixon administration, to destroy present and future generations of Cambodians by destroying our environment. Once nature dies, man also dies.

An American colonel was once quoted as having said that the solution for the 'Vietcong' problem was to 'asphalt over the whole of South Vietnam'. Nothing would grow, nothing would live, the 'Vietcong would wither on the vine'. That is what is being done with napalm in Cambodia.

According to reports from our resistance headquarters, more had been destroyed in two years of bombings of Cambodia, than in ten years of bombing of South Vietnam. (These reports were received before the extermination bombing of the northern areas of South Vietnam started in April 1972.) Destruction of all that lives and grows in Cambodia is carried out systematically by saturation bombing of region after region according to squares on the target maps.

Perhaps this is because the Saigon régime – which has US air power at its beck and call – wants to destroy its 'traditional enemy', not to mention its competitor in natural rubber? Added to this is the madness of Lon Nol. Apart from his certifiable madness, following the stroke which affected his brain, he is also mad with frustration. He was so sure that, once the coup was carried out, he would have no more problems. Nothing would stand in the way of his becoming 'king' of the 'republic'. When he saw that his dream had turned into a nightmare – inevitable victory for Sihanouk and his Khmers Rouges allies – Lon Nol is capable of saying to the Americans: 'Destroy everything. Après moi le déluge!' There is little doubt but that Lon Nol and Sirik Matak were prepared to destroy everything in order to cling to power. They are even more determined when they see they are going to lose. Just as the Americans act when they lose a base – they send planes to destroy everything left behind. In this case they lose a country – so they agree with their puppets to destroy everything inside the frontiers of that country. This is what was going on in the first half of 1972.

An example of the lengths to which they go is the barbarous practice started in 1971 of using planes to dump tons of broken glass in the ricefield mud to slash the feet and legs of our barefoot peasants and their buffalo labouring the mud in the planting season. Man and beast are afflicted by dangerous wounds. This is a fiendish attack against the peasantry and difficult to deal with. The United States, its Saigon puppets and Phnom Penh sub-puppets, are, between them, doing everything possible to jeopardize the country's future for as far ahead as possible.

As for my personal future! I had originally decided to retire as soon as the enemy invaders had been driven off and the traitors totally defeated. I have no desire to wield power any longer and I have repeatedly stated that the future will be in the hands of the young progressives, whose purity of motives and patriotism I have long recognized, but more than ever since we have become united in the resistance struggle. I have had long discussions in Peking with the 'leftist' elements within the government, also with Ieng Sary, mentioned earlier as one of the first Khmers Rouges to start reorganizing the old resistance bases as far back as 1963, and we have come to appreciate each other's motives and aims. With our young progressives, the future of Cambodia will be in safe hands. But, in response to requests from those who are directing the resistance from inside the country, I have agreed to stay on as Head of State. The request has been made in such terms, and with such backing from the overwhelming majority of the people, that it became clear that it was my duty to stay on.

The tasks of reconstruction will be tremendous, and my compatriots would like me to preside over this as a sort of 'working symbol' of that unity which has been forged in the resistance struggle. It may be useful for me to serve as a bridge, for instance, between communists and non-communists; between Khmers Rouges, whom I have come to know so much better, and Sihanoukists. We will need to develop everything that unites us and discard everything that makes for disunity in the work ahead.

I will also place my thirty years of experience in diplomacy and dealings with heads of state and of governments at the service of the nation. There will be visits to be made to many of the twenty-six states that have supported and recognized *de jure* our government.[1] There will be heads of state and other visitors of mark to receive as visitors. But I will never again take over the reins of government, nor will I ever wield administrative power as Head of State. To be the symbol of our unity and of the Khmer nation is satisfaction enough.

My highest reward will be the moral compensation for having led my people to victory in the greatest trial Cambodia has known in our more than two thousand years of history.

1. The number of states which have recognized *de facto* the Royal Government of National Union rose sharply as the result of the Foreign Ministers' Conference of Non-Aligned Nations, held at Georgetown, Guyana, between 8–12 August 1972. Over sixty nations, almost half the membership of the United Nations, accepted the Royal Government of National Union into full membership of this organization. The Lon Nol delegates were sent packing. It was an historic victory for the peoples of Indo-China, when the flags of the Cambodia of the Royal Government of National Union, and of the Provisional Revolutionary Government of the Republic of South Vietnam, were hoisted outside the Conference Hall. I will head the Cambodian delegation to the summit meeting of Heads of State of the Non-Aligned Nations, to be held in Algeria in 1974.

List of Principal Personalities

Personalities are from Indo-China only, and are listed in the order their names appear in the book.

Page 9.   *Prince Norodom Sihanouk* (1922), appointed King of the Kingdom of Cambodia in April 1941 on the death of his grandfather, King Sisowath Monivong. Abdicated in favour of his father, King Norodom Suramarit, March 1955. Head of State following his father's death in April 1960. Prior to this was several times Prime Minister and Foreign Minister. Deposed following a military coup in March 1970. Remains Head of State-in-Exile and President of the Khmer National United Front which leads an armed struggle against the régime set up in Phnom Penh after the coup.

Marshal Lon Nol (1913), Chief of Staff Cambodian army 1955, Minister of Defence 1960, Prime Minister 1966–7, and 1969. Main organizer of the coup of 18 March 1970, retaining the post of Prime Minister until 11 March 1972, when he proclaimed himself President of the Republic of Cambodia and for a few days relinquished the premiership, reassuming this post briefly on 13 March 1972.

Page 17.   *Lieutenant General Sisowath Sirik Matak* (1914), Minister of National Defence and Foreign Affairs 1954–6, Defence and Education 1957–8, Ambassador to Peking 1962–4, to Tokyo 1966–9, deputy Prime Minister 1969–72. Co-author of the March 1970 plot. Prime Minister 11–13 March 1972, when he was dismissed by Lon Nol following student protests.

Page 22.   *Colonel Lon Non*, younger brother of Lon Nol. Organizer of the attacks on the Embassies of the Democratic Republic of Vietnam and the Provisional Revolutionary Government (NLF) of South Vietnam which preceded

the 18 March 1970 coup. Known for his 'strong arm' methods and as a contender for power at the top in case his ailing brother becomes incapacitated.

Queen Sisowath Kossomak Nearireath, the 'Queen Mother', widow of the late King Norodom Suramarit, for many years director of the Royal Cambodian Ballet. Under house arrest since the 18 March coup and refused permission to leave the country. Mother of Norodom Sihanouk.

Page 27. *Samdech Penn Nouth* (1906), 'Elder Statesman', closest adviser on political affairs to Prince Sihanouk. Prime Minister 1948–9, 1952–5, 1958, 1961–2, 1967–9, holder of many other high offices from 1941. Head of the Royal Government of National Union, set up in Peking in May 1970.

Page 28. *Neak Moncang Monique Sihanouk*, wife of Norodom Sihanouk, President of the Cambodian Red Cross Society, member of the Central Committee of the Cambodian National United Front.

Page 32. *General Nhiek Tioulong* (1910), has held many high posts from 1941 onwards, including heading the ministries of Education, Finance, Information, Public Works, Foreign Affairs. From 1954 onwards was several times Minister for National Defence and Chief of Staff of the Royal Cambodian Armed Forces. Retired to France before the March 1970 coup.

Page 37. *Son Ngoc Thanh* (1908), ethnic Cambodian from South Vietnam, Secretary of Buddhist Institute 1937, Prime Minister of puppet government set up by Japanese in Phnom Penh during the Second World War. Arrested for treason by the French when they reoccupied Cambodia, 1945, and sentenced to death. Saved by Sihanouk's personal intervention and eventually permitted to return to Cambodia where he launched a rightist armed movement ostensibly against the French, but in fact against Sihanouk. After failure he fled to Thailand and reappeared years later as head of the Khmer Serei (Free Khmers), a CIA run organization based in South Vietnam and Thailand, with its own armed forces, and avowed aim of overthrowing Sihanouk

and his neutralist régime. Returned to Cambodia as 'special adviser' to Lon Nol, appointed Prime Minister by the latter in March 1972.

Son Thai Nguyen, brother of Son Ngoc Thanh, elected to the South Vietnam Senate in August 1972.

Page 40. *Huynh Tan Phat* (1913), Saigon architect, member Committee of Resistance and Administration, Saigon–Giadinh, during first resistance war against French. Chairman Saigon–Giadinh, National Liberation Front Committee 1961–9, Prime Minister Provisional Revolutionary Government of the Republic of South Vietnam (NLF) at its formation, 10 June 1969.

Page 45. *In Tam*, former governor of Takéo province, acting President of the National Assembly who called for vote deposing Prince Sihanouk as Head of State, 18 March 1970, Successively President of the National Assembly, Minister of the Interior, President of the short-lived Constituent Assembly, one of two candidates to oppose Lon Nol in the presidential elections of June 1972.

Page 51. *Cheng Heng*, former governor of Phnom Penh central prison, Chairman of the National Assembly, who replaced Prince Sihanouk as Head of State after the 18 March coup. In March 1972 replaced by Lon Nol, as President of the Khmer Republic.

Page 55. *General Dap Chhuon*, commander of the Royal Cambodian Armed Forces in Siem Reap and Kompong Thom provinces at the time of the attempted coup in February 1959 in which he was killed.

Page 62. *Khieu Samphan* (1930), Ph.D. French-trained economist, former Minister of Trade, deputy to National Assembly, left for resistance bases early 1967. Minister of National Defence, concurrently Commander-in-Chief of People's National Liberation Armed Forces, May 1970, Deputy Prime Minister, Royal Government of National Union, July 1970.

Hou Youn (1928), Ph.D. French-trained economist, former Minister of Economic Planning, also left Phnom Penh for resistance bases in 1967. Minister of Interior, Communal Affairs and Cooperatives in RGNU, May 1970.

Hu Nim (1929), LL.D. French-trained lawyer, Deputy to National Assembly, held various high posts until 1967 when he also left for the resistance bases. Minister for Information and Propaganda in RGNU, May 1970.

Page 63. *Chau Seng* (1928), headed various ministries in pre-coup governments, including Education and Agriculture, member of the Royal Council, Chef du Cabinet of Prince Sihanouk, went into voluntary exile in France in 1968. Minister of Special Missions in RGNU, May 1970.

Page 65. *Tan Son Hai*, believed to be pseudonym for Son Ngoc Thanh.

Page 104. *Sam Sary* (1917), held numerous high posts 1941–58, including that of deputy Prime Minister, member of the Cambodian delegation to the 1954 Geneva Conference on Indo-China, ambassador to London, recalled June 1958 because of a moral scandal. Involved in Dap Chhuon plot, January–February 1959, during which he fled the country to join Son Ngoc Thanh as deputy leader of the Khmer Serei. Died mysteriously in Laos a few years later.

Page 109. *Prince Boun Oum of Champassac* (1911), former ruler of Champassac, southernmost of three former principalities which formed Kingdom of Laos. Prime Minister and Minister of National Defence of Laos 1949–50 and 1960–62, Minister of Religious Affairs 1966–7.

Page 110. *Son Sann* (1911), French-trained financial expert. Held many high government posts 1946–70, including heading ministries of Finance 1945–56 and Foreign Affairs 1950; Governor National Bank 1954–8, Prime Minister 1967. Under house arrest following 18 March coup, later went into self-imposed exile in France.

King Norodom Suramarit (1896), succeeded his son, Prince Norodom Sihanouk, to the throne in March 1955; died 1960.

Page 114. *Quinim Pholsena*, Laotian politician, founder and chairman of Peace and Neutrality Party, Foreign Minister Royal Laotian Government 1962; assassinated 1 April 1963.

Page 122. *Nguyen Huu Tho* (1910), French-trained Saigon lawyer, arrested by French, 1950, for heading demonstration protesting presence US warships at Saigon. Released after 1954 Geneva Agreement, was founder-president Saigon–Cholon Peace Movement. Arrested November 1954 by Ngo Dinh Diem régime, released later by guerrillas and elected President of National Liberation Front (1962), appointed President of the Republic of South Vietnam (June 1969) at the formation of the Provisional Revolutionary Government.

Page 129. *General Phoumi Nosavan*, rightist Laotian political officer. Held many high posts Laotian government 1959–65, including heading ministries of Defence, Interior, Finance, Culture, deputy Premier (1961–2). Exiled to Thailand, 1965.

1941	*25 April*	Norodom Sihanouk crowned King of Cambodia at the age of eighteen.
1945	*12 March*	King Norodom Sihanouk proclaims Cambodia an independent, sovereign state – while under Japanese occupation.
	October	The French return to try and restore the former 'Protectorate' status to Cambodia, resisted by King Sihanouk.
1949	*8 November*	France accords 'limited independence' status to the Kingdom of Cambodia.
1953	*9 November*	France grants Cambodia complete independence.
1954	*20 July*	The sovereignty, independence, unity and the territorial integrity of Cambodia accorded international recognition in the Final Declaration of the Geneva Conference on Indo-China.
1955	*2 March*	King Norodom Sihanouk abdicates in favour of his father Norodom Suramarit, in order to devote himself to political affairs. Prince Sihanouk announces the formation of the Sangkum (Popular Socialist Community) which he headed and which dominated the parliamentary political life of the country until March 1970.
1959	*21 February*	Final act in the Dap Chhuon plot, with the capture and killing of General Dap Chhuon who headed a plot in which the CIA, Thailand and South Vietnam were involved.

	31 August	The lacquer-box bomb attentat in which Prince Sihanouk, King Suramarit and his wife, Queen Sisowath Kossomak Near-ireath, narrowly escapes assassination.
1960	*3 April*	King Norodom Suramarit dies, provoking a constitutional crisis over the succession to the throne.
	14 June	National Assembly elects Prince Sihanouk as Head of State thus resolving the constitutional crisis.
1962	*23 July*	Agreement based on three-party neutralist government in Vientiane reached at Geneva Conference on Laos, held at initiative of Prince Sihanouk.
1963	*1 April*	Quinim Pholsena, neutralist Foreign Minister of Laos, assassinated.
	1 May	Visit of President of the People's Republic of China, Liu Shao-chi to Cambodia, and discovery of CIA–Kuomintang plot to blow up the official cortège, including Sihanouk and Liu Shao-chi, on the road from Phnom Penh airport to the capital.
	1 November	Overthrow and assassination of Ngo Dinh Diem and Ngo Dinh Hhu, the dictator brothers of South Vietnam, with CIA involvement in the coup.
	20 November	The National Congress of the Sangkum unanimously votes, at Sihanouk's initiative, to 'end all aid granted by the United States in the military, economic, technical and cultural fields'.
1964	*27 October*	Warning by the Royal Cambodian Government and the National Assembly that diplomatic relations with the United States would be severed in the case of further violations by US planes of Cambodian territory.
1965	*1 May*	Bombardment by US planes of villages in the 'Parrot's Beak' area of Cambodia's frontiers with South Vietnam.
	3 May	Sihanouk breaks diplomatic relations with the USA.

_1966_	_11 September_	Cambodia's first 'free-for-all' general elections, in which the Sangkum leadership did not pre-select the electoral candidates.
	22 October	A new government under Lon Nol was approved by the rightist National Assembly which had emerged from the general elections.
_1967_	_First months_	Three prominent left-wing deputies, elected in the September 1966 elections, leave Phnom Penh for embryo resistance bases in the frontier areas.
	April	Armed peasant revolt in Samlaut district of Battambang province against attempts by Lon Nol authorities to expropriate their farms.
	April 30	Lon Nol resigned as Prime Minister, ostensibly due to injuries received during a car accident.
	3 May	Penn Nouth appointed Prime Minister of an 'Emergency Government'.
_1969_	_11 June_	Diplomatic relations resumed with United States in exchange for US pledge to 'respect Cambodia's independence and sovereignty within the present territorial boundaries'.
	1 August	Penn Nouth resigns as Prime Minister for 'health reasons'.
	12 August	Lon Nol replaces Penn Nouth as Prime Minister.
	3 September	Death of President Ho Chi Minh and departure of Prince Sihanouk for Hanoi, as the only Head of State to attend the funeral ceremonies.
	September	Lon Nol leaves for France ostensibly for medical treatment of his car accident injuries. Deputy Premier Sirik Matak takes over as acting Prime Minister.
	27–29 December	Sangkum National Congress at which delegates support Sihanouk's rejection of Sirik Matak's measures to denationalize the banks and the import-export trade.

1970	*7 January*	Sihanouk and his wife, accompanied by Penn Nouth and his wife, leave for Grasse on the French Riviera, where the Prince took a medical cure every two years or so.
	8 March	Anti-Vietnamese demonstrations in Svay Rieng province.
	11 March	Embassies of the Democratic Republic of Vietnam and the Provisional Revolutionary Government (NLF) of South Vietnam sacked, mainly by troops in civilian dress, in Phnom Penh.
	13 March	Prince Sihanouk leaves Paris for Moscow.
	18 March	*Coup d'état* in Phnom Penh in which Sihanouk is deposed as Head of State. Sihanouk leaves Moscow for Peking.
	23 March	Sihanouk issues an Appeal for the formation of a Khmer National United Front and armed resistance to overthrow the Lon Nol–Sirik Matak régime.
	24–25 April	Summit Conference of Peoples of Indo-China held in 'the frontier region of Laos, Vietnam and China' at Sihanouk's initiative to coordinate the struggle of the three peoples. Chou En Lai presides over a banquet to celebrate the Conference and its decisions.
	29 April	South Vietnamese forces invade Cambodia to support the Lon Nol régime after massive uprisings in support of Sihanouk.
	1 May	US forces invade Cambodia from South Vietnam.
	5 May	A Royal Cambodian Government of National Union is formed in Peking, with Sihanouk remaining Head of State, and Penn Nouth appointed Prime Minister. Heading the key ministries of Defence, Internal Affairs and Information, are three left-wing deputies inside Cambodia, Khieu Samphan, Hou Youn and Hu Nim respectively.
	5 July	After three-day trial *in absentia* by a military tribunal in Phnom Penh, Prince Sihan-

271

		ouk is sentenced to death, his wife, Neak Moncang Monique Sihanouk, to life imprisonment.
1971	*March*	The resistance government claims four fifths of the territory and five of the seven millions of the population under its control, including seventy of the country's hundred administrative districts and 751 of the 1,129 villages.
	18 October	Dissolution of the National Assembly by Lon Nol and the institution of government by decree.
	17 December	Lon Nol issues decrees banning political meetings, anti-government demonstrations and the suspension of all constitutional civic rights.
1972	*11 March*	Lon Nol proclaims himself President of the Republic, dismissing Cheng Heng who had replaced Sihanouk as Head of State on 18 March 1970. Sirik Matak named Prime Minister.
	13 March	Sirik Matak dismissed as Prime Minister. Post temporarily assumed by Lon Nol, but later awarded to Son Ngoc Thanh.
	4 June	In elections, the legality of which is denied by Prince Sihanouk and the probity of which is hotly contested by the two opposition candidates, In Tam and Keo An, Lon Nol elected 'President of the Khmer Republic'.